SOCIAL SCIENCE &
NATURAL HAZARDS

Edited by James D. Wright and Peter H. Rossi

Abt Books/Cambridge, Massachusetts

Library of Congress Cataloging in Publication Data
Main entry under title:

Social science & natural hazards.

    Proceedings of a conference held in Washington,
D.C., May 1979, sponsored by Social and Demographic
Research Institute, University of Massachusetts,
Amherst.
    Includes bibliographies and index.
    1. Disaster relief — United States — Congresses.
2. Disaster relief — United States — Political aspects
— Longitudinal studies — Congresses.   3. Disaster
relief — Research — United States — Congresses.
4. Natural disasters — United States — Congresses.
I. Wright, James D.   II. Rossi, Peter Henry,
1921–   III. University of Massachusetts at Amherst.
Social and Demographic Research Institute.
HV555.U6S63   363.3|4|0973   80-69663
ISBN 0-89011-552-4   AACR2

Printed in the United States of America

Designed by Martha Scotford Lange

CONTENTS

INTRODUCTION

James D. Wright and Peter H. Rossi

In May 1979 the Social and Demographic Research Institute (SADRI) at the University of Massachusetts, Amherst, conducted a conference in Washington, D.C., entitled "Social Science and Natural Hazards," the proceedings of which appear in this volume. Attended by over forty scholars and government officials interested in or responsible for the nation's natural disaster response mechanisms, the conference was organized for three primary reasons.

First, the conference was intended as a forum for the presentation of results from SADRI's Disaster Research Program to potential user communities, both government and academic. With funding from the National Science Foundation, SADRI had undertaken two major studies of natural hazards between 1976 and 1979: one focused on the long-term effects of natural disasters on American communities (James Wright et al. 1979), and the other focused on the state and local politics of natural hazard issues (James Wright et al. 1979). As in most such major research projects, the SADRI staff intended to disseminate the research results through the usual academic channels, in professional journal articles and in two scholarly monographs. But we also felt the need for some method that would put the relevant results directly into the hands of potential users, especially those in government action agencies that deal with disaster response. A user's conference seemed just the thing, particularly since the (now defunct) National Science Foundation program, Research Applied to National Needs (RANN-NSF), required that such a conference be given.

Not that we felt the interaction or transfer of information would be one-sided. On the contrary, as the conference proceedings show, we are uncertain in many cases just what the policy implications of the results are, or how they can be properly phrased and disseminated so as to avoid possible misreading. A second purpose of the conference was thus to sharpen our thinking about the conclusions that can be drawn from our results.

Finally, and perhaps of most importance, our experiences in conducting the Disaster Research Program convinced us that the time had long since come to take serious stock of what thirty years of social science research on natural hazards had actually accomplished. With the hindsight of our own studies in the area and having reviewed most of the significant earlier social science studies, we came to feel very strongly that much of the social science disaster research was less informative than it ought to be. In many cases, we felt, the wrong questions had been posed, inappropriate theories and concepts had been brought to bear on the research, and less-than-fully-informative research methods had been followed. It seemed appropriate, therefore, to use the conference as an occasion to air some of our concerns about the social science disaster literature. One result, we hoped, would be an agenda for future studies that would prove more incisive, more informative, and, most of all, more relevant to policy concerns.

All three of the senior staff members on the project (Peter Rossi, James Wright, and Sonia Wright) were very much "outsiders" to the disaster area — outsiders in terms of background, professional interests, and previous research, but most of all outsiders in the sense that we were willing to question key elements of the conventional wisdom that had emerged from the social science literature. Our inexperience was costly in some respects. For example, the research designs for both major studies were based in part on assumptions that later proved inappropriate (as becomes apparent later in this volume). On the other hand, not being part of the disaster "in crowd," we were able to be essentially iconoclastic in our discussion of previous research and in the presentation of our own findings. Our candor was in turn reciprocated by the conference participants, most of whom had been involved in natural disaster research or operations for decades. In the short run, the effect of candor on both sides is a certain abrasiveness in the tone of some comments. In the long run, however, the effect has been, in our opinion, a more frank discussion of the contributions of social science to an understanding of natural hazard phenomena than will be found anywhere else.

The organization of this volume follows the organization of the conference itself. First, results from SADRI's disaster studies are presented and discussed (these presentations occupied the first day of the conference); second, papers on the larger social science disaster literature are presented (these occupied the conference's second day). Part One summarizes the results of the study of long-term community-level disaster effects. Here, as in all other cases, the presentation is followed first by prepared commentary commissioned by us specifically for the conference, then by spontaneous remarks and discussions from the floor. Part Two considers findings and implications from our study of the state and local politics of natural hazards. Papers, comments, and remarks focused on the larger social science disaster literature comprise Part Three. The volume ends with a discussion of the research and policy implications that can be drawn from the conference proceedings. This concluding chapter was *not* presented at the conference itself: it is, rather, an after-the-fact attempt to assess just what was learned at the conference and what, in the longer view, the conference papers and commentary suggest about future disaster policy and hazard research.

We have not attempted to reproduce here a verbatim transcript of the proceedings. All major oral presentations made at the conference were derived from prepared papers distributed in advance to participants; the prepared papers (and not the oral summaries of them) are what appear here. Further, we distributed copies of the transcript to participants, and in most cases we have used their edited (rather than spontaneous) remarks. Some material appears here that was not presented at the conference but which has been written since, in particular, the discussion of implications in Part Four and, in Part Three, Professor Gilbert White's response to our assessment of his research work. Finally, we have heavily edited the entire manuscript for both style and substance. For the most part, then, what appears here is what the participants meant to say or would have said had they had more time to think about it, and not what was actually said during the conference.

REFERENCES

Wright, J. D. et al. 1979. *After the Cleanup: Long-Range Effects of Natural Disasters.* Beverly Hills, Calif.: Sage Publications.

_____. 1979. *The Apathetic Politics of Natural Hazards.* Amherst, Mass.: Social and Demographic Research Institute.

PART ONE

Natural Disasters and Their Long-Term Effects

ARE THERE LONG-TERM EFFECTS OF AMERICAN NATURAL DISASTERS?*

Peter H. Rossi, James D. Wright, Sonia R. Wright, and Eleanor Weber-Burdin

INTRODUCTION

Hardly a week goes by without some attention in the mass media to the damage from and the victims of natural disasters. The damages and injuries wrought by the tremendous forces of nature lead to dramatic news stories and television footage. Disaster victims quite deservedly attract sympathy, with public agencies and voluntary organizations providing quick rescue help and emergency shelter and care. However, last week's damages and victims recede in memory to be supplanted by this week's occurrences. Clearly, floods, tornadoes, and hurricanes excite public interest and enjoy public sympathy, at least in the period immediately after occurrence.

If last week's flood is old news, then what is last year's damage? The immediate aftermath of a natural disaster is usually the focus of considerable attention and proffered help, but what about long-term needs for reconstruction? Are there significant long-term needs resulting from disasters that require more attention than is being given under current American policy?

To be sure, current federal disaster relief and rehabilitation policy in the United States, as expressed in the Disaster Relief Act of 1974 (PL 93-288), shows some nominal concern for the long-term effects of natural disasters. Title V of the act is aimed at providing relief and rehabilitation support to meet the long-term needs of disaster-stricken communities. But this section of the legislation has never been implemented, possibly expressing the federal agencies' concern about whether there are demonstrable needs for such relief and rehabilitation efforts.

*This summary of the Social and Demographic Research Institute's (SADRI's) long-term effects study was originally published in *Journal of Mass Emergencies* 3 (1978): 117-132, and is reproduced here with the kind permission of the journal and Elsevier Publishing Co. The oral summary of the paper was presented at the conference by Sonia Wright.

These are the questions to which the research to be described in this paper is addressed. We have attempted to estimate the long-term effects of the major floods, tornadoes, and hurricanes that occurred in the decade 1960 to 1970, a period chosen because of available data. The effects studied are those that manifest themselves in distorted population, housing, and economic decline (or growth) in small areas — census tracts — within urbanized places and in counties throughout the United States. These estimated changes are calculated using data from the 1960 and 1970 U.S. censuses and from several disaster data bases in a unique, powerful research design, to be described in greater detail later in this paper.

The nature, duration, and magnitude of the long-term effects of natural disasters have been the focus of previous research, almost exclusively in the form of case studies of relatively large disaster events, typically occurring in small settlements (Bates et al. 1963; Cochrane 1975; Erickson 1976; Friesema et al. 1979; Haas, Kates, and Bowden 1977; Barton 1969; Dacy and Kunreuther 1969). These case studies provide rich detail on how some communities have reacted to disaster events, but they all suffer from the chronic problems of case studies. First of all, they focus on events that are quite atypical, usually at the most serious end of the continuum of disaster magnitude. Second, they are all handicapped in being unable to disentangle the events taking place after the disaster that were reactions to it from the events that would have taken place anyway. Thus, the conclusions of some case studies that the disaster events accelerated growth (or brought about a decline) cannot be evaluated, since we ordinarily have no way of discerning what would have happened to the community had the disaster not occurred.

The research we report here is free of some of these deficiencies of case studies. We will present analyses of the long-term effects of all the major floods, tornadoes, and hurricanes that occurred in the period between 1960 and 1970. Furthermore, we have developed a method that will provide estimates of what would have occurred to places experiencing disaster events if the disaster had not occurred. Finally, the disasters we study are serious occurrences, but not all of them swamp the capacities of the places involved; we study the effects of events in large urban places as well as in relatively sparsely settled areas of the United States.

Method

The method employed to estimate the long-term effects of natural disasters takes advantage of the fact that the U.S. Bureau of the Census provides fairly detailed demographic, housing, and some economic data for small subareas within metropolitan places and for all counties. Since two consecutive censuses can be linked (with some error, as we were to learn), it is possible to calculate the changes with respect to these data experienced by such areas over the decade intervening. Those calculated changes represent the outcome of many processes, some of which can be modeled. Based upon our general understanding of change processes for small areas, we can calculate, for each such area, what its expected 1970 state is, given its position in that respect in 1960, and the change processes typical of places that are roughly comparable. If we then identify those areas that have experienced disasters within the decade 1960 to 1970, we can estimate how change processes have been affected positively or negatively by such experiences. Since disasters occur at various times during the decade, we can also see how 1960–1970 change is affected by the timing of the disaster within the decade. Presumably those disasters that occurred late in the decade should show stronger impacts on small area changes than those occurring earlier in the decade.

This general approach was applied separately to all counties in the United States and to all tracts in standard metropolitan statistical areas (SMSAs) that experienced a major disaster, along with all tracts in a control sample of metropolitan areas that did not experience a disaster. The general linear model was applied to the estimation procedure using models of the general form shown below (for tracts):

$$Y_{1970i} = Y_{1960i} + \Sigma b_i T_i + \Sigma b_k M_k + \Sigma b_i D_i + e$$

where

Y_i is some 1960 or 1970 measure for tract i, for example, total tract population, total housing in tract;

$\Sigma b_i T_i$ is a vector of tract characteristics that relate to tract change, for example, land area, location in SMSA, socioeconomic composition in 1960;

$\Sigma b_k M_k$ is a vector of characteristics of the SMSA and region in which the tract is located, for example, SMSA size and growth rate;

$\Sigma b_i D_i$ is a vector of variables indicating whether or not the tract experienced a disaster in the period and of descriptors of such events;

e is the usual stochastic error term.

Similar models were used for counties, with appropriate modifications. Since economic activity measures are ordinarily not available in any detail for tracts and are available only for counties, the economic activity effects of disasters could be estimated only for these larger units.

Although the models used provide a means for estimating disaster effects that are net of other changes occurring either in tracts or counties, the models were unable to separate out the effects of disasters from the effects of public policies that were applied in the form of relief and rehabilitation activities in the wake of the disaster. Hence, the estimates for long-term disaster effects that will be presented later on in this paper are estimates for disasters *and* accompanying endogenous recovery efforts, aid given by political units and private organizations originating outside the disaster-stricken areas, and the resulting reactions of housing markets for both rental and owner-occupied units.

Clearly the worth of the procedure employed is highly dependent on our ability to undertake with some degree of accuracy two important steps. First, we have to be able to match 1960 and 1970 census tracts and counties so data from the two censuses refer to the same spatial areas. Second, we need to be able to pinpoint the location of natural disasters finely enough to be able to detect which tracts and which counties had such experiences in the 1960–1970 decade. The next section of this paper addresses these two issues.

THE CENSUS DATA BASES FOR COUNTY AND TRACT ANALYSES

The decade 1960–1970 was marked by considerable growth in the American population and an even greater growth in its housing stock. Urbanization trends continued and more and more of the American population congregated in metropolitan areas. At the same time, within metropolitan areas, growth and decentralization led to some degree of reapportionment of residential locations. All these trends meant that areal aggregates used by the U.S. Bureau of the Census and designed to reflect the political boundaries of American localities and the population distributions within such boundaries were changed. The consequence for our study was to make it difficult to identify area units that were identical in boundaries from the 1960 to 1970 censuses.

Counties are important political units outside of the New England states and Alaska;[1] hence, these area units are less likely to change than metropolitan census tract areas. Of the 3,141 counties to be found in the relevant portions of the United States, 3,102 comparable county units could be identified, consisting overwhelmingly of exactly comparable counties and a few units made up of combined contiguous counties whose boundaries, when combined, were comparable. Hence, the data base for our county impact analysis consists of the 3,102 counties and county units whose boundaries were essentially unchanged in the censuses of 1960 and 1970.

Much more difficulty was experienced with census tracts, areal subdivisions of metropolitan areas that are created for census purposes. A census-defined standard metropolitan statistical area consists of a county containing a city of 50,000 or more and includes the contiguous counties that

[1]Alaska did not have counties or census tracts in 1960 and therefore was dropped from the analyses.

are urbanized. In a period of rapid urbanization and growth, new SMSAs are recognized by the Bureau of the Census for each new census. The period 1960 to 1970 was no exception. However, since tracts are defined only for existing SMSAs, those places advanced to SMSA status with the 1970 census were not defined as tracts in 1960. Hence, our census tract analysis must necessarily be based on only those SMSAs that were already defined as such in 1960. Since the number of SMSAs for the United States so defined far exceeds the number that experienced a natural disaster in that period, we devised a sample of SMSAs that consists of all the 1960 SMSAs experiencing at least one disaster and a probability sample of all other SMSAs drawn so that the final sample represents the size distribution of SMSAs in the United States.

When an area becomes an SMSA, tract boundaries are drawn according to rough guidelines that direct local census tract committees to observe physical demarcations as boundaries (for example, rivers, major highways, and the like) enclosing roughly homogeneous areas with about 1,500 dwelling units and 4,000 residents. Clearly, a tract first defined in 1940 or even 1960 may have changed a great deal by 1970, while areas that were essentially unpopulated in 1950 or 1960 may now house many thousands of residents. Each decennial census recognizes these changes by redrawing some of the tracts. Of the 10,720 tracts that we finally used in our analysis, 70 percent were exactly comparable in boundaries (or changed in trivial ways) in 1960 and 1970. An additional 12 percent of the tracts represent mergers of groups of tracts (usually pairs) that, through merger, maintain comparable boundaries for the two censuses. An additional 18 percent are roughly comparable, encompassing areas that are 90 percent or more identical from one census to the other. Merged and roughly comparable tracts are precisely those experiencing the greatest amount of change from 1960 to 1970; that is the reason that they were split or merged or that their boundaries were changed. Hence, in the census tract analysis the degree of area comparability has to be taken into account.

Merging the two census files required a great deal of handwork, especially for census tracts. We are confident that the units in our sample are either exactly comparable in area or comparable enough for our purposes when the small degree of incomparability is taken into account.

THE DISASTER DATA BASE

The form of analyses specified by the model presented earlier requires that we be able to identify all the disasters taking place between 1960 and 1970, as well as their location in space and time and their magnitude. Unfortunately, no single source contains all the required information with sufficient specificity. Instead there are a variety of data sources, each of which suffers from more or less grievous faults.

To begin with, literally thousands of events that could have precipitated natural disasters occurred in sparsely populated areas or were of minor magnitude even though occurring in populous areas. For example, the National Severe Storm Forecast Center's tornado file enumerates more than 7,000 tornado events in the decade 1960–1970. The vast majority of these events, however, were not natural disasters, because they inflicted neither injury nor damage. Of this very large number, only 24 were serious enough to elicit a Presidential Disaster Declaration and only 129 were serious enough to warrant a Small Business Administration (SBA) declaration. Clearly, events which have had no short-term consequences for life or property can scarcely have any long-term effects. Similar counts can be made of other types of potentially disastrous events; for example, most riverine floods cause little or no damage because either they are minor in extent or they occur in places where there are few people and little in the way of property.

Second, each of the various sources of data on natural disasters represents a different slice of the total set of events that might qualify as disaster occurrences. One of the more comprehensive files is the tornado file (machine-readable), compiled by the National Severe Storm Forecast Center, which is purported to contain every tornado occurring in the United States since 1945. Although this data base is more inclusive than we need, it contains important locational information (latitude and longtitude to nearest minute of points where each tornado touched land and where it raised again) and damage and injury estimates.

Another set of comprehensive sources is the American National Red Cross Chapter Reports filed with national headquarters. While the chapter reports contain fewer accounts of disaster events, the most serious events are almost certain to be included. Other sources that we used include the files of the Small Business Administration, the Federal Disaster Assistance Administration (FDAA), the National Hurricane Center, publications of the U.S. Geologic Survey—especially the *Hydrological Atlas* and *Water Supply Papers*—flood hazard boundary maps filed with the Federal Insurance Administration, and files of the *New York Times*.

Each of these data sources documents a particular portion of the universe of natural disaster events, provides particular items of information about each event recorded, and is difficult to reconcile with the other sources. Fortunately, when two or more sources cover the same classes of events, each tends to record most faithfully the most serious occurrences.

Finally, with the exception of the tornado tape, most of the data sources are at best vague and at worst silent on an important characteristic of disaster events. They do not record precisely where the disasters took place, a characteristic that is quite critical for our purpose of identifying small areas that experienced disaster events in the period 1960 to 1970.

TABLE 1 **Counties and SMSAs Experiencing Natural Disaster Events, 1960–1970**

Area	Total Number Experiencing at Least One Event	Number Experiencing Tornadoes*	Number Experiencing Floods*	Number Experiencing Hurricanes*
Counties	1,140 (37% of all counties in census data base)	677	516	137
SMSAs	56	33	35	8
Census tracts	1,102	505	419	260

*Since the same natural disaster event could have affected more than one county, SMSA, or tract, these figures represent a considerably smaller number of separate and distinct disaster events.

We used the disaster data bases in two ways. First, we needed to enumerate all the disaster events that were serious enough that their long-term effects might conceivably be measurable; that is, the amount of damage to property or to persons had to be more than simply minimal. We were surprised to learn how trivial were most of the events that were recorded. Employing a definition of "serious" that would mark off about the top twentieth of disaster events,[2] we arrived at the enumerations shown in Table 1 separately for counties and for SMSAs. It should be noted that the criterion used was not very stringent; we were concerned that too high a threshold would leave us with few natural disaster events to study.

A second use of the disaster data base was to locate in precise terms the occurrence of the natural disaster events within metropolitan areas, in order to identify which census tracts were likely to have been affected. The tornado tape provided by the Severe Storm Forecast Center was most useful for this purpose, since it provided the latitude and longitude to the nearest minute of the beginning, end, and major bends in each tornado's path. Yet even this information was not as accurate as we desired; accuracy to the nearest minute meant that the path's location was accurately identified to within

[2]See Wright et al. (1979) for a complete enumeration of the criteria of seriousness employed. One criterion (in the use of the American National Red Cross Chapter Reports) was that damage from the disaster reported had to exceed 50 in the following index:

$$\text{Damage index} = \text{twice the number of houses destroyed} + \text{the number of houses with major damage}$$

plus or minus one mile—a relatively large measurement error when calibrated to the average size of a census tract (eight square miles). The hurricane tape provided by the National Hurricane Center also contained detailed locational data on the eye of each hurricane and its position at frequent time intervals. However, since hurricanes are rather diffuse phenomena, this information had to be supplemented with data from the Small Business Administration's home loan program.

Locational data on floods posed the most serious problem. Detailed maps showing the extent of flooding for the major urban floods of the 1960s do not generally exist; the few exceptions, such as certain *Hydrological Atlases*, were found to be unusable for other reasons (for example, only a small portion of the total flood area was mapped). It was therefore necessary to rely upon Flood Hazard Boundary Maps outlining the 100-year floodplains for the areas in question, picking those floodplains containing addresses for which Small Business Administration home loans had been given as a consequence of the floods in question.

The locational data upon which the census tract analyses are based are obviously only approximately correct. We are most confident of the data on tornado damage in tracts, but it is likely that we have included tracts that were not affected. The errors of overinclusiveness are probably greater for hurricanes and floods.[3] It should be noted that the consequences of these errors are to water down the estimates of effects to be presented later in this paper, since areas have been included that did not actually experience disaster events. This underestimation applies primarily to the analysis of disaster effects on census tracts; we are quite certain that we have correctly calculated the effects on counties.

THE LONG-TERM EFFECTS OF NATURAL DISASTERS ON COUNTIES

In most areas of the United States counties are important (and sometimes the only) units of local government, providing in many cases police protection, medical services, educational services, and emergency rescue and relief. Even in metropolitan areas, such as Los Angeles and Chicago, county governments provide a significant number of local urban services, and in rural areas counties are often the only local government body able to provide essential services. In short, counties are important political units and often important economic units as well.

---

[3]For one event for which we were able to get accurate maps showing the exact extent of flooding, our estimated flooded tracts correlate 0.7 with those shown to be flooded on the presumably more accurate maps. It should also be noted that the analysis presented in the next section is not substantially changed if we use the actual flooded tracts instead of our estimated flooded tracts.

For our purposes, we have identified 3,102 counties (or combinations of counties) for which we have census data for both 1960 and 1970. Because counties are relatively large geographic units, we are quite certain that we have been able to identify correctly those hit by natural disaster events in the decade 1960-1970. However, by the same token, it seems unlikely that we will be able to find long-lasting disaster effects, because counties are large enough to obscure, possibly, those enduring effects that are characteristic of the smaller areas within them that have been affected by the disasters in question. The damages and injuries inflicted by the typical flood, hurricane, or tornado have occurred to so small a proportion of the structures, enterprises, and households located within typical counties that it is not likely that these events have been a serious threat to the total resources of the counties in question.

To discern the effects of disaster events on counties, we employed the model described above. The results of the application of this model to the percentage changes (1960-1970) in housing stock and population are shown in Tables 2 and 3. The county characteristics that we have included in the model are measures of the composition of the population in the counties; certain economic variables, such as median household income and proportion unemployed in 1960; and measures of the housing stock in the counties.

The regression coefficients (b_i) shown in Tables 2 and 3 should be interpreted as follows: a unit change in an independent variable is accompanied by a change in the percentage growth in population or housing that is shown by the value of the corresponding b. Thus, in Table 2 a shift upward of one year in the median age of all persons in a county is accompanied by a 0.122 percent increase in the housing stock. The value R^2, shown at the bottom of the tables, represents the extent to which the characteristics used in the model account for the percentage changes in housing or population in the decade in question.[4] In addition, the right-hand columns of Tables 2 and 3 contain significance levels for b, a measure of the extent to which the b in each, row differs significantly from zero. Thus, an entry of 0.000 in this column indicates that there are fewer than one in a thousand chances that a coefficient of that size could have been drawn by random sampling of circumstances in which the "real b" was zero.

While there may be some interest in all the coefficients listed in Tables 2 and 3, our primary concern is with those associated with the three types of natural disasters. Note that these coefficients are not large enough to be

---

[4]Thus, R^2 of 0.38 in Table 2 indicates that 38 percent of the variation among counties in percentage change in housing may be accounted for by the variables shown in that table. Clearly there are other processes that account for such changes that are not presented in Table 2, including such artifactual differences as errors of measurement in either independent or dependent variables.

TABLE 2   *Regression of Percentage Change in Total County Housing Between 1960 and 1970 on Disaster Hits and Selected County Variables*

Independent Variable	Dependent Variable Is Percentage Change in Total County Housing, 1960 to 1970*		
	b	Standard Error	Signif-icance
Area of county (square miles)	0.000	**	0.850
% nonwhite (1960)	-0.020	0.021	0.352
Median age of all persons (1960)	0.122	0.071	0.089
Median family income (1960)	-0.002	**	0.000
% unemployed (1960)	-1.038	0.117	0.000
% in manufacturing (1960)	0.253	0.026	0.000
% in trade (1960)	0.101	0.085	0.235
% built after 1949	0.916	0.032	0.000
County in SMSA***	8.495	0.803	0.000
Flood hit	0.417	0.785	0.531
Hurricane hit	2.001	1.435	0.163
Tornado hit	0.810	0.693	0.243
Intercept	-10.837	2.890	0.000
R^2 =	0.384		0.000
N =	3,078		

*Percentage change = $\dfrac{\text{total county 1970 housing} - \text{total 1960 housing}}{\text{total 1960 housing}} \times 100$

**Standard error too small to record.

***Any time during decade or by 1975.

significantly different from zero; that is, *there are no discernible effects of either floods, tornadoes, or hurricanes on the changes in population or housing stock experienced by counties in the period between 1960 and 1970.*

We also analyzed the effects of natural disaster events on other characteristics of counties, including housing value, rent, age composition, educational level of population, and family income. In the interests of simplicity of presentation, these tables are not included here.[5] While there were a few instances in which the disaster coefficients were large enough to be statistically significant, no coherent interpretable pattern emerged. In short, there appear to be no firm findings that indicate that natural disasters have any effects on counties that last for an appreciable period of time.

[5]A full analysis of these potential disaster effects is presented in Wright et al. (1979), chapter 6.

TABLE 3 *Regression of Percentage Change in Total County Population Between 1960 and 1970 on Disaster Hits and Selected County Variables*

Independent Variable	Dependent Variable Is Percentage Change in Total County Population, 1960 to 1970*		
	b	Standard Error	Signif-icance
Area of county (square miles)	0.000	**	0.199
% nonwhite (1960)	-0.046	0.021	0.030
Median age of all persons (1960)	0.455	0.072	0.000
Median family income (1960)	0.001	0.000	0.028
% unemployed (1960)	-0.252	0.119	0.034
% in manufacturing (1960)	0.191	0.026	0.000
% in trade (1960)	0.148	0.086	0.084
% built after 1949	0.867	0.032	0.000
County in SMSA***	9.904	0.814	0.000
Flood hit	-1.245	0.796	0.118
Hurricane hit	2.562	1.454	0.078
Tornado hit	0.306	0.703	0.663
Intercept	-37.002	2.930	0.000
R^2 =	0.395		0.000
N =	3,078		

*Percentage change = $\dfrac{\text{total 1970 population} - \text{total 1960 population}}{\text{total 1960 population}} \times 100$

**Standard error too small to record.

***Any time during decade or by 1975.

The expectation we stated in the beginning of this section — that no direct and lasting effects of natural disaster events would be found on the level of counties — has been borne out. For the entire set of counties, it is clear that there are no significant effects of disasters on growth trends in either population or housing. There are several reasons for this finding. First of all, the damages and injuries directly attributable to the disasters are very small in relation to the population bases and housing stocks of the counties. Even in rural counties, where the ratio of damage to stock may be regarded as largest,[6] this ratio is apparently too small to expect that the task of reconstruction would absorb significant proportions of county resources. Second, disaster policies on the federal, state, and local levels in effect during the

---

[6]In Wright et al. (1979) separate analyses are presented for counties of different population sizes. In each size class natural disaster effects are essentially zero.

decade of the 1960s may have been sufficient to provide enough additional support for reconstruction to dampen considerably the lasting effects of natural disaster events on counties.

In short, the general thrust of the findings presented above lead to the following conclusions as the most plausible interpretation: *disaster events occurring within counties in the period between 1960 and 1970 have no discernible consistent effects that survive more than a very short period of time.*

THE LONG-TERM EFFECTS OF NATURAL DISASTERS ON CENSUS TRACTS

Compared to counties, census tracts are very small in population and area. If size were the only determinant of discernible long-term disaster effects, we should be able to discern such effects when we shift to census tracts as the unit of analysis. This section presents the results of the application of our general model to intercensus tract changes for the period 1960 to 1970.

The specific model used was constructed with the following considerations in mind. First, changes in a tract during the period 1960 to 1970 are partially a function of the characteristics of the tract at the start of the period. In particular, it is necessary to take into account the 1960 level of the characteristic being studied; for example, tracts that were heavily populated in 1960 are likely to still be heavily populated in 1970. In addition, one must take into account 1960 housing characteristics, the 1960 socioeconomic composition of the tract, the location of the tract in the SMSA, and so on.

Second, trends in a particular tract are likely to reflect changes that are occurring in the SMSA in which the tract is embedded. Thus, a tract in Dallas is likely to share in the overall growth patterns of Dallas, just as a tract in Worcester, Massachusetts, is likely to share in the general decline of that city.

Third, binary dummy variables were used to represent whether a tract was hit by a natural disaster of a given type during the period 1960 to 1970. More elaborate specificatins of disaster events were also tried but with no resulting enhancement of our understanding of the effects of natural disaster events.[7]

Finally, variables were entered into the model that captured the degree of merging and uneven matching that was necessary to make the 1960 and 1970 tract files compatible. Since such adjustments were made most often for tracts in areas experiencing large growth or decline, these variables were

---

[7]See Wright et al. (1979). Alternative specifications of the disaster variable included measures of the amount of damage or number of injuries resulting from the event, as well as interactive terms that weighted damage by the time the disaster occurred in the period 1960 to 1970. Since these alternative specifications did not materially change the results presented later in this section, we opted for the simpler binary dummy representation of disaster hit.

especially important in removing artifacts of method from our estimations of disaster effects.

The direct impact of a natural disaster event is visited upon the physical structures, land, and inhabitants of the areas impacted. Destruction of residential dwellings, stores and factories, public utilities, and public facilities and injuries and deaths suffered by inhabitants constitute the direct impact of a natural disaster. Consequently, we can expect that at least a major indicator of long-term disaster effects would be alterations in the growth patterns of an area's housing and population. Certainly the destruction of dwellings lowers the population-carrying capacity of an area, at least temporarily. Deaths and injuries directly lower population levels and can possibly make an area less attractive as a place to live in. Clearly, were nothing else to happen, the expected impact of a natural disaster event would be to alter the growth patterns in housing and population in a downward direction, that is, fewer houses and persons than would otherwise be expected. Of course, the occurrence of a disaster does cause other things to happen, including relief and rehabilitation measures, along with reconstruction of the damaged physical structures of the area.

On the average, five years have elapsed between the occurrence of a serious disaster and the taking of the 1970 census,[8] with some events occurring as much as ten years earlier but none less than a year. In that period much could have happened to restore the status quo ante and possibly to catch up with general local growth trends. Hence, all we can discern in our data is whether the tracts that were subject to tornado, flood, and/or hurricane events showed growth trends in the period between 1960 and 1970 that were more than, less than, or the same as trends in tracts that did not suffer such incidents. Tables 4 and 5 present our findings with respect to population and housing growth trends.[9]

Population growth trends are analyzed in Table 4. Obviously, the most important predictor of a tract's total population in 1970 is the same tract's population in 1960. The regression coefficient, 1.09, associated with this variable indicates that, *ceteris paribus*, tract population grew by 9 percent from 1960 to 1970. The remaining coefficients can be interpreted directly in terms of the numbers of people over and above that expectation that are associated with each of the tract characteristics shown. Thus, for each

---

[8]Since the disasters were not uniformly distributed among the years intervening, this estimate may be as much as six months to a year off.

[9]Note that the form of analysis for tracts differs from that employed for counties. In Tables 2 and 3 the regression equations predict the percentage change in population and housing stocks, while in Tables 4 and 5 the equations are predicting the absolute size of housing and population stocks, a difference in approach made necessary by the fact that there is much less continuity in population size for tracts than for counties.

TABLE 4 *Regression of Total Population (1970) on Disaster Hits and Selected Tract and SMSA Characteristics*

Independent Variable	Dependent Variable Is Total Population in Tracts, 1970		
	b	Standard Error	Signif-icance
Total tract population (1960)	1.090	0.009	0.000
Median age, 16 and over (1960)	-44.000	5.600	0.000
Median household income (1959)	0.095	0.017	0.000
% housing built before 1940	-16.300	1.290	0.000
Number of trailers (1960)	5.360	0.580	0.000
% nonwhite (1960)	-12.050	1.370	0.000
Tract area (square miles)	9.880	0.896	0.000
SMSA population in 1960 (000's)	0.084	0.013	0.000
SMSA population change (1960-1970)	21.900	3.410	0.000
SMSA % unemployed (1960)	-67.400	25.200	0.008
Exactly comparable tract 1960-1970*	-769.100	80.200	0.000
Ring City tract	-444.100	21.500	0.000
Central City tract	-767.600	75.400	0.000
Tornado hit	224.700	142.800	0.116
Flood hit	239.100	156.600	0.127
Hurricane hit	250.600	198.000	0.206
Intercept	2850.500	254.200	0.000
R^2 =	0.706		0.000
N =	10,654		

*"Exactly comparable tract" is a binary variable taking on the value of 1 if the tract in question was identical in 1960 and 1970 or formed over a group of tracts that, as a group, had identical boundaries in 1960 and 1970.

additional year in the 1960 median age of persons sixteen and over, there are forty-four fewer persons than predicted in tracts in 1970.

The reader's attention is directed toward the coefficient for "exactly comparable tract," a measure that marks whether a tract (or group of tracts) changes boundaries in between the two censuses. Tracts whose boundaries did not change (and hence are exactly comparable) were most likely to decline in population, by an estimated 769 persons.

As one might expect, the determinants of tract housing stock, as shown in Table 5, are quite similar to those for population, as shown in Table 4. It should be noted that the housing stock in the 1960–1970 period was growing at a faster rate than tract population—13 percent as compared with 9 percent.

TABLE 5 *Regression of Total Tract Housing (1970) on Disaster Hits and Selected Tract and SMSA Variables*

Independent Variable	Dependent Variable Is 1970 Total Tract Housing		
	b	Standard Error	Signif-icance
Total housing (1960)	1.130	0.008	0.000
Median age, 16 and over (1960)	-12.310	1.740	0.000
Median household income (1959)	0.036	0.005	0.000
% housing built before 1940	-6.240	0.398	0.000
Number of trailers (1960)	2.000	0.178	0.000
% nonwhite (1960)	-2.580	0.422	0.000
Tract area (square miles)	3.850	0.276	0.000
SMSA population in 1960 (000's)	0.016	0.004	0.000
SMSA population change (1960-1970)	6.390	1.050	0.000
SMSA % unemployed (1960)	-20.120	7.780	0.010
Exactly comparable tract*	-245.450	24.720	0.000
Ring City tract	-115.190	29.530	0.000
Central City tract	-206.800	23.250	0.000
Tornado hit	64.650	44.000	0.142
Flood hit	72.210	48.260	0.135
Hurricane hit	103.200	61.030	0.091
Intercept	906.900	76.400	0.000
R^2 =	0.711		0.000
N =	10,654		

*"Exactly comparable tract" is a binary variable taking on the value of 1 if the tract in question was identical in 1960 and 1970 or formed over a group of tracts that, as a group, had identical boundaries in 1960 and 1970.

At the bottom of Tables 4 and 5 are shown the coefficients for each of the three types of natural disasters. Although all the coefficients are positive, none of them is statistically significant. As in the case of counties, *there are no discernible net effects of natural disaster events on growth trends in housing or population stocks for census tracts in the period 1960 to 1970.*[10]

Additional analyses were performed on subsets of tracts. No particular pattern was shown for tracts from SMSAs of different sizes, indicating that disasters had negligible effects in small-sized metropolitan areas and in

[10]To make certain that these results are not artifacts of the difficulties experienced in matching tracts, the analyses were run separately for exactly comparable tracts, with results essentially the same as shown in Tables 4 and 5.

larger ones as well. Stratifying tracts by median family income in 1960 (an indicator of socioeconomic level), we found that high-income tracts (approximately the upper third in median income level) appear to be favorably affected by floods in that they have significantly higher growth rates than would be expected on the basis of their other characteristics. No explanation comes to mind for these counterintuitive findings; perhaps all they indicate is that residential locations on the floodplains of urban places are attractive sites and hence are likely to have both higher income households and higher growth rates.

Regressions with tract characteristics other than housing and population were also run, but no particularly strong patterns emerged. Drastic alterations in income, age structure, and housing value were not associated with any of the three types of disaster events.[11]

The results of our analyses of the long-lasting effects of the three types of disaster events on both counties and census tracts can be succinctly summarized: *for the period 1960 to 1970, natural disaster events occurring in counties and census tracts had no discernible effects that materially altered population and housing growth trends.*

IMPLICATIONS FOR DISASTER RESEARCH AND DISASTER POLICIES

Our attempt to assess the long-term effects of natural disasters has led to a number of conclusions about the existing data bases that are available to the research community for the study of natural disasters in the United States, about the nature of the distributions of such disasters for what may be called a typical decade in recent U.S. history, and finally about natural disaster relief and rehabilitation in the United States.

Existing Natural Hazard Data Bases

The data bases upon which this report was constructed were not collected, obviously, for the purposes to which we put them, and hence our experiences with trying to use them were frustrating. The ideal natural hazard data bases would most likely have been far beyond the agencies' capabilities — and certainly far beyond their interests — to produce. Yet certain steps could be taken by the agencies in question that would, at minimum cost, make their data bases more useful to researchers.

The first step is to computerize existing data bases in a form that would facilitate the transfer of information among agencies and from agencies to researchers. Although most agencies have either done this or are in the process of doing it, it is important to stress that computerization can be done in ways that restrict outside-the-agency applications and that such forms

[11]Some statistically significant disaster effects were found, but their substantive significance in most cases was slight.

should be avoided, if at all possible. For example, the excellent American National Red Cross Chapter Reports are currently on tape in a form that makes it easy for the Red Cross to get hard copies of its reports but difficult for anyone else to use the computer tapes for research purposes.[12]

A second step that could aid future disaster research considerably would be for agencies to standardize data bases. Standardized procedures, formats, codes, and so forth should be used whenever possible, including the adoption of such general procedures as the Federal Information Processing Standards codes for states, counties, and other places.

The most pressing need for standardization is in defining and recording the actual location of disasters. The data bases, with the exception of the National Severe Storm Forecast Center's tornado tapes, do not allow one to locate disasters with any precision, even within such gross categories as counties and municipalities. Of course, part of the problem lies in the ambiguous location of some disasters, especially hurricanes, but damage and injuries located by counties would be a serious improvement over current imprecision.

A third step that could be taken is to centralize records, requiring the development of a new institution that would serve as an archive with the mission of collecting, cataloguing, and disseminating data on the incidence, location, and sequelae of natural hazards. Although it is clear that such an archive would be of immense utility to researchers, it would also directly serve policy purposes and thus justify the considerable start-up and maintenance costs involved. For example, hazard risk assessment would be considerably strengthened by better historical records on the risk experiences of communities and larger areas. If disaster location could be recorded in fine detail, the disaster experience of local communities could be used to bolster arguments for disaster-mitigating land use management and structure construction standards.

The Distribution of Disasters by Severity and Size

It should now be abundantly clear that many events routinely labeled "natural disasters" are not really disasters in any literal sense of the word, especially when regarded from the perspective of communities, states, and the federal government. This is *not* to state that the occurrence of a natural disaster event is trivial to the individuals, households, firms, and possibly neighborhoods that have directly experienced the impact, a topic to which we return shortly.

This point is made dramatically if we consider damages and injuries from floods. In the 1,612 counties for which at least one Red Cross Chapter Report exists for the decade 1960–1970, we may note that *over the entire decade* the average affected county experienced losses that amounted to less than one

[12]Specific details about this and other data bases are given in Wright et al. (1979), chapter 5.

person killed and about twelve injuries, with four dwellings destroyed and twenty-two dwellings suffering major damage. Similar average losses were experienced by counties that had experienced a tornado event. Even the most serious hazard, hurricanes, produced decade-accumulated injuries and damages amounting to 1.4 deaths, 179 injuries, 42 dwellings destroyed, and 137 dwellings damaged. What long-term disaster effects could be expected from such events in counties with an average population of 78,000 people and an average of 25,000 dwellings in 1960? For the typical disaster-stricken county, loss of life from automobile accidents exceeds loss of life from natural hazards by a ratio of 50 to 1; the loss of property due to natural decay exceeds the loss of property due to natural hazards by approximately twice that magnitude. No one would seriously maintain that automobile accidents and natural decay have long-term effects on counties.

Of course, these events are not trivial from the point of view of the victims involved, and there may be quite serious long-term effects on the health and economic well-being of the households and firms that have been the direct victims of even the smallest natural disaster events. The contrast is with the community as a whole, for which the effects of disaster events are relatively slight.

Three important conclusions stem from this contrast between the individual and social viewpoints. First, in assessing the likely effects of natural disasters on various units, it is essential to consider the magnitude of the losses involved in terms of the resources at the command of the unit in question. The losses experienced by an individual or household are large in comparison to that unit's resources, while for a city, county, or state, the ratio of losses to available resources is small. The larger such an *impact ratio* (ratio of damages to available resources), the greater the need for outside help.

Second, although we are skeptical that communities need any long-term recovery assistance, no such implications should be drawn for individual, household, and business victims. We do not know from this analysis whether or not individuals, families, and businesses need long-term disaster assistance.

Third, the preceding points are addressed primarily to *average* disasters, not to extremely severe disasters — the Betsy or Agnes hurricanes, a Topeka-sized tornado, or a Denver-sized flood. For these extreme disaster events, the impact ratios are high; that is, damages and injuries are inflicted on a large proportion of the persons and structures in the area in question. For example, we estimate that, as a result of the Topeka tornado, the ratio of damaged dwelling units to total dwellings was about 1 to 10.[13] Of course, we

[13]Note that the Topeka tornado is so far out on the distribution of tornado events during the decade 1960-1970 that it must be regarded as a one-in-a-thousand-years tornado for metropolitan areas subject to risk. Given the number of SMSAs in tornado-prone portions of the country, a Topeka-sized tornado can be expected once every two or three decades.

are not sure what values of the impact ratio indicate the need for long-term rehabilitation measures, but we are sure that only when this ratio is high does it make sense to look for such long-term needs.

It should also be noted that the impact ratio is affected by both its numerator and denominator. This means that the same physical event experienced by a small community and an SMSA may have much more serious effects for the small community. Indeed, that is why so much attention has been given in the disaster literature to events that have occurred in small towns, for example, Xenia, Rapid City, Conway, and Buffalo Creek.[14] Catastrophic events occurring in larger places—events on the order of the 1906 San Francisco earthquake—can hardly be understood with any degree of sureness by extrapolating from the experiences of a Xenia or Buffalo Creek disaster event.

National Disaster Policy
Wholesale revisions of our national disaster policy appear to come about in reaction to the severe events that are statistical outliers, not to what might be called the "average, once-a-month" American disaster. We believe that our research, which presents a rather good description of the average disaster, establishes at least one clear finding: the average, once-a-month American natural disaster does not look like Topeka 1966, it does not look like the Thompson Canyon flood, and it does not look like Agnes or Buffalo Creek. This finding raises the question of whether it is wise to base national disaster policy on the statistically rare event.

In the ideal, but never realized, case of unlimited resources, policies based on an assumption of the worst imaginable situation are reasonable and defensible. In such an ideal world every airport could be prepared for a Canary Islands type of aircraft accident, every hospital could be prepared for the aftermath of a nuclear holocaust, and every city could be prepared for a Topeka tornado or a once-in-a-thousand-years flood. But in view of all the other demands on resources, the question can be raised: how big a disaster is it rational and efficient to prepare for? Perhaps the most reasonable policy is simply to admit in advance that such rare catastrophic events cannot be prepared for and to expect that special measures would have to be taken ad hoc if such events were to occur.

There are several reasons for this suggestion. First, probably no set of relief and rehabilitation measures would be fully adequate to handle what might be called "extreme value" events, mainly because no policy could possibly

[14]Because events entailing a large impact ratio are very rare for large places and relatively rare even for smaller places, statistical studies of long-range disaster effects are unable to say much about what happens when the impact ratio is very large. We are forced to conclude that research on the long-range effects of severe natural disaster events will have to be restricted to case studies for some time to come, with all the implications for generalizability that this method implies.

anticipate and resolve all the relief and rehabilitation problems that events of this magnitude would pose. Second, because such events are rare, it makes sense to tailor relief and rehabilitation measures to the specific place and specific type of disaster that would take place. Thus, a superforce hurricane hitting Miami might require different types of relief and rehabilitation measures than a superforce earthquake occurring in Los Angeles, because Miami and Los Angeles are different places and also because hurricanes and earthquakes leave behind different sequelae. Finally, federal disaster policy should not be overhauled every time a new catastrophe comes along and then applied in the interim to the average, once-a-month disasters. We should have a federal disaster policy that is tuned to the needs that are generated by the average disaster and applied to those events alone.

A final implication of the distributional characteristics of natural disasters is that the perspective on the natural disaster problem varies with the level of aggregation involved. A local community's perspective may be conditioned largely by its own historical experiences with natural disasters, most likely *not* including a major serious event (at least not within the memories of persons currently living), because such catastrophes are extremely rare for any given place. Catastrophes are not as rare when viewed from the national perspective, since the experiences of local communities when aggregated to the national level represent a formidable problem indeed. What this implies is that policies that are designed to deal with the national disaster problem and that appear to be rational and effective from that viewpoint may be seen as burdensome, irrational, inefficient, and perhaps even counterproductive from the viewpoint of the communities to which they are applied. No better example of this difference in perspective can be cited than the Flood Insurance Program. From a federal viewpoint, the program has much to recommend it. From the viewpoint of a specific community whose recent history does not include a hundred-year flood, the policy may appear to be capricious and inequitable.

This last point suggests that federal disaster relief and rehabilitation policies have to consider not only the costs of policy to the nation as a whole but also the costs to local communities. Costs imposed upon local communities without corresponding perceivable benefits may lead to the deterioration of national policy in the United States as its impact upon local communities becomes felt.

REFERENCES

Barton, A.H. 1969. *Communities in Disaster: A Sociological Analysis of Collective Stress Situations*. Garden City, N.Y.: Doubleday.

Bates, F. L. et al. 1963. *The Social and Psychological Consequences of a Natural Disaster: A Longitudinal Study of Hurricane Audrey*. National Research Council Disaster Study No. 18. Washington, D.C.: National Academy of Sciences.

Cochrane, H.C. 1975. *Natural Hazards and Their Distributive Effects.* NSF-RA-E-75-003. Boulder, Colo.: Institute of Behavioral Science.

Dacy, D.C. and Kunreuther, Howard 1969. *The Economics of Natural Disasters: Implications for Federal Policy.* New York: The Free Press.

Erikson, K. 1976. *Everything in Its Path: The Destruction of Community in Buffalo Creek.* New York: Simon and Schuster.

Friesema, H.P. et al. 1979. *Aftermath: Communities After Natural Disasters.* Beverly Hills, Calif.: Sage Publications.

Haas, J.E., Kates, R.W., and Bowden, M.J. 1977. *Reconstruction Following Disaster.* Cambridge, Mass.: MIT Press.

Wright, J.D. et al. 1979. *After the Cleanup: Long-Range Effects of Natural Disasters.* Beverly Hills, Calif.: Sage Publications.

Commentary

Howard Kunreuther

I like this study a great deal: it was extremely well done and provides a new perspective on the losses and consequences of disasters that complements the case studies undertaken in the past. Three principal points related to the long-term effects of disasters have been presented. First, except for statistically rare events, there are no discernible long-term population and housing impacts on communities struck by natural disasters. Second, legislation is based on the statistically rare and unusual event rather than on the average disaster. This is inefficient and we might want to consider making policy changes. Third, the data available to analyze natural hazard impacts are not very good. On the basis of these three general findings, the authors provide a specific set of policy recommendations and suggestions for future research. Here I analyze each of the findings in turn and then evaluate their implications for policy.

LONG-TERM IMPACTS

In assessing long-term impacts on the community, we have to distinguish between the aggregate macro-level effects and the more detailed micro-level effects. As the authors emphasize, the study did not look in detail at the micro-level (or individual) effects; it was designed to investigate higher order macro-level effects. In future research perhaps it will be possible to blend both analytic levels. On the macro level it seems to me that everything SADRI is saying is correct — as a matter of fact, if one looks at some specific disasters, maybe even some rare ones located out on the statistical tail, SADRI may actually be underestimating some potentially *positive* long-run effects.

Let me provide a few examples from the 1964 Alaskan earthquake. Alaska was excluded for a variety of reasons from SADRI's data base, but it is one of those case studies where we do have a good deal of information about what happened after the disaster, so we can probe effects on the micro level (that is, effects on specific communities). The first example is Seward, Alaska. Seward is a community that was decimated by the Alaskan earthquake: the per-capita damage was about $19,000. After the earthquake, a decision was made to rebuild this small and declining community (the population declined from about 2,000 to 1,500 after the quake), despite the fact that Anchorage and Whittier would have been able to absorb most of Seward's shipping business. In fact, a good deal of money was poured into the community, and, as a result, Seward was far better off after the disaster than it had been before. This decision was made on political and social, rather than on economic, grounds.

As a further illustration, consider the following quote from a newspaper story about what happened in Anchorage a year after the earthquake:

> With its first post-quake Christmas approaching, the city's merchants have taken a close look at Yuletime spending and find the current business picture as bright as the twinkle in Santa's eyes. The consensus is that business this Christmas season in Anchorage promises to be the best ever despite the big shake of March 27.

Here and in at least some other cases, then, a community that has had severe damage turns out to be much better off after the disaster than it was before. This factor may not be easily captured by SADRI's aggregate data analysis (for example, postive effects in communities like Seward might be offset by negative effects in other communities, producing SADRI's "no effect" finding in the aggregate), but it would obviously be important to consider in designing meaningful legislation.

On the micro level there may be very serious effects experienced by portions of the population. An example comes from the work of Joe Vinso (forthcoming), who spent considerable time in the Wilkes-Barre area trying to gain a better understanding of individual recovery from a flood. He found that low-income and elderly people were having an extremely difficult time. Many of them had owned their houses outright and were very proud that they did not have an outstanding mortgage. As a result of the flood, they found themselves in a much higher debt/asset position than they deemed desirable. They had suffered serious destruction to their homes and had to ask themselves whether they should take advantage of the liberal relief provided by the federal government.

What happened in this particular case was very surprising. Many people did not want 1 percent low-interest loans, because they did not want to be saddled with debt at the age of seventy. When asked why they wouldn't want a loan, they gave very simple answers, such as, "I would like to die solvent." This example again illustrates that once we look at micro or individual effects, we may have to ask ourselves what policies are appropriate for dealing with disasters.

The SADRI study concludes that the average disaster is not going to cause much difficulty to communities and that this should be reflected in legislation. At an aggregate level this may be correct. However, when we look at the effects disasters have on specific groups, there may be more cause for concern. As SADRI points out, the impact ratio to a community as a whole may be small, but it may be very large for specific groups of people within the community, as shown by the Wilkes-Barre case study. Legislation must thus reflect trade-offs between efficiency questions (which relate to resource allocation problems at an aggregate level) and equity questions (related to distributional impacts on specific groups). Efficiency questions are concerned with the average disaster. Equity questions are concerned with micro-level effects. SADRI's study has provided insight into the problems of efficiency, but we need considerably more and better data on equity impacts (such as damages suffered by different socioeconomic groups) before policies can be revised. For example, if we want to see how the low-income group compares to the high-income group, then we will have to collect and analyze entirely different kinds of data. In this connection, one of SADRI's findings is especially interesting: floods seem to have positive effects in high-income tracts and negative effects in low-income tracts. This is a suggestive finding that could be pursued further: why does this happen and what are the policy implications? A similar point can be made about the types of damage to the community itself. What is the proportion of damage to the residential sector, the industrial sector, and the public sector? Damage concentrated in a particular business in the community may call for different legislation than damage occurring in an affluent residential sector, as in the Alaskan earthquake. There, most of the damaged structures were owned by high-income groups, and it is not clear whether they really needed the liberal relief that was provided. In summary, we need more detailed studies of the socioeconomic groups affected by disaster and the type of damage to the community in the industrial, residential, and public sectors.

THE NATURE OF DISASTER LEGISLATION

The second principal recommendation coming from SADRI's study is that disaster legislation should be based on average events rather than on statistically rare events, as is currently the case. It may not be easy to implement this policy recommendation, because average disasters are low-salience events for Congress, as well as for states and communities.[1] Until now, Congress has not had much stake in disasters: it is less concerned about having efficient legislation to meet average disasters than about reacting to the statistically rare catastrophe in politically useful ways—responding with sympathy votes and passing special relief legislation. It costs Congress nothing politically and is helpful to the affected region. In other words, pressure is placed on Congress by the local communities that are hit by big disasters—statistically rare events, to be sure, but highly salient once they occur.

Is there any realistic hope of changing these tendencies? I think not, because there is no reason for Congress to pass legislation designed to meet the needs of areas hit by average disasters. Since ad hoc legislation is not very

[1]The salience of disaster issues to state and local decision makers is discussed in Part Two of this volume.

attractive, how can we improve the situation? One way is to incorporate explicit distributional criteria, as well as efficiency criteria, into legislative objectives. Certain groups will be severely affected by a disaster and will demand relief. If we recognize this fact in designing legislation, we may have more efficient legislation.

THE AVAILABLE DATA BASE

Let us now turn to the third point raised by SADRI's study, namely, that the data available to analyze natural hazard impacts are not very good. I agree! There is a clear need for improving the disaster data base. Major disasters, such as the Alaskan earthquake, are notable exceptions to this generalization. In the case of Alaska, substantial data were collected by researchers and government agencies. These efforts were coordinated by the National Academy of Sciences and the National Research Council in a major effort to look at the physical as well as socioeconomic impacts of the disaster. The Corps of Engineers has published a number of studies on major disasters, and studies of short-run responses to disasters have been supported by the National Academy of Sciences–National Research Council's Committee on Disaster Studies. (Gary Kreps discusses this research in Part Three of this volume.) Some of these studies are extremely useful in giving us insight into potential long-term impacts, but considerably more and better data are needed.

The National Flood Insurance Program (NFIP) offers an opportunity to analyze the impacts of floods and hurricanes on communities throughout the United States with its data on flood insurance claims. As more businesses and individuals in flood-prone areas purchase insurance, either because they are required to do so or because they are more aware of the coverage and its benefits, the data base will become richer and exhibit fewer systematic biases than it does now.

IMPLICATIONS OF FINDINGS FOR POLICY

Establishing a Natural Hazards Data Base

Although most people would agree that we need a better data base, there is probably much less agreement on what kind of data base we need. I would contend that we need more micro-level data in order to gain a better understanding of the real impact of natural hazards and to enable us to link the case studies with the types of longitudinal studies that SADRI advocates. Some of the data collected by SADRI might be useful for more detailed or extended analysis. For example, the Small Business Administration (SBA) loan data base helps one gain an understanding of how different socioeconomic groups recover from a disaster, what the impact of the disaster is on different age and income classes, what happens to them, what happens to victims who do not take advantage of SBA loans, and so forth. The Red Cross data may provide us with a better indication of what is happening on the micro level as well.

The National Science Foundation can play a role here. In recent years it has supported a number of studies in which data have been collected from field surveys. These data have yielded considerable information on the behavior of individuals and the impact of disasters on communities. Recently the National Science Foundation has supported other empirically based studies on disasters. For example, it has provided generous funding to the University of Pennsylvania for an extensive field survey in flood- and earthquake-prone communities to gain a better understanding of the insurance purchase decision and knowledge of hazard mitigation and relief measures. These data complement the statistics from federal, state, and local longitudinal studies, providing additional data that may be very useful. There is a need, as SADRI suggests, for a data base clearinghouse, which could document and coordinate information collected by different research projects and agencies concerned with disasters.

Designing Meaningful Legislation
Future legislation should be sensitive to the distributional impact of disasters. Following a disaster, the American public and its representatives are concerned with assisting poor, unfortunate victims. It is not likely that this fundamental and generous impulse will change in the future, whether or not the conference participants feel it is fair or rational. But rather than reacting to future disasters, Congress can anticipate this response. Legislation can be passed now that responds to two questions. First, what should be done to help different socioeconomic classes of victims in disaster-stricken communities? Second, what preventive and hazard mitigation measures should be taken to alleviate the potentially high cost to the federal government of large-scale relief?

With respect to the first question, current legislation offers special provisions to low-income groups as part of the Disaster Relief Act Amendments of 1974 (Section 408). It would be useful at some point to learn from the Federal Emergency Management Agency how well this legislation is working. If, in fact, low-income groups are well taken care of, then Congress may not need to pass new legislation. The Red Cross has provided assistance to low-income victims or people who cannot afford to get SBA loans. Earlier studies have revealed that the SBA is not a source of relief to many of these low-income people either because they do not know about the program or because they cannot afford to pay back the loan. These are the people who need the most help, but SBA will make disaster loans only if the victim is considered a good financial risk. Special grants to cover public sector damage and to cover the economic impact to communities suffering severe industrial losses are the kinds of measures that are needed, and it may be that this type of relief will have to be tailored to specific communities, as SADRI suggests.

I would suggest that we be more explicit about the purpose of disaster legislation prior to the statistically rare event. Otherwise we are going to find ourselves back in the same box at the end of any disaster. We will find Congress responding with the same kinds of measures that it has responded with in the past. To measure the basis for loans or relief to certain classes of victims, income tax forms or other kinds of explicit documents that are on hand may be useful in designing legislation that at least has a chance of being implemented.

With respect to hazard mitigation and preventive measures, a good case can be made for legislation. Empirical evidence from SADRI's political study (see Part Two) suggests that local and state governments don't care a great deal about disasters. For this reason, the concept of hazard mitigation measures and preventive activities is not likely to sell well in Peoria. The challenge for Washington is to make the issue sufficiently salient so that the financial burden is transferred from the federal government to local and state constituencies. Today the federal costs of disaster relief are very large. This fact has been noted in SADRI's reports and others on the subject. Local and community preventive costs are not large on the average, but after a disaster the costs can be substantial. The problem can be stated rather simplistically: people don't want to take action before an event. They don't want to take action because they misprocess information. Prior to a disaster, everyone says, "It's not going to happen to me, so why should I worry?" Communities respond in this manner, so do potential victims, and until recently the federal government has shared this attitude. After a major disaster, all these groups are burdened with large debts. Then victims and communities plead for financial assistance and the government responds with special legislation.

The federal government and Congress should begin to design legislation that explicitly reflects this ex ante–ex post trade-off. By recognizing that prior to an event (ex ante) people don't care, but after the event (ex post) they do, the legislation can reflect these different time perspectives. To do this accurately requires data on socioeconomic groups and communities. It requires an understanding of the decision processes of individuals and of the institutional arrangements associated with disasters at federal, state, and local levels. Only then can we design the kind of legislation that transfers the burden of relief from the federal government to the states and local communities.

The government has two main mechanisms for doing this today. NFIP utilizes a carrot and stick approach. The carrot is the subsidized insurance offered to residents currently living in flood-prone areas; the stick is land use regulations and other mitigation measures required of communities participating in the program. The principal problem with this tool is that people generally do not want to buy flood insurance until they've been hit by a flood. Amendments to NFIP now require homeowners with federally financed mortgages to purchase coverage if they reside in hazard-prone communities enrolled in the program. The communities most likely to be pressured into joining the program, if they haven't already done so, are those that have recently been hit by floods. In these areas residents are demanding insurance. Aside from the education process associated with a graphic event, such as a disaster, there is a need to provide residents with better information about why they should protect themselves through insurance. Then we will have a chance to see some of these mitigation measures actually adopted by residents of the community as a means of self-protection.

The second way of transferring part of the burden to state and local governments is through cost sharing, where a portion of the expenses of a federal project are underwritten by the states and local communities. For example, there is increasing pressure for state and local governments to contribute larger amounts for flood control and structural measures. On the other side of the coin, the federal government might consider sharing part of the costs of hazard mitigation and prevention measures in much the same way that tax credits are given if families adopt energy-saving measures. For example, a partial tax write-off for flood proofing would stimulate states and communities to think about ways they could inform people of these opportunities.

Finally, let me suggest some positive steps the research community could take to study the long-run impacts of disasters. We do need more analyses of micro-level scenarios, for example, scenarios that structure a community on a much more detailed level, with data on the characteristics of socio-economic groups and the community's industrial and residential bases. Using this information, we can begin to understand what the likely impact of alternative disaster policies will be. In order to do this, however, we have to have good descriptive models of choice for short- and long-run behavior following a disaster.

The SADRI study has made us more aware of the importance of linking prescriptive and descriptive models. Now user agencies and the research community must take the next steps and focus on ways in which the SADRI findings can be used to improve future disaster policies and lead to further and better studies in this area.

REFERENCES

Vinso, Joe. Forthcoming. Financial Implications of Natural Disasters: Some Preliminary Indications. *Journal of Mass Emergencies*.

Discussion

Robert K. Leik: I have a question about your data. It is obvious you have large variances on the households, populations, and so on affected by these disasters. Could you give some indication of the upper ranges: the worst events, in terms of injury, death, and destruction, that are contained in your analysis?

Sonia R. Wright: The worst tornado is Topeka 1966, which destroyed 820 houses and did major damage to another 1,010. The worst hurricane in the study is Betsy, which destroyed or damaged over 15,000 homes in New Orleans. And the worst flood is the 1965 Denver flood, which damaged about 1,000 homes.

Leik: That is really a skewed range, though. Most of your disasters are much less destructive.

S. Wright: Absolutely. For instance, the tornado analysis is based on more than 1,000 tornadoes occurring in the decade, and of these, 46 percent do damage of less than $5,000, 74 percent less than $50,000, and so on. Topeka is definitely an outlier.

Let me also make a point in response to Howard Kunreuther's commentary. We are not saying that existing disaster policy has to be changed because it is designed to deal with the outliers. I think all we can say on the basis of our data is that whatever policies existed in the 1960s seem to have worked in the sense that we do not find any long-term effects. This may or may not have implications for the policies in force today. Our data force us to think critically and logically about present policies and their effects, but the data do not demonstrate any such effects, or lack of them, directly.

Peter H. Rossi: I also have a comment on what Howard said, something that doesn't appear in any one of our reports. Clearly, the work we did does not address the micro level, as he refers to it; that is to say, it does not disaggregate down to the level of individuals, households, or firms, and the like. And, having found on the macro level (census tracts and counties) that there were no discernible long-term effects, we cleverly went back to NSF and proposed a micro-level study, a kind of disaster victimization study: what are the damages, injuries, and the like that are experienced by the victim population? Let's not look just at SBA loans and Red Cross handouts, because we don't know how selective FDAA, SBA, and the National Red Cross are when they make relief decisions. We need to know total damage, the amount that is covered, the distribution of coverage, the bias in coverage, the asymmetry in coverage, and so on, as it exists under present policy. NSF has cut back funding for social science research on natural hazards. But some sort of direct study really is the next step, and I think Howard is perfectly right to point that out.

Daniel O. Price: Going back to your data, I am bothered, for example, by Table 4, where the dependent variable is total tract population in 1970 and where one of the independent variables is the population in 1960 and another is tract population change from 1960 to 1970. It seems to me that you have roughly the same variable on both sides of the equation. Also, I am bothered by possible multicolinearity. For instance, does "hurricane hit" have any relationship to tract population change from 1960 to 1970? If so, you've given the 1960-1970 population change the credit, not the hurricane. In other words, you have not given the hurricane (or other disasters) first crack at its effects.

S. Wright: The first variable in Table 4 is the total tract population in 1960. That is a control variable, and with that variable in the equation, the coefficients are interpretable as the net *change* over the period. Now, obviously, we must control for the 1960 population when analyzing 1970 population as the dependent variable. Second, the population change variable expresses 1960-1970 change in the *SMSA population,* not in the tract population. These are clearly not the same thing. Finally, multicolinearity is not a serious problem in these equations. All our programs were run on a computer package that routinely prints the determinant of the matrix, and we looked at that before we did anything else. The determinants are all within the allowable range.

Price: In the regressions did you put in, say, hurricane hit as a first-order inclusion level ahead of some of these others?

S. Wright: No. When we separated out only the hurricane-prone areas at both the county and SMSA levels, there was again no colinearity problem. The effects were always the same. We also tried to separate out the multiple hits, and again there were no effects.

Price: I'm also concerned about whether the significance levels were corrected for finite population. You have a very large proportion of the total population in your sample so these significance levels are probably all biased.

S. Wright: The tables do not have a finite population correction. I don't think that we have as large a proportion of the total population as you imagine.

Price: Well, it's at least 10 percent, isn't it?

S. Wright: Even at 10 percent, we are running thousands of regressions and looking at thousands of coefficients, so if you just disregarded Type I errors, you would probably end up with the same findings.

Price: You might. I think your conclusions are probably true; I am just not sure the data bear them out.

Joseph F. Coates: Suppose your data had worked out quite contrary to what you found — suppose in all cases you had an unequivocal effect. Could you describe for us what this would have meant? Just run through a little scenario about what an effect would have amounted to. You see, my client has great difficulty understanding numbers of the sort that you've presented. If you could describe what it would have meant to find an effect, and then say this, as a minimum, *didn't* happen, it would make things clearer.

S. Wright: One might suppose that all the effects were negative. Then what we would have concluded is that, between 1960 and 1970, there were population or housing declines as a result of disaster events, holding all else constant. But it is hard to answer the question, because we don't find many statistically significant effects.

Coates: Yes, but I'm asking you to say something about how close your findings are to the thresholds. It seems to me that is a far more interesting way to present the data. The question is, have you just missed the thresholds; that is, if you had only slightly larger effects, would they be statistically significant, and if so, would that change the story?

Price: Considering the figures in Table 4, for example, if your hurricane hit had been significant, you would have concluded that being hit by a hurricane increased the tract population by 250 people. In other words, the question is not statistical significance but practical or substantive importance.

S. Wright: The lesson from what we found is that all effects are positive but not significant; the effects shown in all tables are consistently positive. That they are not statistically significant only means there is some probability that the effects occur by chance alone.

Price: I don't think Coates is worried about the positive and negative so much as the order of magnitude. Your results suggest that being hit by a natural disaster causes an increase of a little over 200 people per tract and about 75 to 100 additional housing units. Are effects of this magnitude, even if statistically insignificant, something to worry about?

Rossi: The issue is: how big is big? From a substantive or policy viewpoint, a difference of 250 people and 75 structures in a tract of 4,000 people and 1,000 structures may or may not be something Congress should be concerned about in formulating policy.

Howard Kunreuther: I think it's even deeper than that. It seems to me Coates is saying, suppose you found effects amounting to 1,000 or 2,000 people. What would you then conclude? What policy recommendations would follow? The client wants to know what the effects mean for the actions to be taken.

Roy Popkin: Would it have made a difference if Hurricane Camille had happened in 1963 instead of 1969? As it was, it was one of the two worst hurricanes in the century, but it was at the tail end of your census period. Do you think that if Camille had struck several years earlier, you might have found substantially different results?

S. Wright: Camille is at the head, not the tail, of the period. If anything, we expected that the effects would be *more* pronounced the closer to 1970 the disaster occurred (for example, shorter available recovery time until T_2). As for hurricane effects in general, the growth in coastal areas during the period, even adjusting for other conditions or characteristics of the counties and tracts, was quite overwhelming and simply swamps any effect of a hurricane that destroys five houses, or even twenty-five or fifty-five in a given county.

Henry Quarantelli: Before we accept that this study shows there are no long-term macro-level effects, I'd like to point out that it taps a very limited range of phenomena — basically, certain demographic and economic features. It ignores (necessarily so, given the data base) consequences in all other institutional areas, health, politics, and so on. So before we agree with Kunreuther that we've got to look at the micro level, consider whether we should leave the macro level yet. SADRI's study examines only a very limited range of possible macro effects. (And their finding, by the way, is not very surprising. Studies of the rebuilding of cities after World War II found exactly the same thing in Germany and Japan. So what SADRI finds has basically been found before in disasters of considerably greater magnitude than natural disasters.) In short, I don't want to leave the macro level before somebody looks for other kinds of effects.

A second point: there is the notion that, according to this study, threats of disasters have no effects, because not enough homes are damaged, too few people are killed, and so forth. But disasters sometimes have effects even when they do *not* occur. An example is Three Mile Island, a potential disaster that did not occur but that I suggest is going to have fundamental impacts on American society. Also consider hurricane- and flood-prone areas that are frequently threatened. Maybe they never actually experience the disaster, but that does not mean they don't experience the consequences of the continual disaster threat.

My third point rephrases a point that Kunreuther raised. He said that people don't want to take action before a disaster strikes. I think this is empirically incorrect: if one looks at the history of disaster planning in this country, it is a different world now than it was even a decade ago, so somebody's doing something somewhere along the line. But, more important, there are obviously conditions under which people in groups take action and there are other conditions under which they don't. In general, they will take action if they feel threatened. One should try to specify the conditions under which this proposition holds.

Finally, while this of course was not the focus of your study, there can be serious disaster effects at levels higher than the community. The community is not the highest macro level; above it is a super-macro level (for example, the federal government) that disasters often influence.

Kunreuther: Can I get a clarification on what you [Quarantelli] meant when you said there were changes over the last ten years in how people behave? What exactly do you see happening?

Quarantelli: For example, ten years ago, relatively few American communities had disaster plans or emergency operations centers (EOCs). Now most American communities have communitywide disaster planning of some sort. The FDAA data show, I think, that there are EOCs now in a great majority of communities.

Hirst Sutton: I am anxious to know what implications Kunreuther's comments have for SADRI's preliminary report. SADRI seems to welcome the opportunity for another grant to pursue the so-called micro study, the victim study. Is it not hazardous to disseminate the present findings, implying no new policy needs, until something like the victim study is done?

Rossi: The report emphasizes that we are not discussing micro-level phenomena, such as people, firms, classes, and sectors. We are talking about the need for a policy that deals with disaster effects on neighborhoods, municipalities, and counties.

James D. Wright: When we began this project, we assumed these were policy-relevant units. But clearly others are also relevant. Anyone who derives a contrary conclusion from the report simply has not read it. In retrospect, now that these results are in, it seems obvious that many of the micro-level questions are probably far more important, or should be, in policy formulation. Perhaps it is the measure of our success that this was *not at all* obvious when we started the project.

Our report does suggest implications for the micro study. The concept of the impact ratio implies that the effects of disasters on individuals and families will be serious and negative.

Sutton: Some of Kunreuther's comments about hazard reduction measures may prove self-defeating. Perhaps we really don't accomplish much betterment through some of these approaches in other areas. Has revenue sharing in general been a good idea? Are we any better off trying to use these approaches in the hazard area? Kunreuther recommends shifting some of the burden to state and local levels, but the administration of disaster programs has become increasingly complex and centralized, and the programs themselves now encompass everything from terrorism to civil defense to natural and man-made disasters. Many of these phenomena are clearly beyond the capacity of local government to deal with and result from national and international policies and resources decisions, about which local government has very little to say. So why should they be made to pay?

Gary A. Kreps: My interpretation of Kunreuther's point is that the micro-level studies can examine equity issues in a way that SADRI's study cannot, that is, through evaluation studies of the equity of postdisaster assistance. The problem Quarantelli raises concerns the proper subject of the evaluation. Should we study Small Business Administration loans or the distribution of mental health services or mobile homes, or what? What are the *specific* equity issues we need to examine, and how do the local priorities here mesh with federal priorities? Equity has a different meaning at each political level.

Kunreuther: If this study says there really are no serious, enduring impacts of disasters on communities, legislatures and others thinking about what steps to take next may misread the message as: we don't have to worry about disasters. That is the research community's information-processing problem. My feeling is that this may well happen to SADRI's study unless the report says boldly that there are other serious research issues still outstanding. And what, after all, are the stated implications of the report? That we need better data. We all agree on that. That we need to understand distributional effects in communities. Again, we all agree. That many disasters are smallish events with few enduring effects on whole counties or tracts. There is relatively little here about what should or should not be done on a policy level. SADRI's stated policy implications seem appropriately modest.

Ugo Morelli: I am concerned about the lack of current data. We are examining the results of a study, trying to draw some fairly significant conclusions from data that are nine to nineteen years old. In the 1960s we had much different legislation and a different set of expectations. Disaster victims today seem to expect more from federal, state, and local government than they did in the 1960s, and certainly government provides more. So if further research is to be done in this area, we need to do it using more current data.

A second point that has not been previously made: one possible reading of the no-effects finding is that impact areas in U.S. communities for 1960–1970 disasters have been thoroughly rebuilt in the same small-area location, the tract. Your study thus documents, very specifically, that we are perpetuating the hazard risk in the process of reconstruction. The report should emphasize that this phenomenon was occurring in the 1960s and continues today. Often areas are rebuilt three or four or five times, always after the same hazard losses in the same physical area. Many of us suspected this, and now we have documentation for it.

Michael Ornstein: Kunreuther's presentation refers to the "trade-off" between equity and cost. I wonder whether there is any necessary trade-off here. The implication of trade-off in this context is that more expensive programs will necessarily be more equitable, which seems unlikely. And it is also not at all clear that disaster relief is the best way to try to achieve large measures of social equity anyway. Another consideration is that if the federal government is paying for disaster relief out of its general tax revenues, the relief system cannot be more equitable that the tax system as a whole. Finally, shifting the hazard responsibility to local jurisdiction might be more equitable, but it might also be much less equitable. Perhaps a better reason for this shift is that, if the costs are borne by local jurisdictions, they may become more likely to take risk-mitigative action. As long as all relief is federal and there are no local costs, then there is no incentive to mitigate the risk, whereas if the local jurisdiction bears the cost, there is such an incentive.

Kenneth Prewitt: I would like to raise some questions about the purpose and advisability of the so-called micro study. First, I doubt that the equity/efficiency distinction should be superimposed on the macro/micro distinction, as we seem to be doing. A given disaster policy could be either inefficient or inequitable at any level from individuals up, so these concepts are independent.

More pointedly, there may be individual-level disaster effects, which a micro study could explore, and there may be community-level effects, which the SADRI study explores. But there is a level of effect which has not been explored in this data base, and indeed probably could not be explored in any extant data base, that is, effects on the system as a whole. We have a very intertwined national economic structure, with communications, transportation, and economic systems criss-crossing the nation.

When a disaster hits at a particular point, its costs may ripple through the rest of the system in subtle and diffuse, but not uncostly, ways. For example, I have been associated for the last several years with a national survey organization. When a disaster hits one of our sampling points, it costs us money. We have to absorb that cost or pass it on, if possible, to the survey client. Sooner or later, somebody pays. Thus, there is a network of institutions that somehow absorb the costs of disaster; they sustain effects of some sort that probably should be studied. Perhaps we are making a mistake to think exclusively about a data base for the micro level. Perhaps we should think about a very complicated national accounting system that would detect the ways in which hazard costs are absorbed by, and strain, various institutions in the society.

Hal Cochrane: I have been working on your impact ratio concept recently in a study of housing markets in disaster communities. I found that for Hurricane Betsy there was no impact at all: there was no change in the housing market in the postdisaster period. But when I looked at smaller places, such as Xenia and Rapid City, I did see an effect, which makes some sense, given the notion of impact ratio. I have also looked at large earthquakes around the world and tried to assess their impact on national economic performance. Here too I have found effects: they do not last very long, only two or three years, but in certain instances there is a reduction of about 10 percent in the gross national domestic product. I thus suggest that SADRI's focus on *long-term* impacts ignores possible short-term disruptions, which can in fact be sizable and disruptive. These short-term disruptions also show up in the housing study, with effects lasting one and a half to three years. SADRI's ten-year time frame, that is, might miss an important class of disaster effects.

Coates: Your macro conclusions seem quite dramatic and have potentially large policy implications. For the record, then, could you just state the five or six most important macro concerns that your study is *irrelevant* to?

J. Wright: As Morelli points out, the study is irrelevant to any policy in effect after 1970, which effectively means all current policy. The study is also irrelevant to any short-term effects, such as those Cochrane has just discussed. As he says, there may be disruptions of one and a half to three years in housing markets or some short-term disruption in economic production that our study would never pick up. The study is irrelevant to effects on variables other than those in the 1960 and 1970 censuses. Community integration, morale, and prevailing levels of mental health are examples. Finally, the study is irrelevant to the effects of disasters on aggregations smaller than census tracts — city blocks, families, particular firms, individuals, and so on.

Frederick L. Bates: Many of the comments have asked, essentially, whether there really is an effect that you are not measuring. I would like to accept that your results are valid, that there *is* no long-term effect, and ask what this means. Why is there no effect? What does the finding say about the hazard policy and practices employed in the 1960s? Your findings show that impact areas are effectively restored within ten years. But which policy, which practice, which set of activities, leads to this restoration? Perhaps public policy has negative effects that individual efforts overcome. Many other processes can be imagined that would ultimately produce SADRI's no-effect finding. Many of us seem to be worried that you have closed this field of research once and for all, whereas, in fact, you have opened up a much larger set of more precisely formulated questions. And maybe the least interesting question is whether or not there is an effect. Perhaps the most interesting question is how the noneffect is produced. The SADRI study does not tell us which policies or organizational practices produce the noneffect.

Annabelle B. Motz: I am concerned about the variables used in the analysis, for example, "percent in manufacturing." My observation is that in the past decade, in areas that were flooded, in particular, many small businesses were driven out, and manufacturing became concentrated in the hands of a few firms. That kind of effect, although obviously important, is not reflected in a variable such as percent in manufacturing. Also, there may have been important political changes in these communities that your results do not reflect. Have you looked at the most important variables?

On the other hand, I commend SADRI for getting census tract data on disaster impact areas. This should help us move on to the next step: looking at just what part of the community is hit — the industrial sector, the commercial sector, or the residential sector — and how the ensuing effects might vary across sectors.

Leik: It is always easy to suggest that other variables be included, but I wonder if it would be possible to analyze contiguous but unhit tracts, that is, tracts next door to the hit. That would provide a kind of natural control group. Also, would it have been possible to get data on the influx of relief dollars into the hit area?

J. Wright: At best, down to the county level, and then only very imprecisely. Allocating damage or relief monies to the level of census tracts is impossible.

Rossi: On Leik's first point, we experimented with respecifying the hit — enlarging it, narrowing it — to see the impacts associated with different definitions. Nothing occurred. The suggestion to use adjacent tracts as the control for natural growth is well taken, but we accomplished the same end with the general growth model we employed. That model, in effect, gives us expected population and housing values for any tract — values that reflect the general growth trends for the SMSA, region, and so on.

S. Wright: Appendix C in *After the Cleanup* reports on one experiment we did on hit specifications. In this case we compared the hit, as designated by our methods, to the true hit, as designated by a large-scale, highly detailed map of the empirical flood. The regression coefficients for the hit dummy are essentially the same under both specifications.

J. Wright: Also, in this one case where we did have a detailed and accurate map of the actual flood area (for the 1969 San Bernardino and Riverside floods) our methods produced an underinclusive hit; that is, the hit shown by our methods was narrower than the true hit. Our assumption was that it would go the other way, so we were very pleased with this outcome.

Thomas E. Drabek: I have a question about the disasters you decided to include in your analysis. Footnote 2 of the paper gives the severity criterion you employed: the sum of twice the houses destroyed, plus the number with major damage, had to exceed fifty. So in a census tract, the smallest level of analysis, if ten houses were destroyed and thirty had major damage, the disaster would be included. My question is, did you really anticipate that over a ten-year period you might detect some effect for that kind of small, one-shot impact? In other words, is this really a study of *disasters*?

J. Wright: The criterion is even looser: since the threshold applies to whole counties, not tracts, the damage index of fifty would usually be dispersed among many tracts. And the answer to your question is clearly no: most of these events are *not* disasters. That's the conclusion we reached after a year and half of work: most of these things are modest ripples.

Drabek: Did you try to shift your threshold for some of the analysis to look at the effects of real disasters?

Rossi: In some analyses we entered variables reflecting the gross seriousness of each disaster. In these regressions neither the hit dummy nor the continuous seriousness variable yielded significant coefficients. We also did some individual analyses of the most serious disasters, including the Topeka tornado. These analyses also did not show us very much.

Coates: Is there not, then, a problem of misleading advertising in the title of your paper? You are dealing not with disasters at all, but with a series of routine, natural events that are of no real public policy consequence.

J. Wright: Most of the hits in question are either SBA declarations, or presidential declarations, or both, and nearly all elicited a Red Cross response. So there is clearly *some* policy relevance. We have analyzed roughly the upper 5 percent of the severity distribution. Now if your point is that even the upper 5 percent lops off a significant share of relatively trivial phenomena, then you have only restated a main conclusion of the report. If we looked just at the true catastrophes of the decade, we would end up, again, with three or four case studies.

Bates: Maybe the implication of this discussion is that we do not yet know what a disaster is. Perhaps what we really need is a better classification system, a taxonomy of hazard events that differentiates between the routine phenomena you have investigated and the true catastrophes. I think we would all agree that we cannot research the effects of disasters on any variable at any level of aggregation until we can state precisely what a disaster is.

PART TWO
The State
and Local Politics
of Natural Hazards

THE POLITICS OF
NATURAL DISASTER:
STATE AND LOCAL ELITES*

James D. Wright and Peter H. Rossi

INTRODUCTION

The environmental hazards to which human civilization is prey are among the most awesome forces to be observed on the surface of the planet. Slight movements of the earth's crust create earthquakes so powerful that large structures are toppled like so many dominoes. Tornadoes, of which there are perhaps 1,000 per year in the United States, shatter houses with consummate ease and lift cars, mobile homes, cattle, and other objects miles into the air and scatter them haphazardly over the landscape. The forces associated with hurricanes drive the sea itself hundreds of yards onto the land, sweeping away beaches, highways, and structures. A raging flash flood, such as the infamous Big Thompson Canyon flood, will scour the earth down to bedrock, at the same time removing any accretions of human activity that happen to have been on the surface. Compared to the total energies released in even a moderate earthquake or hurricane, the most devastating explosives devised by man are puny. At no time is the frailty of human existence so apparent as in the aftermath of a natural disaster.

The magnitude of such events, the energies involved, and their intrinsic unpredictability make the possibilities for controlling the events severely limited. There is little technology can do to prevent the rains from falling or the winds from blowing, and there is nothing we can do that will seriously alter the geology, hydrology, or meteorology of the earth. Our response to environmental hazards must therefore, of necessity, assume one of two forms: either we take steps to avoid disasters in advance, or we develop measures to deal with their effects in the aftermath. Controlling, much less preventing, the events themselves is well beyond present and any likely future technology.

*This summary of the Social and Demographic Research Institute's (SADRI's) disaster politics study constitutes the first chapter from the final report, *The Apathetic Politics of Natural Hazards*. The oral summary was presented by James Wright.

Solutions to the problems posed by environmental hazards, in short, require more than convenient technological "fixes," and it is for this precise reason that there is a politics of natural hazards in the first place. In the end, we deal with the problem, if at all, by influencing the behavior of individuals, groups, and communities vulnerable to the risk of these hazards, so our solutions must be inherently political, not technological. If we cannot prevent rivers from flooding, perhaps we can prevent people from locating in flood-prone areas; if we cannot prevent the winds from blowing, perhaps we can persuade people to build structures that withstand severe winds; and if we cannot prevent the earth from quaking, perhaps we can at least minimize the inevitable havoc by limiting the development of areas with high seismic risks. In sum, while we cannot prevent or control the events themselves, we *can* control, at least in principle, their impact on human activity and civilization.

Unfortunately, many of the political solutions to the problems of environmental hazards that we might imagine come into direct and immediate conflict with other legitimate human values. We could, for example, eliminate the loss of life and property from flood by evacuating low-lying areas contiguous to rivers. Yet virtually all the major cities in the nation are built up around rivers, because, historically, cities depended on the rivers for commerce and transportation. Evacuating the people and property living in flood-prone areas, while obviously possible, would require nothing less than complete transformation of the social and physical ecology of the contemporary American urban scene. Likewise, we could avoid the hurricane hazard by depopulating coastal areas from Texas to Maine. Yet, in Florida alone, there are some 7.5 million people living in coastal counties and thus facing some level of hurricane risk. We could greatly lessen earthquake hazard in San Francisco by removing parapets, cornices, and old hazardous structures, but in so doing we would likewise destroy much of the city's elegance and charm. Whenever we take political steps to deal with environmental risk, in short, we find potential conflict and the need for compromise and trade-off. We trade some degree of safety from hurricane off against the fine luxuries of oceanfront living, or we trade some degree of safety from flood off against the costs of abandoning an expensive urban infrastructure, or we trade some degree of seismic safety off against the obvious attractions of San Francisco and Los Angeles. And while the options open to us are typically clear-cut, the "best" choice among them often is not. As in all other problem areas requiring essentially political solutions, then, dealing with environmental hazards poses a transparent potential for conflict and rancor.

The study whose results are reported here was undertaken to assess the current political environment surrounding the management of natural hazard risk, especially at the level of state and local governments. There are many measures any state or local community could take to lessen the risk its citizens face from environmental hazards. Some states and communities have already taken many of these steps and are quite advanced in their environmental risk management; other states and communities have taken some steps; still others have done practically nothing at all. What accounts for the variation across states and localities in their willingness to deal with environmental hazards? In virtually every state and every local community we find some partisan groups actively working toward hazard risk mitigation goals, other groups in active and contentious opposition, and still other groups for whom the entire issue is a matter of little or no concern. How do the major sectors of state and local power structures line up on these issues? What degree of political influence does each group bring into the battle? As we discuss later, the policy options open to governments for dealing with natural hazards are relatively few in number (at least at the conceptual, if not operational, level). Which of the available options tend to be preferred among the political influentials and elected decision makers who will ultimately formulate, implement, and enforce state and local policies in this area? And where, finally, does environmental hazard fall on the agenda of state and local political concerns? Is this a high-priority item, something state and local decision makers are worried about, or are there more pressing concerns that occupy the bulk of their political attention? These and many related questions constitute the substantive content of the research reported here.

Our conclusions are based primarily on a survey that we conducted in the summer of 1977. All told, we surveyed more than 2,000 political elites in a sample of 20 states and 100 local communities across the nation. Respondents were chosen for the survey because they occupied positions of influence in state and local government or because they represented partisan groups with putative interests in the management of environmental risk. Thus, at the state level we interviewed governors; state legislators; planners; state geologists; civil defense directors; and representatives of real estate, development, insurance, and banking interests, as well as many others. At the local level our respondents included mayors and city managers; local legislators; bureaucrats in planning and zoning offices; flood control officials; public works officials; Red Cross and civil defense representatives; realtors; developers; bankers; and private sector interest groups, such as the League of Women Voters, the chamber of commerce, and the local taxpayer's association. In no sense did we attempt to obtain a random sample of state and local decision makers, much less of the general public. Our respondents were chosen quite purposively: they represent those sectors of state and local power structures that are directly responsible for formulating relevant legislative initiatives or maintain the state and local disaster preparedness and response mechanisms or have some stake, direct or indirect, in the issues posed by the management of environmental risk.

Likewise, the states and local communities that we studied were sampled with probabilities proportionate to the total population at risk from floods, tornadoes, hurricanes, and earthquakes; states and communities with larger populations and higher levels of natural hazard risk were proportionally more likely to fall into the sample. Because of the uncertainties involved in calculating hazard risk, it is difficult to be very precise about the characteristics of the ensuing state and community samples; a reasonable guess is that the twenty states in the analysis contain perhaps three-quarters of the total American population living at risk from these four natural hazards.

In sum, the study we have undertaken deals quite directly with the most influential people in the hazard risk area, people who either are or can be expected to become active in risk management issues, representing the states and localities that themselves present potentially the most serious natural hazard problems.

What *are* the policy options open to political decision makers as they consider the problem of environmental hazards? While there are no doubt hundreds or thousands of specific policy measures that might be implemented, the range of generalized approaches to the problem is quite restricted. On the increasingly attractive principle that the best government is the one that governs least, the most basic policy option is no policy at all or, what amounts to the same thing, a policy that allows individuals to assume whatever level of environmental risk they wish, as determined by their behavior in the free market for space, unrestricted by the interventions of local, state, or federal government. This policy emphasis asserts, in short, that people have the right to locate in hazardous areas if they want to, so long as they are willing to live with the consequences of that decision. A person who invests in General Motors makes a bet that the company will prosper; if this proves to be a good bet, the individual profits; if it is a bad bet, he does not; and in either case it is his, not the government's, business. Likewise, a family that chooses to live in the floodplain makes a bet that the probable return period for a destructive flood is more than the probable lifetime of their structure; again, they win if this is a good bet and lose if it is not, and in either case it remains none of the government's business. One is hard-pressed to imagine a more appropriate forum for this viewpoint than the eminently conservative *Wall Street Journal*, which opined in the issue of May 15, 1978, that the federal government "must develop the philosophy that he who lives on the beach is a fool and the public isn't responsible for his foolish act." Or, one might add, in the floodplain, on the fault line, or on the landslide-prone hillsides. The "free market" approach to environmental risk management asserts, in short, that the government is not responsible for protecting people from their own stupidity.

Unfortunately, the matter is not quite so clear-cut as this. Lack of information, as well as stupidity, can cause people to locate in hazardous areas. "Hazardous areas" are themselves difficult to define; even at the present state of the art, hazard risk mapping is an inexact science. Unscrupulous operators can find ways to dump hazardous properties on naive and unsuspecting buyers. And even the most risk-aversive individuals cannot avoid environmental hazards altogether; the rains and winds and geology and so on are ubiquitous across the earth's surface, and no one can live entirely free of their possible untoward effects.

For these and other complicated reasons, the free market, when it has been allowed to do so, has historically tended to place enough people and their properties in areas of high environmental risk that over a sufficiently large area (say, the United States) or long time span (say, a decade), some sizable fraction of the population has necessarily and inevitably suffered catastrophic losses because they happened to be in the path of a horrifying, unpredictable, and largely uncontrollable event. And while it is easy enough to be tough-minded about these things before the fact, it has proven extremely difficult to maintain this attitude in the aftermath of a serious disaster. Who among us would feel comfortable telling a family that was just wiped out by flood that it is their own fault or that they ought not to have lived there in the first place? The impulse to come to the assistance of families and communities ravaged by disaster, to aid and comfort to the extent possible, and to help in their restoration seems fundamental in the human experience.

Providing relief and rehabilitation assistance in the aftermath of a disaster is thus the second major policy option for dealing with environmental hazards. Historically, victims of disasters have turned to governments for postdisaster aid, mainly because only governments command the resources necessary to deal with the aftermath problems of a serious disaster event. And, for the most part, governments have responded generously, at least in modern times. In the United States the history of a formal, sustained disaster relief policy can be traced to 1950 and the passage of the Disaster Relief Act (PL 81-875) in that year. Prior to that legislation, there was, for all practical purposes, no ongoing federal disaster policy to speak of (excepting, of course, a policy of building flood control structures in high-risk areas, which dates to the Flood Control Act of 1936), certainly none that would compare with the increasingly comprehensive disaster relief policies that followed. Prior to 1950, the major source of postdisaster assistance was that supplied by the American National Red Cross, a private voluntary association operating under federal sanction. Such federal disaster legislation as there was in the pre-1950 era was invariably ad hoc in nature, consisting mainly of bills passed in the immediate aftermath of major catastrophes, with provisions applying just to the particular disaster.

In the quarter-century following PL 81-875, "the Federal government has assumed a leading role in disaster relief" (Kunreuther 1973, p. 4). The document entitled "Digest of Federal Disaster Assistance Programs," which merely lists (with brief descriptions) the disaster assistance programs

currently operated by the federal government, runs to 126 pages! The legislation described therein reflects a history of increasingly liberal benefits for an
increasingly broadly defined victim population, with the policy emphasis on
relief, assistance, and rehabilitation in a disaster's aftermath.

These policy trends culminate in the Disaster Relief Act of 1974
(PL 93-288), the enabling legislation for most of the present federal disaster
relief effort. PL 93-288 provides, among many other services, $250,000
grants to each of the fifty states to conduct studies of their hazard problems,
direct grants of up to $5,000 for individuals and families suffering loss in a
disaster, low-cost Small Business Administration (SBA) loans for losses not
covered through the grant-in-aid provision, grants to local communities to
rebuild damaged public works, mental health counseling for disaster
victims, and so on. The operant principle underlying these policies is that
victimized individuals, businesses, and communities should be restored as
quickly and fully as possible to their predisaster conditions.

The basic effect of policies emphasizing government assistance in the
postdisaster period is to lift the burden of environmental risk from the
shoulders of the individuals and communities that, through their behavior,
have assumed it, and spread that risk evenly over the entire taxpaying
population. Through the mechanism of postdisaster relief, in short,
environmental risk is socialized, and all individuals, whether or not they live
at risk, assume some share of the total burden. Because of this, the argument
is increasingly heard that such policies pose perverse and counterproductive
incentives: in brief, postdisaster relief provisions punish risk averters and
reward risk takers; the wise and cautious, that is, are made to pay for the
folly, shortsightedness, and simple bad luck of others. Thus, these policies
encourage the rehabitation of hazardous areas after disaster has struck,
because they absolve individuals from any responsibility for the risk. The
message these policies are alleged to convey is that one can freely build and
rebuild in hazardous areas, because the government will always be there to
shoulder the losses whenever disaster strikes again. The possibility of these
kinds of perversities has caused many policymakers at all levels of government to consider alternative strategies for managing natural hazard risks.

A third option, of course, is to do what one can to contain or control the
hazard in the first place. This is possible, at least to some extent, in the case of
water-borne hazards (if not air- or earth-borne hazards) and has typically
involved the construction of so-called structural mitigations, such as dams,
levees, channels, seawalls, and other like structures that would contain
excess water and prevent ensuing floods. As noted above, this approach to
the management of flood risk has been an element of federal hazard policy at
least since the New Deal. The appeal of the approach, of course, is that it
entails a technological "fix" that works by itself, with or without a specific
behavior on the part of individuals or communities. This approach has the

additional advantage, typically, of involving large construction projects that create numerous employment opportunities, and sometimes they simultaneously solve other serious problems as well, such as problems with community water supplies or lack of recreational opportunities. So these structural mitigation approaches have historically proven very attractive as techniques for managing water-borne hazards.

But here too there are serious potential problems, including the untoward environmental effects of such large-scale structures. More important, such an approach may pose many of the same perverse incentives that are posed by postdisaster relief policies. By definition, flood control structures of any type encourage, rather than discourage, habitation of the floodplains. Further, any such structure must be designed to some standard, the standard being the largest disaster event that can be contained by the structure. And while it may protect admirably against events at or below the design standard, it may exacerbate the destruction caused by events that *exceed* the design standard, and sooner or later, of course, a flood bigger than the design flood is bound to occur. For this reason, enthusiasm for structural approaches to water risk mitigation has begun to wane, at least in some federal policymaking circles.

Unwilling to do nothing, as the free marketeers would counsel, yet equally unwilling to live with the possibly counterproductive consequences of structural mitigation measures or policies emphasizing postdisaster relief, policymakers have begun to consider so-called nonstructural mitigation measures as possible supplements or alternatives to the more traditional approaches. Chief among the nonstructural options is land use management in areas of high environmental risk. Here the term "land use management" is broadly construed to include not just standard planning and zoning practices but also building and construction standards. The general idea behind this approach is to prevent development in hazardous areas in the first place or to assure that the structures that are built are designed to withstand environmentally hazardous events.

Nonstructural hazard risk mitigation is the new wave in natural disaster policy. Prominent examples are the National Flood Insurance Program (NFIP), the Coastal Zone Management Program, and the Earthquake Hazards Reduction Act of 1977, all of which emphasize land use management. The present and likely future commitment of the nation to these nonstructural approaches to the management of environmental risk is evidenced quite emphatically in a recent communication from President Carter to four of his cabinet officials:

> For many years, nonstructural measures to reduce flood damage have not been given as much emphasis...as structural measures. Nonstructural alternatives are often more cost-effective and less environmentally damaging

than structural measures. Therefore, there is a need to emphasize nonstructural measures, including land acquisition, with existing Federal Programs
where consistent with primary program purposes. To accomplish this objective, I am directing your respective Departments to utilize existing programs
to encourage the use of nonstructural floodplain management practices.

On the surface, these nonstructural approaches have much to recommend
them; beneath the surface, they reveal many of the same problems that
plague other approaches. We have discussed this issue elsewhere and merely
summarize here.[1] Federal land acquisition, as suggested in Carter's memo-
randum, was tried experimentally in Rapid City after the devastating 1976
flash flood. Basically, the government attempted to purchase the entire
floodplain at predisaster values, the cost of which worked out to some
$12,000 *per capita*, that is, for every man, woman, and child in the city.
So the land acquisition alternative is not a cheap one. And there is a related
problem, especially in cities: when some areas of a city are declared off limits
to development for hazard risk management or any other purposes, the
alternatives are then either to build elsewhere or not to build at all. For areas
that are already heavily developed, which includes, obviously, most cities,
the first alternative adds to urban sprawl and the second amounts to a no-
growth policy. Most cities will find both these options equally unattractive.

There is yet another problem, one that relates directly to issues posed by
our research. Nonstructural approaches to hazard risk management, unlike
most other approaches, require the active cooperation of state and local
governments. The right to regulate the uses of land is left by the Constitution
to the states; most states, in turn, delegate these authorities to local government bodies. Thus, one cannot take a land use management approach to
flood or earthquake hazard unless local communities can be persuaded to
pass and then enforce the relevant legislation. Enforcement, in turn,
requires a heavy administrative commitment: maps designating hazardous
areas must be drawn and information about them disseminated, zoning laws
must be passed and protected from the incessant nibbling of variances and
appeals, inspection cycles must be frequent, offenders must be punished. In
short, the effectiveness of these nonstructural or land use approaches turns,
almost entirely, on the zeal with which local governments administer and
enforce them. Here it is appropriate to interject the observation that local
government often seems incapable of effectively administering virtually any
human service, and there is no a priori reason why hazard risk management
would be an exception.

The choice among available policy options in the hazard risk area, in
short, is not an easy or clear-cut one. Some options seem coldhearted and

---

[1]See Rossi, Wright, and Wright, "Social Science and Natural Hazards: *Assessment of
Research on Natural Hazards* Reassessed in Light of the SADRI Disaster Research
Program," in Part Three of this volume.

cruel, others appear to increase rather than decrease the overall level of hazard risk, and still others depend for their effectiveness on the actions of government units that may be unenthusiastic or even hostile. What course, then, *should* the nation steer as it formulates its environmental hazard policies?

Our evidence on how state and local political influentials feel about this topic is that most are greatly attracted to traditional policy approaches. Of the options we presented to them, the most favored is that emphasizing structural mitigations, and the second most favored is that emphasizing postdisaster relief. Nonstructural approaches, in contrast, are rejected by a small majority, as is an approach emphasizing compulsory, government-subsidized hazard insurance. Thus, among the political influentials in our sample, traditional policies are preferred over the new policy directions. It can also be mentioned that the free market approach, while rejected by a clear majority, was strongly favored by one-tenth of the respondents, and was appealing at some level to more than one-third. So there is a sizable minority view among state and local elites that the federal government might just as well stay out of the hazards area altogether, and a substantial majority believe that traditional policies of structural mitigation and postdisaster relief represent the most appropriate policy responses. The distinct lack of enthusiasm for nonstructural measures among the persons who will eventually have to implement and enforce them does not, in our view, bode well for the future of such policies in the United States.

At the same time, the survey offers considerable evidence that natural hazard issues are not especially salient in most states and communities at the present time. There are, at any given instant, a handful of communities and states that have just suffered a serious disaster, and in many of these communities and states hazard risk management is a high-priority item. But, for obvious reasons, the largest share of communities and states will *not* have had a recent serious disaster experience, and these areas are much less concerned about environmental hazards. A second important finding is that the majority of our respondents tell us they could take an exact opposite position on the management of hazard risk (for example, they could switch from opposition toward to support of postdisaster relief approaches) and thereby do no serious harm to their political positions. The attitudinal data, in short, appear to be much firmer than they actually are; most elites in states and local communities seem free to move around on these issues, more or less as they please. So the potential opposition to new wave measures, as noted in the previous paragraph, is just that — a potential whose realization, we think, will depend very much on how the issues are phrased and how the policy options are presented.

The preference for traditional over nonstructural approaches is not uniform across the elites in the sample; some groups prove predictably more favorable than others to nonstructural mitigation concepts. In general, elites most favorable to such approaches include what we call "hazard specialists"—persons whose positions involve them quite intimately and directly with environmental hazards (such as civil defense or Red Cross personnel). A second supportive group consists of what we call "supralocal" or "suprastate" elites—persons in the states and local communities whose primary interests or constituencies lie elsewhere. Supralocal elites include the Regional Alliance of Local Government, the local Red Cross, and the local chapter of the League of Women Voters; suprastate elites are state representatives of the Farmer's Home Administration, the Small Business Administration, or the Federal Insurance Administration. Again, the outlooks of hazard specialists and these supra elites are reasonably distinctive: they tend to favor nonstructural mitigation concepts and to oppose more traditional risk management policies.

At the opposite pole, we find representatives of the real estate and development sectors to be consistently most opposed to nonstructural approaches and to favor strongly more traditional policies.

Between the hazard specialists at one pole and the developers at the other lie most of the major opinion leaders to be found in state and local governments—executives, legislators, the media, business interests, and so on. None of these groups is as enthusiastic about nonstructural mitigation as the hazard specialists; likewise, none seems as clearly opposed to such measures as real estate and development interests. Their outlooks on the management of hazard risk are, for the most part, uncrystallized; a good bet is that they will move in whatever direction the political winds are blowing. In any case, it seems reasonably clear that the ultimate fate of hazard management policies at state and local levels will depend much more on how these (largely undecided) elites eventually view the issue than on the present lineup of political forces.

Our most compelling direct evidence of the low salience of hazard management issues is that, for the most part, political decision makers in the states and local communities do *not* see environmental hazards as a very serious problem, particularly in comparison to the many other problems that these government units are expected to be doing something about. We asked each respondent to rate the seriousness of eighteen potential state and local problems, including five environmental hazard problems. In all states and communities the most serious problems reported are inflation, welfare, unemployment, and crime; the least serious (at least in the minds of our respondents) are fires, floods, hurricanes, tornadoes, and earthquakes. It is an interesting fact that, in the aggregate, pornography is seen as a somewhat *more* serious problem than any of these natural hazards; only "race relations" and "too much economic growth" are considered less serious than floods (rated as the most serious of the five hazards we asked about). (Parallel data for the population of nine cities in California suggest that the general public shares this view of the relative seriousness of natural hazard problems.) From these results it would seem to follow that environmental hazard problems will *not* compete very strongly against other state and local problems for a share of finite and dwindling resources.

As with the policy preferences, the seriousness attributed to hazard problems varies across elite groupings, again in the predictable manner. Hazard specialists tend to see these problems as relatively more serious, real estate and development interests as less serious, with other elites arrayed in between. An interesting finding is that hazard specialists also tend to *understate* the seriousness of nonhazard problems, relative to the seriousness attributed to these problems by other groups. Thus, the hazard specialists tend to inflate the seriousness of problems that most elites see as rather trivial (namely, the hazard problems) and deflate the seriousness of other problems that most elites regard as the most serious problems facing the community or the state.

In general, the best predictor of the seriousness attributed to hazard problems is prior experience with disaster; this holds at all levels of aggregation. Thus, respondents who have personally experienced a flood see flooding as a more serious problem than those who have not; likewise, at the aggregate level, flooding is seen to be a more serious problem in states and communities that have recently experienced one than in states and communities that have not. However, neither prior experience with disasters nor the seriousness attributed to them predicts policy preferences, contrary to what one might have expected. The apparent lesson is that disaster experience raises the salience of hazard management issues and causes persons to take the problem more seriously, but it does not create any firm consensus on what policy options to pursue. An interesting implication is that it may prove most difficult to implement new wave hazard management measures in states and communities with the most serious hazard problems. In states and communities with little or no disaster experience the salience of the issue is so low that virtually any measure could be instituted without opposition; in states and communities with extensive disaster histories everyone may agree that "something must be done," but they may not agree on what.

Another interesting pattern is that problems in general, and hazard problems in particular, are considered more serious by state elites than by local elites; in other words, the seriousness attributed to the problem seems to vary by the level of political aggregation, such that seriousness increases among larger political units. Why this might be is not hard to understand. The disaster problems of any given state are an agglomeration of all the specific disaster problems of each of the communities in the state, just as the federal disaster problem is an agglomeration of fifty state disaster problems. Thus, *objectively*, virtually any problem becomes more prevalent and hence more serious the larger the political unit from whose perspective it is viewed. But the further implication in this case—not a comforting one—is that different political units may well have sharply differing views on how a hazard risk ought to be managed. From the federal perspective, for example, the flood problem may be serious enough to warrant large-scale, highly intrusive, even rather expensive risk mitigation measures; from the local perspective, these measures may appear to be capricious, inequitable, and possibly even counterproductive. In some cases, then, conflict among the different levels of government over how to manage environmental hazards may well be inherent in the nature of the problem itself.

A key, if obvious, implication of this point is confirmed by data from the survey on the victimization of individuals, communities, and states by the four major natural hazards. As would be expected, states are more prone to victimization by any of these disasters than are local communities, if only because they present larger targets in the first place. Further, the estimated return probabilities for another serious disaster in the next ten years are everywhere higher among states than among local communities. Thus, compared to communities, states regard their hazard problems more seriously, are more likely to have been hit by a serious disaster in the recent past, get hit by serious disasters more often given that they are hit at least once, and have higher expectations for a repeat disaster. These results make it plain that hazard management is a far more pressing issue for state governments than for local governments; by implication, it is more pressing at the federal level than at the level of any particular state. One possible consequence of this pattern, which tends to be confirmed in the historical record, is that policy innovations and directives will originate at higher governmental levels, typically the federal level, and then be imposed upon lower levels. This pattern, we believe, does not augur well for the future of those risk management policies, such as nonstructural mitigation, that depend critically on the cooperation and active support of lower level governments.

Among individual respondents, we find that victimization by hurricane is the most common form of disaster experience, partly a function of the large number of coastal states falling into the sample. Next to hurricanes, floods represent the most common form of personal disaster experience, followed distantly by tornadoes and earthquakes. All told, roughly 90 percent of the sample had experienced at least one of the four major disaster types at some point in their lives, and, of these, about half had suffered personal losses because of the experience. These results, of course, reflect lifetime disaster experience in the sample; in any given decade roughly 12 percent report suffering a disaster-related loss. Interestingly, the victimization rates estimated from these survey data exceed equivalent rates estimated from official disaster agency records by factors ranging from 3 to 8, depending on the disaster type. This suggests that a large fraction of the total disaster-victimized population does *not* receive direct disaster relief or assistance.

Each respondent reported not only on his or her personal disaster experiences but also on the major disaster experiences of the last decade in his or her community or state. At the state level, the data reflect much ambiguity among respondents as to whether the state had experienced a serious disaster or not. In about half the cases, but only half, we get 80 percent or more concensus among the elites on the state's disaster history over the previous decade; in roughly an additional third of the cases we get at least 60 percent consensus; and in the remaining cases we get no concensus at all. The lack of consensus, we think, indicates only that different respondents have different standards for what constitutes a serious disaster, and subsequent analysis tends to confirm this hunch. As one would guess, hazard specialists have rather low criteria and thus tend to report a serious disaster, even when most elites in the state do not; likewise, real estate and development interests have high criteria and tend to deny that a disaster is serious, even when most elites in the state confirm it. (Interestingly, no similar pattern was found among local elites; and there is generally more consensus among local elites about their disaster histories anyway.)

As one would expect, given the sampling strategy, most of the well-known and highly publicized disasters of the 1967-1977 decade are represented in the disaster histories of the states and communities in the sample. Among the major disaster occurrences reported by our respondents are the Lubbock tornado and the super-outbreak of tornadoes in 1974; the San Fernando earthquake of 1971; the Big Thompson Canyon flood, the 1973 Mississippi floods, and the 1976 Tulsa flood; and Hurricanes Eloise, Carmen, Beulah, Celia, and of course, Agnes—this latter being the most devastating and expensive natural disaster in the nation's history. Several dozen less well-known, "garden variety" natural disasters were, of course, also reported.

Respondents who reported a serious disaster occurrence in their state or community were asked their opinions on whether the disaster in question had had long-term effects on the community (or state). For the most part, these data tend to confirm findings from other studies of this topic (for example, Friesema et al. 1979, Wright et al. 1979): most respondents reported that most disasters did *not* have long-term effects. Flood disasters, particularly large and recent ones, constitute the main exception; many respondents reported long-term economic and, especially, policy effects of recent major floods. Still, of the eleven states reporting a serious flood in the last ten years, a majority of respondents cited a lasting economic effect in only six; the same proportion held for a long-term policy effect. Tornadoes and hurricanes are usually seen as having no long-term effects at all, except for very recent events, where the physical effects of the disaster sometimes remain noticeable.

The archetype of the new wave in federal disaster policy, of course, is the National Flood Insurance Program, first instituted in 1968 and substantially revised into its present form in 1973 and 1977. Because of the prominence of NFIP in the nation's current disaster policy arsenal, a substantial portion of the survey dealt with feelings about and reactions to the program. As of the summer of 1977, well over 90 percent of the elites at both state and local levels had at least heard of NFIP. (In contrast, about 90 percent of the California population sample had *not*.) Although most elites had at least heard of NFIP, knowledge about community participation in the program was, in general, substantially lower. Whatever the level of knowledge, however, the general run of opinion on NFIP among elites is highly favorable: nearly 90 percent at both state and local levels expressed favorable or very favorable opinions. It should be noted that favorability toward NFIP per se is very much higher than favorability toward the risk mitigation concepts that NFIP contains. As we mentioned earlier, a majority of our respondents disagree to some extent with a nonstructural mitigation emphasis, and even more reject a policy emphasizing compulsory hazard insurance, yet both are central to the NFIP policy. We have no firm explanation for this disparity; our guess is that many state and local elites have only a dim understanding of just what NFIP is all about, even though they may have at least heard of the program.

In general, respondents, communities, and states with the most favorable opinion of NFIP are those with the most extensive prior experiences with water-borne hazards, those who regard flood and hurricane problems as relatively more serious, and those who tend to agree most strongly with the NFIP risk mitigation concepts. Also, consistent with earlier results, hazard specialists at both state and local levels tend to favor NFIP somewhat more than do real estate and development representatives at both levels. Indeed, the skepticism of real estate and development elites toward NFIP comes through rather sharply in all analyses. One final pattern of some interest, given an earlier theme, is that state elites generally have more favorable attitudes toward NFIP than do local elites, even though local communities are assigned a critical role in NFIP, whereas states have a minor or non-existent role.

Although NFIP has been highly controversial in a few communities (especially in Missouri and Texas), most local elites who have at least heard of the program feel that their community's flood problem is serious enough to justify participation. Most also feel that NFIP is "fair" to the parties most directly affected, especially to homeowners living in flood-prone areas. (Real estate and development representatives, of course, feel that NFIP is less fair to all parties than do other elite groupings.) We also asked local elites from participating communities what kinds of problems NFIP had created. Most mentioned at least one or more NFIP-related problems; over the total sample of local elites from participating communities, the average respondent mentioned 3.76 problems. Consistent with all previous results, real estate and development elites mentioned far more problems on average than did other respondents. Most commonly mentioned were problems with the various maps that NFIP requires and the fact that homeowners have not expressed much interest in purchasing the insurance. Other problems often cited in discussions of NFIP—for example, that the local floodplain regulations are often "appealed" and "varianced" to death, or that the program causes ongoing development projects to be abandoned—were mentioned by only a few of our respondents. Finally, despite the controversy over NFIP in the Congress and in some local communities, only about one-tenth of our respondents reported that NFIP has sparked "much" controversy in their communities, and some 40 percent reported that it had sparked no controversy at all. Although flood insurance specialists in the Federal Insurance Administration no doubt see things differently, NFIP is *not* viewed as being (or having been) highly controversial by the local elites in currently participating communities.

Local elites in participating communities also expressed generally positive opinions about NFIP's probable effects. Over 90 percent, for example, agree that persons in flood-prone areas can now "feel more secure" knowing that flood losses will be protected through insurance, and some 70 percent feel that consciousness of flood hazards in the community will increase "now that flood-prone areas have been mapped." Most respondents also feel that the NFIP restrictions on building and development in floodplains are "about right" (rather than too strict or too lenient). In all cases, of course, real estate and development representatives are more skeptical than other respondents. Finally, about 85 percent of the respondents feel that NFIP will have a strong effect or at least some effect on construction and development in flood-prone areas over the next twenty years. (Interestingly, real estate and development respondents are just as likely as all other respondents to agree with this view, which is perhaps why they are opposed to the program in the first place.)

Many of these elite outlooks are also reflected in a special adjunct survey conducted in nine communities in the state of California, the same nine communities that are represented in the elite sample. Thus, for these nine communities, we have parallel data from 20 to 25 local elites and from a sample of 100 local residents. On all points where a direct comparison is possible, there is substantial (indeed, rather impressive) agreement between residents and their political elites. Communities with high proportions of elites favoring traditional hazard management policies also have high proportions of residents favoring the same policies. For any particular community, elites and residents also tend to agree rather closely on (1) the seriousness of hazard problems in the community, (2) the community's previous experience with natural disasters, and (3) the likely return probabilities for a repeat disaster in the next ten years. In the contemporary lingo of political sociology, there is thus a high level of "concurrence" between elites and masses, at least in California, on hazard management issues.

Thus, as among elites, California residents favor policies emphasizing postdisaster relief the most and favor the free market position the least. However, residents seem somewhat *more* in favor of nonstructural mitigation approaches than do elites (although this may just reflect differences in how the questions were worded).

The California sample was also asked about the status of various types of hazard-mitigating legislation in their particular communities (for example, whether the community had laws governing construction in areas of flood or seismic risk, or whether there were special building code provisions governing construction of buildings). Few respondents have any knowledge at all of these matters; those who do are as likely to be incorrectly informed as not.

For the most part, California residents (as well as elites) do not consider their natural hazard problems as among the most serious problems they face. Again, with the exception of drought, pornography was seen to be a more serious community problem than either floods, fires, or earthquakes. Of these three hazard types, fires were considered the most serious and floods the least (reflecting, perhaps, only that much of Southern California was burning while the survey was being conducted in the field). That earthquakes are seen by California residents to be substantially *less* serious than even pornography is, we think, a truly stunning result.

Our attempts to predict seriousness ratings and policy preferences by the California sample reveal a weak but rather interesting pattern: in general, renters, low-income respondents, and persons who have lived in the state only for a short while give greater support to nonstructural mitigation approaches and see hazard problems, especially floods, fires, and earthquakes, as more serious than do older, more affluent, and longer term state residents. Our interpretation of this finding is that the longer one has lived in the state, the more jaded one becomes about all matters related to environmental hazards; we think, in other words, that the data reflect the well-known psychological process of denial.

Although natural hazards are not seen as very serious community problems in the state, they do appear to be a source of some personal worry or concern. Many respondents seem especially concerned about the ability of local emergency services to handle the aftermath consequences of a serious disaster event. The most widespread concern is that hospitals would not be able to care adequately for all the victims, and there is a nearly equal level of concern that essential community services (such as water, sewage, and gas) would be disrupted for an extended period.

Despite their apparent concern, Californians have done little to protect themselves and their families from the possible effects of environmental hazards. First, at the time of the survey hardly anyone had even heard of NFIP, so virtually none of the respondents had yet protected themselves from flood hazard through the purchase of flood insurance. A much higher proportion (but still only about a quarter of the total) had at least considered getting earthquake insurance, which is generally available throughout the state, but only about one-tenth actually carried earthquake insurance on their property at the time of the survey. Further, about a quarter of the sample has chosen to live in some sort of high-risk location or structure — on the side of a hill, for example, at the base of a canyon, in an area surrounded by dry brush and timber, or in a mobile home; this tally does *not* include any count of persons living in floodplains or near fault lines or similar areas of disproportionate seismic risk. In the same vein, some 40 percent of the households in the sample are without a first aid kit, nearly 60 percent do not have a fire extinguisher in the house, and more than 80 percent have not installed a smoke or fire alarm.

Our concluding analyses attempt to piece together what might be called the political sociometry of environmental risk management at state and local levels by posing the following kinds of questions: who in the community (or state) is active in these issues, who is important to have on one's side, which elites are in frequent contact with which other elites, what positions have various sectors of the elite taken on these issues? At the local community level, the groups perceived as most active on issues involving "local natural disaster legislation or regulation" include, first, local elected officials, such as mayors and councilmen; second, persons responsible for managing local community infrastructure, such as planners and public works officials; and, third, hazard specialists, such as civil defense personnel, police and fire chiefs, and the local Red Cross. The chamber of commerce and local media were also seen as beng relatively active on these kinds of issues. In general, the highest levels of activity (for all groups) were reported in communities where hazard issues are considered most serious (as indexed by the aggregate "seriousness" ratings given to hazard problems), as would be expected. The data also reveal some clustering in activity levels across communities: in some communities, in other words, certain sectors of the elite are more active than in other communities. Further, the factors apparently affecting the level of activity vary from one elite sector to another. Real estate interests and public officials, for example, are most active in communities with the most salient disaster problems; local political leaders (that is, Republican and

Democratic party leaders), in contrast, react less to disaster seriousness and more to the level of local controversy surrounding hazard management issues.

Activity, of course, is only one aspect of the political sociometry; power is another. To get at varying levels of power and influence, we asked the local respondents to tell us who they would like to have on their side if they were trying to get "something enacted...on some issue concerning natural disasters." Using responses to this question we found that mayors and city councilmen are the most influential, as would be expected. Following closely are the local media. A majority of respondents also reported that they would like the local civil defense director and the chamber of commerce on their side. No other group was mentioned in this connection by more than 50 percent of the respondents. Interestingly, only a third mentioned leading industries, only 25 percent mentioned land developers, and only 22 percent mentioned the local real estate board. Also of some interest, only 29 percent of the respondents mentioned themselves as potentially important or influential.

We also asked respondents which elite groups they were in "more or less regular" contact with and found that patterns of contact tend to follow patterns of influence. Thus, groups mentioned as contacts by more than half the sample include, as above, mayors and city councilmen, the local media people, and the chamber of commerce. (The city planner, police department, public works, and fire department were also each mentioned by half or close to half the respondents). In general, individual patterns of contact with different groups vary mainly as a function of position: private sector respondents typically reported less contact across groups, public sector respondents more. For example, only about a third of the respondents reported regular contacts with bankers, land developers, or industrialists, whereas more than 70 percent claimed regular contact with members of the local city council. Hazard specialists, in particular, seem to be well outside the inner network: only 37 percent of the respondents reported regular contact with civil defense and only 23 percent reported regular contact with the local Red Cross director.

Which groups in the local community are perceived by our elites as generally favoring nonstructural mitigation approaches to the management of hazard risk? In the main, the answer is, "Hardly any." Indeed, only one group, the city planning department, is seen by at least a majority of our respondents as favoring such approaches (cited as favoring such measures by 54 percent). Others perceived as supportive of these measures by at least a third of the respondents include city councilmen, the mayor, public works officials, local conservation groups, and the civil defense director. Other groups in the community, of course, may well support such measures; it is just that our respondents don't know about it. This finding again confirms that these issues are generally not highly salient in most local communities.

The degree to which local elites are seen to favor such measures varies substantially across communities. The highest perceived elite favorability (weighted, in this case, also by the activity and importance of each group) is registered in cities with the most extensive historical experience with disasters.

A final question in the sequence asked respondents which groups influenced their own (the respondents') opinions about hazard management issues. By this measure, the most influential elite groups are again mayors and city councilmen, the local media people, city planners, the civil defense, and, surprisingly, local conservation groups. All these groups were mentioned as influential by a third or more of our respondents. In contrast, traditionally influential elites, such as bankers, industrialists, and land developers, were mentioned by relatively few respondents.

All analyses thus suggest that local elected officials—mayors and city councilmen, in particular—are the genuine "key" people in the local community when it comes to environmental risk management issues. They are seen as the most active groups, those most important to have on one's side, those most influential in respect to the views of others, and those favoring land use and building code regulations to protect against the risk of natural hazards.

A parallel set of analyses at the level of states shows that, as in the local communities, activity in the hazard area is dominated by elected officials: the governor, state house and senate leaders, and chairs of relevant commit-tees. State agencies regarded as active by the majority of the respondents include the director of civil defense, the state planning agency, the U.S. Corps of Engineers, and the National Guard. In the private sector groups considered active are insurance firms, the construction industry, conserva-tion groups, and the Red Cross director.

State public officials appear to be most active in states where the preponderance of both state and local opinion favor nonstructural mitigation measures and where NFIP is relatively popular. Public officials are also most active in the heavily populated states. The business and real estate sectors, in contrast, are most active in states with the most extensive disaster histories. The business cluster is also most active in the least prosperous states, as indexed by median household income. Finally, disaster agencies are active in states where there is some opposition to the idea of state regulation of land use in high-risk areas.

Power to affect natural disaster legislation is also firmly in the hands of elected officials on the state level. The important actors in terms of getting things done are the governor, the party leaders in the two houses of the state legislatures, and the two relevant legislative committees. Backing from other public agencies or organizations in the private sector is not regarded as important by the majority of key persons interviewed.

The majority of state elites apparently do not favor land use regulation in risk areas or tighter building codes to reduce damage and injury. Conservation groups, the state planning agency, the governor, and the civil defense director are the only ones seen as favoring such measures by more than a third of the respondents.

Paralleling the analysis of local communities, a favorability score weighted by activity and importance was calculated for each group and particularly the committees in legislature that deal with disaster mitigation legislation, are connected with the general business interests of the state, expressed through the leading financial institutions and the state chamber of commerce. Three other identifiable clusters are real estate groups, business groups, and disaster agencies. The correlates of favorability also show that the densely populated, highly urbanized, and prosperous states have active and influential elites who favor nonstructural mitigation. Interestingly, a state's experience with disasters appears to be quite irrelevant.

The other major dimension of the structure of power and influence in states is the contact levels among groups and key persons. Unsurprisingly, respondents report frequent regular contact with elected state officials. Again, the clusters of contact involve elected officials, business and industry (including real estate interests), and disaster agencies. The only predictors of regular contact with these groups are the respondent's position and past activity in other business, professional, or civic associations. None of the characteristics of the state show consistent effects.

One last issue concerns how respondents are themselves affected by the relevant actors in their states. Interestingly, conversation groups are the only ones regarded as influential in this sense by a majority of key persons. Other influential groups are the governor, local officials, the state planning agency, civil defense, and the Corps of Engineers. The clustering of these patterns of influence is very clear: some key persons are oriented (either postitively or negatively) to elected officials, others to business and industry interests, and others to disaster agencies.

In view of the prominent role that local communities must play in regulating land use for hazard risk management and the paramount importance of local elected officials in the political sociometry of the local community, we also conducted a special subanalysis of the factors influencing the hazard management outlooks of the 383 local elected officials in the sample (Diggins, Wright, and Rossi 1979). For this analysis, we constructed a measure of the local "balance of power" on hazard management issues from the responses given by local officials to the questions, "Who is active, who is important, who is influential in shaping your own views, and who are you in regular contact with?" Each group named received a score of "1"; scores were then summed across the four variables and multiplied by +1 if the group is seen as *favoring* nonstructural mitigation approaches and by − 1 otherwise; the ensuing group-specific scores were then summed across all elite groups in the local community. The resulting index thus measures the local balance of power on the issue. Once normed for the number of elite groups in each community, the index takes on a positive value if active, important, and influential elites in the community tend to favor nonstructural mitigation, and a negative value if the active, important, and influential elites tend to oppose such measures.

The key finding is that this power balance index is the single most important variable predicting the hazard management views of local elected officials — more important than any measure of the objective seriousness of the community's natural hazard problem, more important than the officials' subjective views of the seriousness of the problem, more important even than any social or ideological characteristic of the officials themselves. Also of some interest, the effect of the power balance measure was greatest in the substratum of communities where disaster salience was high. Thus, in all communities, but especially in communities with the most serious disaster problems, local elected officials respond first and foremost to their sense of where the local balance of power on the issue lies.

A SUMMARY VIEW OF OUR FINDINGS AND THEIR IMPLICATIONS

The preceding parts of this chapter have condensed a large number of specific findings and hinted at their implications for our understanding of both the politics of state and local natural disaster policies and the prospects for adopting nonstructural mitigating measures. There are some recurring themes throughout our findings that need highlighting. In addition, we ought to bring out what we believe to be their implications more strongly. This concluding section of the chapter has these two purposes in mind.

It should by now be more than abundantly clear that for most local communities natural disasters are down toward the bottom of the list of problems that are pressing for solution. The salience of such problems for state elites is somewhat higher but is also relatively low on the list of problems that need urgent attention. The implications of these findings are twofold. First, they should be interpreted as neither optimistic denial on the part of state and local elites nor merely a case of blind ignorance. The fact of the matter is that the other problems faced by communities are simply more urgent, and more predictably so, than the possible consequences of low-probability events. Second, because low levels of importance are accorded to natural disasters, the politics surrounding public policies will be the politics of low-salience issues, ones whose course it is difficult to forecast, especially if concern were somehow to increase. We will return to the implications of such low-salience politics later on in this section.

There is very little sentiment for blaming the victims of natural disasters for their folly in placing themselves in the way of tremendous natural forces. Sympathy and willingness to extend aid clearly dominate the stance taken by all elites. In addition, the elites endorse traditional measures—structural fixes and postdisaster relief and rehabilitation measures. Only large minorities are in favor of land use management, stricter building codes, and compulsory, subsidized hazard insurance. Furthermore, their opinions are not seen as political liabilities or political advantages, as one would expect given that the politics of natural disasters is scarcely an urgent item on any state or local agenda.

The implications of these findings are unclear. On the one hand, the status quo in public policy is endorsed, but lightly held, yet equally featherweight is the endorsement of nonstructural mitigation measures. This ideological casualness suggests that elites can perhaps be swayed one way or the other, depending on changes in the status quo or changes in the level of conflict over such policies. In this respect, it is significant that the NFIP receives so much approval as a program, even though the larger policy underlying it receives only minority endorsement. NFIP is the status quo, and, at least for the time being, it is an innocuous program with few vociferous opponents. On the other hand, there is some slight crystallization of opinion on disaster policy: hazard specialists are the protagonists of nonstructural mitigation measures,[2] and those who buy, sell, and develop land and buildings are the most opposed to such measures. This cleavage is scarcely a fault line, since the hazard specialists seemingly have little in the way of a following among other elites.

In short, neither ideology nor group structure is well crystallized as yet. Elite members hold contradictory or ambivalent beliefs without feeling much pressure to become consistent in their views. Similarly, groups do not line up consistently on one side or the other within a community or state, nor are there strong and consistent trends that transcend locale.

Another indicator of the politics of low salience is the fact that so many elite members see public officials as the key actors in deciding disaster mitigation policies. Unlike other areas of social policy where contending groups may influence the outcome, in regard to disaster mitigation policy, legislators act on their own, because no one pressures them to take one side or the

---

[2] A recent letter transmitting a report of a conference on earthquakes and related hazards from a hazard specialist organization provides a dramatic demonstration of how distorted organizational perspectives can be, as in the following quotation: "In the days since the conference [held in November 1977] earthquakes, their related hazards and all natural hazards have continued to become important items on the agendas of state, local and federal governments."

other. Note also that public officials are sensitive to the directions in which political winds blow, but since the latter are scarcely more than light zephyrs in most places, public officials can take their own tack.

What does all this mean for someone who would like to advance toward the state of affairs wherein nonstructural mitigation is adopted as the policy of choice? Our findings have two implications. First, there is neither strong opposition nor strong advocacy even though the balance of opinion is somewhat opposed to such measures. This situation presents many favorable opportunities, especially if the balance can be tipped the other way without arousing opposition. Second, our findings are not very helpful for constructing a strategy that will help to tip the balance. The amorphousness of elite opinion and accompanying mass opinion provides few clues to the details of the social map. It is difficult to locate both potential friends and potential foes.

Indeed, that is the characteristic of low-salience issue politics. Small, highly articulate groups with strong beliefs can often hold up the adoption of policies that majorities favor only lukewarmly, as we saw in the 1960s with water supply fluoridation. As local communities move from the emergency phase of NFIP to the regular phase, one can easily envisage floodplain dwellers and landowners forming such groups and bringing the program to a halt in place after place. Low-salience issues also present opportunities for change. When interest groups care little and the mass is apathetic, administrative or legislative initiative can easily dominate public policy.

But perhaps the clearest lesson we can draw from our survey of elites is that it is too early to tell. Our survey was taken too early in the history of the development of a movement and its diffusion throughout state and local communities to sustain clear predictions of the future.

REFERENCES

Diggins, W. F., Wright, J. D., and Rossi, P. H. 1979. Local Elites and City Hall: The Case of Natural Disaster Risk Mitigation Policy. *Social Science Quarterly* 60, no. 2 (September): 203–217.

Friesema, H. P. et al. 1979. *Aftermath: Communities After Natural Disasters*. Beverly Hills: Sage Publications.

Kunreuther, H. 1973. *Recovery from Natural Disasters: Insurance or Federal Aid?* Washington, D. C.: American Enterprise Institute.

Wright, J. D. et al. 1979. *After the Cleanup: Long-Range Effects of Natural Disasters*. Beverly Hills: Sage Publications.

Commentary

Kenneth Prewitt

I start with two comments, one supporting, one more critical of, the research. The supportive comment refers to the discussion of the long-term effects study. When postresearch commentary is about the appropriate level of analysis, or the number of variables included and excluded from the model, or the specification of the model, it is likely that the research has produced nonintuitive findings. Stated differently, had we asked ourselves prior to the initiation of this research whether the study would find differences in housing structures or population movements following serious disasters, the answer would generally have been "yes." I have been a member of the Social and Demographic Research Institute's (SADRI's) advisory committee from the beginning, and as I recall the advisory committee conversations, none of us suggested that there were serious design problems or that the model would fail to pick up differences. Much that seems obvious now was not obvious when this project was started.

My second comment is less supportive. The research team has written not only the papers and reports we have been discussing but also a series of smaller papers, one of which is a very interesting critique of White and Haas (reproduced in Part Three of this volume). Their criticism of White and Haas is that they write dramatic scenarios but fail to assign probabilities to them. SADRI's study provides the probabilities, announces that they are very low, and then expresses dismay, if you will, because nobody pays much attention. We find a politics of low salience, a politics of indifference, a politics of periphery. Perhaps the SADRI research team has fallen into the same trap that they accuse White and Haas of falling into. In their paper on White and Haas they write: "As we suggest throughout this paper, these consciousness-raising efforts of White and Haas sometimes work at cross-purposes with the more strictly scientific goals...." As I read through SADRI's important material, I find that there are points at which the researchers' interest in advising on political strategy (not just policy, but political strategy) works at cross-purposes with their strictly scientific goals. And that creates, at least for me, some inconsistencies in the analysis.

I first read the long-term effects material some years ago, in preparation for a meeting of the advisory committee. The night before this meeting in Amherst, on a lovely winter evening, I had a drink with Pete Rossi. I asked him, "How do you intend to do a serious political study of a nonhappening?" This was before the survey data were collected. The answer to that snide comment was 600 pages of report.

So now I ask again, how did they do a serious political study of a nonhappening? They partially do it by a sleight of hand. They move quickly from analysis of marginal distributions to analysis of correlations. The marginal distributions demonstrate low seriousness, low salience, and an endorsement of the status quo. But then they use correlational analysis to try to tease out something about a political process that is introducing an innovative policy, nonstructural mitigation. That's a substantial challenge. It's difficult under the best of circumstances, I believe, to uncover a political process from survey data. It's particularly difficult if the political process is not being displayed in bold relief, but instead is submerged, hidden at the edges of things. Part of what they have done is move very quickly from an analysis of distributions, which establishes the context within which politics takes place, to an attempt to ferret out the politics themselves. My overall reading of the manuscript is that the authors do a much better job of establishing the context within which the political process is taking place than actually describing the political process.

What type of politics did they find? I take slight issue with their title. I do not think the authors found an "apathetic" politics. I think they found the politics of a peripheral issue. It's a very interesting peripheral issue, because it's an issue that ceases, often dramatically, to be peripheral when a disaster occurs. When a major disaster occurs there is attention, focus, preoccupation with the disaster itself and with some public response to that disaster. The issue is forced on our attention *when* a disaster occurs, not if a disaster occurs, because, as the authors make very clear throughout the research report, statistically a disaster will occur sooner or later.

What kind of politics occupies the political space when the disaster occurs? It is a politics driven by two public demands: first, the public says, "We want relief"; and second, "Try not to let it happen again." And this becomes the context within which the political leadership has to generate a response to public conditions. That is, SADRI's report is about the nonhappening, but the real politics of disaster response, I think, takes place when a disaster occurs. We have a tension between what happens when one occurs and what happens the rest of the time when one has not occurred.

Probably, the demand, "Don't let it happen again," varies in nature across different kinds of disasters. I do not attempt to distinguish among kinds of disasters, except in a very general way, namely, does the disaster follow the people, or do the people follow the disaster? A disaster that follows the people—toxic waste removal, nuclear siting, Three Mile Island—occurs when the disaster condition is created where people have already decided to make their livelihood, establish their residences, and so forth. In these cases there is more than a peripheral disaster politics. The disaster issue is already at the level of at least some intermediate attention. In contrast, when it's a matter of people following the disaster, that is, settling in floodplains or building on fault lines, then we have a politics of the type addressed by SADRI's research.

The research, then, as I understand it, is about the level of support for the established policy of structural mitigation and relief versus the level of support for an emerging policy of nonstructural mitigation. I do not find much attention to the way in which the policy of nonstructural mitigation has come onto the agenda. We are presented with it, as something to deal with. But we don't have any sense about the evolution of that policy. It is a policy that is in some conflict with the more established policy of structural mitigation and relief.

I turn now to the findings and describe them in somewhat different language in order to make a series of points. The first finding is that the status quo is endorsed, although there is some room for maneuvering. I would interpret that as suggesting the possibility of a gradual, if modest, addition to traditional policies—not a replacement for, but a gradual addition to. I will get to the reasons for that shortly.

Second, the authors report, with respect to the emerging policy of nonstructural mitigation, that there is tension between two categories of people, which I label somewhat differently than they do. In one category is the "commercial class" and in the other are "social engineers." The commercial class is composed of developers, real estate interests, and so forth. The social engineers are what they call the hazard specialists. Paren-thetically, I observe that in the U.S. leadership in general one can find the struggle between a commercial class and the social engineers. It is a struggle being played out in a large number of policy arenas, especially in regulatory policy. In the present case we find the commercial class (the developers, the real estate interests) on the one side, and the social engineers (those who would use the levers of government to intervene in order to solve social problems) on the other side, with the critical actors (that is, the authoritative officials) somewhere in the middle, moving with the prevailing opinion.

Descriptively we are presented with a trimodal distribution: an intense minority at both ends, pro and con on the issue of nonstructural mitigation, with a mode in between—the authoritative officials somewhat indifferent but willing to move either way depending on community conditions. This finding strikes me as eminently reasonable. It is exactly where I would expect to see that group of authoritative officials, ready to move with the power balance in their particular community. Superimposed over that trimodal distribution is a much larger distribution heavily clustered around indifference, which describes the general public.

In trying to sort out the implications of this picture, it is necessary, conceptually, to multiply peripheries. We start with a peripheral policy issue, one of lower salience than everything from pornography to unemployment. The hazard specialists are in turn peripheral to the political system. We start with a peripheral issue, move to a peripheral coalition, and then ask what kind of policy is likely to emerge. This is the framework within which we turn to the findings on the substance of the political process.

The finding that most impresses us is counterintuitive, and therefore critical. It is not the finding we expected. The objective conditions of exposure to risk do *not* determine who falls where on what particular policy formulation. The seriousness of a hazard to the community is not a key determinant of who takes what kind of position, what kinds of coalitions form, what kinds of policy responses are generated, and so forth. To quote from the SADRI report: "At both the individual and the aggregate levels, disaster experience, however major, is not sharply related to hazard management innovation." "Experience, it appears, is not only not the best teacher, it is no teacher at all." "Public officials are more active in urbanized, heavily populated states. However, they are apparently not responding to disaster risk." "Neither perceived risks to the community nor the respondent's experience with and losses from floods have a significant effect on attitudes of officials toward land use and building code standards for disaster mitigation." One finds many similar statements throughout the report. The objective conditions, the levels of risk, do not seem to influence what people think about the various policy measures.

However, one thing does seem to be rather sharply affected by the objective hazard risk — the subjective (or perceived) seriousness of the hazard. It is of interest that neither philosophical positions, nor levels of activity, nor attitudes toward particular kinds of policy responses are affected by the actual occurrence of hazards, but the perceived seriousness of hazards is so affected. This relationship gives me some confidence. It is the one thing I would expect to be most related to objective conditions. Here the finding is: "as was the case in individual-level data, the strongest correlates of hazard seriousness ratings by far are the state's previous ten years' experience with the disaster type and the aggregated estimated return probabilities." If there has been a serious disaster, people think there's a serious problem.

However, thinking there's a serious problem does not in turn affect an elite's disaster philophy, which is rooted in different social and political processes. I am comfortable with the authors' measure of disaster philosophy; they demonstrate to my satisfaction that it is highly intercorrelated with a whole series of other measures. These are not random responses. There is a package of responses with respect to philosophy, with respect to attitude, with respect to policy positions, which cohere as some sort of belief system. But the "policy belief system" is not affected by the seriousness attributed to a hazard. This rings true to me because of the earlier distinction between the social engineers and the commerical class. These disaster philosophies are part of a broader array of political ideologies in American society.

I review these findings because it is at this point that we encounter a major inconsistency in the logic of SADRI's argument. We start with the assertion that the seriousness of disasters does not explain the distribution of beliefs and actions among key sectors. But there is a puzzle: we still have not explained the emergence of a new and innovative policy. Why is nonstructural mitigation suddenly on the agenda? Why are we talking about it? We have an issue that is peripheral. We have the absence of any serious public pressure to bring about this particular policy. So what explains it?

This is the point at which I find an inconsistency in the argument. To summarize quickly, the policy innovation is introduced by the federal government. The following explanation is given: most of the impetus for new policy directions in the natural hazard area, it appears, will have to come from the federal government, because it is primarily at this level that the problem is serious enough to warrant large-scale mitigation efforts. Thus, at the highest level of aggregation it *is* the seriousness of the problem that affects the likelihood of a policy being adopted.

SADRI argues that this is rational. A federal dollar spent for flood prevention projects has an expected return of one dollar, in the sense that the problem that the dollar is expended to solve is certain to occur. Federal investments in hazard management are more rational than state investments, state investments are more rational than local community investments, local community investments are more rational than investments on the part of individuals. That is, as one aggregates the cost of a disaster from individual to community, from state to nation, at some point it becomes rational for the political system to respond with an innovative new policy. And this is the message, as I read it, of the report — that, indeed, it is rational for the federal government to be responsive, because that's where the costs are clearest, and this factor drives the likelihood of policy.

I am not sure I impute as much rationality to the federal government as the authors do. I am not trying to be flippant, just questioning whether the evidence warrants this particular conclusion. Indeed, there is a counterinterpretation, one that is not inconsistent with some of the findings the SADRI authors report. The counterinterpretation has to do with the importance of this policy to bureaucratic interests. Several signs in the report suggest that this is an alternative explanation, including the findings that specialists inflate the seriousness of disasters relative to other actors, and that they inflate the seriousness of disasters in comparison to other kinds of problems society is facing. It's a fairly common finding that people who work on a problem think it's more important than they think other problems are, and that they think the problem they work on is more of a problem than other people think it is. The war is always being won or lost in one's own theater. Further support for the alternative explanation is that state political structures, but not local communities, have what are described as hazard coalitions. No doubt we also would find such coalitions at the federal level. Indeed, the authors at one point observe, in a very persuasive passage, that hazard management functions are more specialized and more differentiated at the federal than at the state level, and at the state than at the community level. This high degree of specialization, preoccupation, and sensitivity to the seriousness of the issue within the bureaucracy that has a responsibility for the problem area is, in my judgment, a better explanation for the emergence of the new policy than the one advanced in the report.

The central proposition in the report is that the seriousness (cost, concern, attention, and so forth) with which decision makers approach disaster issues appears to organize much of the politics of the issues. Seriousness in turn is sensitive to level of aggregation. But I wonder if one would not want to make "structural differentiation" the underlying concept. That is to say, where there is differentiation and therefore hazard specialists, a politics emerges that differs from the politics where there is no differentiation. To be sure, there is more differentiation the higher the level of aggregation, but perhaps the correlation is less than 1.00. At a minimum, there should be variation within states and within communities with regard to differentiation. Differentiation may be even more pronounced in some communities than in some states.

I conclude with a question: why should we care whether or how a given policy innovation will occur? Linked to this question is another: how seriously are we to take this research? I think we should care and we should take the present research seriously. In a nonsalient policy area there is a temptation, in this society as in others, to export the risk into the future. Let the next generation worry about solving it. No matter how serious the risk, there is the presumption that someone will be around to clean it up, to pay the costs. There is a strong charitable impulse in our society. Because there will be human suffering when disasters hit, there will be efforts to alleviate suffering. Knowing that these efforts will occur, and faced with an already crowded political agenda and limited resources, our society is tempted to export the risks if at all possible. There is another, related reason to take the research seriously. As the authors make clear, there is enormous lead time between the introduction of a new policy and its effect. There is a very long lead time between the introduction of something like nonstructural mitigation and its possible effect upon the consequences of disasters. With the possible exception of the bureaucratic interests of social engineers, nothing in the immediate political environment is going to bring about this particular policy innovation. If, therefore, the costs of failing to introduce this innovation are known to be high, and the probability that future citizens will have to pay those costs is close to 1.00, then research that attempts to understand the impediments to that policy cannot but be significant well beyond its contribution to sociological analysis.

Commentary

Frederick L. Bates

After the Cleanup and *The Apathetic Politics of Natural Hazards*, by Wright, Rossi, and associates, constitute landmark studies in the field of natural hazards and will set a new standard for disaster research. This is true for several important reasons. First, *The Apathetic Politics of Natural Hazards* focuses directly on the politics of disaster, a subject little researched by past investigators, especially through the use of systematic research methods. As a consequence, this study fills an information void and furnishes a useful foundation for future policymaking.

Second, the national scope of both studies sets them apart from most research performed in the field of natural hazards. As the authors pointed out, disaster research in the past has been peculiarly dependent upon case studies performed in small communities. We have never had a national assessment of the long-term effects of disasters and the way key individuals in the power structure view these events and policies related to them.

Third, the methodology employed in executing these two studies is among the most sophisticated and rigorous yet employed in disaster research. As a consequence, it will set a new standard in this respect. Furthermore, in order to perform the research involved in *After the Cleanup*, a number of valuable data sets have been assembled and put into a form that will be useful to disaster researchers for some time to come.

Fourth, in executing and reporting this research, the authors have maintained a level of objectivity toward disaster issues rarely encountered in this field. Because of the dramatic nature of disasters and their power to elicit human sympathy, disaster research has all too often resulted in findings based as much on emotional or ideological grounds as on data. This research, in contrast, is coldly objective and, as a consequence of this and the methods employed, seems to have a more factual basis than most.

LIMITATIONS OF THE RESEARCH

Because these are landmark studies and because they are likely to have profound long-range effects on the future of both disaster research and disaster policy, it is important to examine them critically and to keep in mind their limitations. There is a danger that the substantive results of both studies might be misinterpreted by the unsophisticated reader. *After the Cleanup* seems, on the surface, to demonstrate that natural disasters, taken as a category of events, are relatively unimportant since the research shows there are few, if any, discernible long-term effects. To some this may mean that research on disaster is really not needed in the future. The results reported in *The Apathetic Politics of Natural Hazards* demonstrate the low importance placed on disasters and natural hazards as issues requiring policy solutions by leaders and citizens alike. It might be concluded that research on this topic in the future should have low priority. Actually, these studies point to the need for more research rather than less, but the type of research needed in the future will be quite different from that performed in the past.

In order to understand this point, it is important to realize the limitations of the methodology employed in both studies. While both used advanced and rigorous research methods and were executed with a degree of professional competence rarely encountered, there are many questions left unanswered simply because the research was not directed toward answering them. For example, *After the Cleanup* employed census data and data from other sources that locate disasters geographically and assess their impact through documentary evidence. Results are therefore limited to conclusions that can be drawn from these data. Essentially, the study focuses on geographic units (census tracts or counties) as the objects of study and asks the question, what long-range impact upon these units can be discerned? Geographic areas are obviously not individuals or families or businesses or other corporate units. This research simply does not address itself to the question of long-range effects on units other than geographic areas. The conclusion that territorial units show no long-range effects should not be interpreted to mean that other victim units, such as families, or corporate bodies, such as businesses, would not show long-range effects if studied. This is simply not a question addressed by the research. In order to round out our knowlege of long-term effects, additional research is needed that focuses on units other than geographic areas and follows them through time.

In *The Apathetic Politics of Natural Hazards* the method employed is survey research addressed primarily to attitudinal or opinion data. Such data do not indicate actual political behavior or the process of policy formation. Instead, they measure the "attitudinal climate" in which such behavior takes place. While the study is authoritative with respect to that climate, more research is needed to delve into the actual process of policy formation as a behavioral phenomenon.

THEORETICAL IMPLICATIONS

One of the impressive things about the research reported in the two studies is the way research results dovetail to offer a rather elegant, empirically based theory that seems to account for attitudes and policy preferences with respect to disasters and disaster mitigation policies. The authors have done an excellent job of bringing out the interrelations among their various findings through the use of a kind of actuarial framework. This framework employs probability theory and the concept of risk side by side with the measurement of attitudes and opinions. Thus, the important findings and accompanying conceptualization can be stated as a series of propositions as follows:

1. The probability of an individual experiencing and suffering loss from a disaster is very low compared to suffering losses from other threatening experiences.

2. The probability of a territorial unit experiencing a disaster and suffering loss from it varies with the level of political aggregation: the larger the territorial unit (starting with an individual household and extending through census tracts, counties, and states to the national level), the higher the probability that a disaster resulting in losses will occur during a given time period.

3. The amount of aggregate loss suffered within a territorial unit varies directly with the level of political aggregation: the larger the unit, the larger the aggregate loss.

4. Discounting the effects of occupational specialization and special social and economic interests, the rating given to the importance of disasters as a problem and the commitment to various disaster mitigation policies will vary with an individual's perception of the probability of a disaster and of the amount of loss threatened by it.

5. Therefore, it is to be expected that concern over disasters, and interest in disaster mitigation, will be strongest at the highest levels of political aggregation and will be weakest at the lowest levels. Thus, federal and state officials will tend to rate the problem of disasters higher in level of seriousness than will local or individual citizens.

6. If one wishes to explain policy preferences, after taking all of this into account, one must consider the special interests of persons in disaster mitigation issues that stem from their occupational biases or from economic interests. Persons with occupations associated with disaster relief, rehabilitation, or mitigation will tend to rate the importance of the problem higher than other individuals. Those with economic interests that may be benefited or threatened by particular mitigation policies, such as land use management, will tend to rate the importance of the problem higher or lower than average and will express policy preferences in line with their economic interests.

In other words, attitudes and opinions toward disasters and toward disaster mitigation policies are based upon people's perceptions of the probabilities of loss from a disaster. These probabilities vary with the level of political aggregation. Furthermore, attitudes and preferences are a function of special interests that modify the perceptions of probability.

Almost all of the research results reported by the Social and Demographic Research Institute (SADRI) are comprehensible given this framework. It is impressive that this research demonstrates that individual estimates of disaster probabilities strongly parallel the factual material in *After the Cleanup*. This seems to mean that the attitudes of citizens and of elites are essentially rational and are not, as many disaster specialists believe, based on a head-in-the-sand denial of the problems associated with natural hazards.

RESEARCH NEEDS AND POLICY IMPLICATIONS

The research summarized in both *After the Cleanup* and *The Apathetic Politics of Natural Hazards* highlights the need for certain new directions for investigation in the field of disasters and natural hazards. Both studies deal with a wide range of disaster types, which themselves vary considerably in magnitude and point to an urgent need for a better classification system for disasters. The term "disaster" lumps under a general heading a wide variety of events stemming from an even greater diversity of causes. It also subsumes under a single heading great variation in the magnitude of damage and loss associated with these events. In the study of long-range effects, SADRI discovered that events classified as disasters by disaster action agencies vary from small and almost insignificant to cataclysmic. In order to deal with this great variety and at the same time to study earthquakes, floods, tornadoes, and hurricanes, the authors created a scale to measure the extensiveness of the disaster, based on the number of structures destroyed and the number with major damage. They then proceeded to study only those events that fell above a certain point on the destructive scale. Even so, the disasters studied vary considerably in magnitude. As a consequence, the results, which demonstate insignificant long-range effects, apply to a rather wide range of so-called disasters.

In their research on the politics of disaster the authors sought to determine the attitudes held by elites toward natural hazards and hazard mitigation policy. Here again they were forced to deal with floods, tornadoes, hurricanes, and earthquakes as undifferentiated entities in terms of their actual impact on human communities. Lacking a widely accepted classification system that categorizes events such as hurricanes or earthquakes in terms of their disastrous results, the authors based their study on interviews that elicited attitudes toward earthquakes and hurricanes in general. What is needed to add precision to research on disasters is a classification scheme that categorizes natural or man-made hazards according to their disastrous consequences for human populations. In short, disasters need to be classified using a system somewhat similar to those employed to classify canoe rapids, gale conditions, and Richter scale numbers.

Floods, hurricanes, tornadoes, and earthquakes become disasters only when they affect human populations and result in destruction of property and loss of life. If a classification system were created, a Class 1 disaster would be considered one with maximum impact upon human populations, while a Class 10 disaster might be one with minor human effects. The authors suggest a basis for such a classification scheme in their use of a damage index and in their examination of the proportion of a community's resource base that is adversely affected by a natural hazard.

If such a classification scheme could be worked out in terms of the magnitude of the disaster, then a number of beneficial results would follow for both research and policymaking. For example, generalizations concerning disasters and their long-range effects could be stated in terms of the class or level of disaster to which the results apply. Furthermore, research difficulties stemming from the relative rarity of disasters as human events could partially be compensated for, since it might be possible to classify all disasters as Class 1, regardless of the disaster agent, for certain purposes. This would increase the size of the available sample. In some respects the reconstruction process for a given class of disaster might display similar problems regardless of the initial disaster agent. Tornadoes, hurricanes, floods, and earthquakes with similar destructive results might therefore be lumped together in order to expand the sample being examined.

As the SADRI research demonstrates, peoples' attitudes toward disasters are such as to give them relatively low salience compared to other problems. Furthermore, attitudes toward different mitigation policies vary considerably from one population unit to another, depending upon the group's economic and political interests. Some favor structural mitigation, while others are more responsive to nonstructural mitigation. It is possible that different policies should be adopted for different classes of disasters. Providing nonstructural mitigation measures with respect to Class 1 disasters might be more acceptable to a wider range of people than providing such measures for all classes of disasters. Furthermore, at the bottom of the scale of disaster seriousness, it is quite possible that the most acceptable policy is a "free market" solution.

The difficulty at present is that theories of disaster and the conceptualizations that apply to this field are based upon extreme cataclysms rather than upon "garden variety" disasters. This has resulted in confusion both in research and in policymaking. SADRI's research offers a firm foundation upon which to build an empirically based disaster classification system that will be useful to both researchers and policymakers.

The study of elite attitudes and opinions with respect to disaster mitigation policies demonstrates the relatively low priority placed on natural hazards as political issues in local communities and even at the state level. It further demonstrates the relative unpopularity of nonstructural mitigation measures as compared to structural solutions to disaster problems or to traditional relief and rehabilitation policies. While this research reveals much about the political climate that surrounds the political process involved in instituting and implementing disaster policies, it does not touch directly upon the political process itself. This was not, of course, an objective of the research, since it focused mainly on attitudinal and opinion data.

This study should be followed by research on the actual policy formation and implementation process in selected real communities that represent different degrees of exposure to various natural hazards. Even though the priorities are low, the politics do exist and policy issues do arise and are solved in real communities. More direct knowledge of the actual political process that operates within the climate of relative apathy would add not only to our understanding of disaster policy formation and implementation but also to our general knowledge of the politics of low-salience issues.

One interesting set of findings reported in *The Apathetic Politics of Natural Hazards* shows that respondents were more receptive to the idea of disaster-related insurance than they were to the nonstructural mitigation measures tied to it in federal programs. For example, there seems to be a general coolness toward land use management as an approach to solving problems associated with floods on the part of a number of the elite respondents. Another interesting finding is that the citizens surveyed in California are not confident of the ability of local service organizations, such as fire and police departments, hospitals, and public utilities, to deal with a major disaster in their communities. It is also noted in this study that a high proportion of respondents are in favor of relief and rehabilitation measures.

All of this suggests that research in the field of disasters could be reoriented to deal more directly with policy issues that cut across various areas of public service, only one of which is natural hazards. For example, studies of emergency service organizations and of the problems they face in preparedness and actual operations might receive greater support and have more generalizable results than studies focused exclusively on the roles these organizations play in natural disasters. Fire and police departments, hospitals, and public utilities and insurance companies, to mention only a few, have roles to play not only in natural and man-made disasters but in connection with other problems of public interest as well. Furthermore, the problems faced by reconstruction and rehabilitation organizations, in offering assistance to disaster victims, are the same problems faced by most organizations engaged in some form of public assistance. Research on the process of rendering assistance to victim populations in general could add not only to our knowledge of disasters but also to our understanding of other public policy issues. For example, the ideas of equity that people hold with respect to public assistance programs probably cut across various substantive areas, only one of which concerns natural hazards. Research on the subject of equity would be of value to all organizations that distribute any form of public assistance to any population.

In short, disaster research in the future should be joined more closely to research related to other fields of public policy where common organizations, facilities, services, or methods are utilized for multiple purposes. This might result in greater support for the research and also in better application of the results to policy formulation.

SUMMARY

The research reported in both *After the Cleanup* and *The Apathetic Politics of Natural Hazards* answers many questions concerning the long-range effects of disasters and the political climate surrounding disaster mitigation efforts. The two studies provide an excellent background against which to rethink and reorient both disaster research and disaster policy agendas. I hope that everyone interested in this field will think through these implications and take advantage of this landmark research in reorienting their efforts.

Discussion

William Petak: Concerning nonstructural mitigations, your presentation lumped building codes and land use approaches together. Did you deal with those separately in the analysis?

James D. Wright: Yes, in some portions, although the relevant "disaster philosophy" item combines land use and building code approaches as one policy option.

Petak: I have a problem with that: I think you would get a different response to land use than to building codes, because land use is a more emotional issue. Also, what's a "structural mitigation" for earthquakes?

J. Wright: If building codes, performance standards, and the like are treated as nonstructural, as we have done, then I suppose there are none.

Petak: Why, then, do you compare favorability toward structural versus nonstructural approaches among the 900 respondents in earthquake country?

J. Wright: The question on structural mitigations in the California survey dealt specifically with water-related hazards. Keep in mind that even in "earthquake country," in terms of year-in and year-out loss of life and property, floods are a far more serious problem than earthquakes.

Joseph F. Coates: In the questions dealing with importance, did the respondents have an opportunity to distinguish among objective importance, subjective importance, importance to them as political figures, importance within the local and state government community, and so forth? What does "seriousness" mean in this context?

Peter H. Rossi: The question asks them to judge the seriousness of various problems in their local communities or states. This rules out "serious to you." The question poses the community, or the state, as the frame of reference. Otherwise, the seriousness score is some overall rating, with seriousness defined however the respondent wishes. Similar types of ratings are frequently done in other areas, for example, seriousness of crimes. Perceived crime seriousness, by the way, is closely related to average sentences, to the amount of damage or injury, and so on. This is also true of our hazard seriousness variables.

Henry Quarantelli: As a matter of clarification, did you ask only attitudinal, perception, and opinion questions, or did you ask about some behavioral items also?

J. Wright: Mostly opinion questions. We asked some items of fact, for example, whether a state or community had existing legislation for hazard mitigation land use, whether there were local building codes that people would have to meet if they wanted to put up a building in a floodplain, and other things of that nature. The findings are that, by and large, people (both elites and masses) are unaware of or grossly misinformed on the status of these legislative measures in their states and local communities. Also, the California data do contain information on behaviors such as buying insurance and having a fire extinguisher. Finally, we have detailed factual information on prior experience with disasters.

Petak: Regarding the California data, were respondents asked questions specific to earthquake and specific to flood, or did you lump them together?

J. Wright: We had specific questions.

Petak: You say there is high concurrence between the elites and people generally in the seriousness attributed to these hazards. Were you able to determine whether the elites were *influencing* the people or *responding* to them?

J. Wright: That would make us rich and famous! The correlation is there, very clearly in the nine communities, but my hunch is that it is spurious, the seriousness scores in both cases being a function of the community's prior experience with disasters, the nature of the risk, and so on. All these will, of course, be the same for elites and masses in each community.

While I have the floor, let me also respond to Prewitt's concern for the evolution of the nonstructural mitigation emphasis. Bascially, there has been an increasing recognition that other kinds of policy emphases pose certain perverse incentives. Structural mitigations, for example, encourage people to move into hazardous areas. Postdisaster relief tends to socialize risks, lets people be insensitive to hazard risk when they build structures, and so forth. The current emphasis on nonstructural or land use approaches reflects a concern that previous policy emphases may well have increased, rather than decreased, the level of population at risk from hazards.

Both Prewitt and Bates emphasize that our report is better on political context than on political process. We plead guilty! Why? Because with just a few exceptions, there is no process to study at any particular moment. Our victimization data, for example, show that among the hundred communities, there were no more than two or three reasonably serious disasters in the preceding year. To be sure, in those two or three communities the seriousness attributed to the hazard is very high, and so here there may be a process to study. Elsewhere, for the most part, there is not.

When we designed the elite survey, the great Western drought had not yet begun, so there were no drought questions. When we were designing the California population survey, drought was *the* big problem, so we added a question on drought seriousness. In the summer of 1977, in the middle of the worst Western drought in this century, the resident population ranked drought second only to inflation in seriousness. This and many of our other findings make it clear that there *is* a process, but one that is very much event-determined. When disaster strikes, then a political process is activated, but in the interim that process essentially disappears. And so, for most of the communities in our sample, we are not able to tap into it. Most of our communities, that is, are "in the interim," between their last disaster and the next one.

Finally, to respond to an earlier question, our seriousness measures are very strongly correlated with all measures of disaster experience, both subjective and objective. The 1960–1970 disaster experience data used in the long-term effects study are very good predictors of attributed hazard seriousness. Also, the seriousness indicators are strongly correlated with the estimated return probabilities. I agree with Coates that we are not exactly sure what seriousness is. But whatever we have measured, it correlates strongly with everything it ought to correlate with, which suggests it is a valid measure.

Claire B. Rubin: Several people have described your results as counterintuitive. I think they are also counterexperiential. A recent report by the National Governor's Association discusses thirty case studies based on site visits to disaster-stricken communities. Several questions were asked about structural and nonstructural mitigation measures that were taken after disaster struck. The results show that a fair number of mitigation steps were taken, and in the majority of cases the implemented mitigations were even stronger than had originally been planned. This suggests that local officials are taking steps toward nonstructural hazard mitigations despite the opinions you have tapped.

J. Wright: Eleven of the twenty states represented in our sample show a clear majority consensus on a serious flood in the previous ten years, and of the eleven, six report definite effects on public policy regarding flood hazard. Responses to the open-ended questions concerning policy changes typically mentioned some sort of risk mapping, increased awareness of or interest in the flood insurance program, and so on. So clearly, some states and communities do innovate in the disaster aftermath. I do not think it is inconsistent with the main thrust of our findings if in thirty communities that have recently been hit by a serious disaster, there is a higher level of hazard-mitigating activity than in, say, American communities as a whole. Also, I would need to know about the sample. If, for example, the study is based on Prewitt's social engineers, it will give a different picture than if based on a sample such as ours — that is, a broad spectrum of the local power structure.

James Kerr. The study Rubin notes did find that mitigation measures taken in response to disasters were stronger than planned. But this is not inconsistent with SADRI's findings, and the SADRI findings are broadly replicated in the recent J.H. Wiggins report: Quoting briefly from the last page:

> Current evidence suggests that problems other than those associated with natural hazard exposure are currently assigned a much higher priority by policy makers. Public and policy maker understanding of natural hazard consequences and alternatives are generally low level. Jurisdictions exhibit substantially less than optimal capacity to engage in expanded hazard management. No easily indentifiable political constituency emerged. . . .

Ugo Morelli: I too am puzzled: I hear about results showing that mitigation for natural hazards is a low-salience issue. I hear the same thing in Utah, in California, and in Boston. And yet we know that in those states and in that city risk mitigation is being undertaken. I think it would be very interesting if we could explain how, in spite of the low importance accorded this issue, innovations are nonetheless introduced.

J. Wright: There is more on this in the full report. At the state and federal levels it is a bureaucratic process; at the local level it is an ad hoc process. There are agencies at the local level that deal with these problems. But disasters are not their exclusive function. At the state level there *are* hazard coalitions that are pushing for innovations.

Morelli: Are there other nationwide survey rankings of some of these issues? How would they compare with your results?

J. Wright: The only one would be the Gallup poll, which asks respondents to state the most serious problem facing the nation today. The patterns are very similar — most people pick bread-and-butter economic concerns unless there is a war. Inflation, unemployment, and the like are at the top among both elites and the general public.

Thomas E. Drabek: Are there any comparable data on households or elites that give ratings of other issues, such as abortion? We need a context to interpret the findings. Can we consider them in the context of public attitudes on other issues relating to federal regulation? My question, in other words, is whether you have measured "disaster philosophies" in themselves, or whether you have just picked up a more generalized hostility to government regulations.

Rossi: One could look through the archives of public opinion polls over the last twenty years for data on public attitudes toward things involving federal regulations. But we have not done this, and nothing in our data base per se provides the context you are looking for.

Drabek: It is, I think, a very important insight that the politics of low-salience issues are so different from "normal" politics. We need to know more about transformation processes in the community: how the issue becomes highly salient when the disaster hits. It seems to me that this substantive area is extremely important, and yet the literature has not attacked it very well.

J. Wright: The question is, what makes Tulsa a Tulsa? Why do some communities, but not others, seem so anxious to innovate in this area? Unfortunately, we don't have that many Tulsas in the sample, so we cannot say much about it. There is some kind of political process triggered when disasters hit. What the components of that process are, who is mobilized, who is activated, how the issue bounces up and down on the agenda — we do not have a very good feel for these questions, most of all because we do not have enough recently affected communities in the sample.

Rubin: Perhaps one of the problems of assessing the implications of SADRI's research is that there aren't any state or local officials here. It would be interesting to hear their perspective on your findings. Did you have state and local officials on your advisory committee?

Rossi: No, we had representatives from associations of state and local officials. We aggregated one level up! As to the "perspective" of state and local officials on our findings, I should emphasize that their perspectives on these matters *are* our findings.

Howard Kunreuther: Have you looked at the past experience of political elites during their term of office? We know that political elites are in office for a relatively short time — too short, perhaps, for them to think seriously in time frames relevant to the mitigation of hazard risk. Have you begun to investigate that at all?

Sonia R. Wright: Not directly. In some analyses we controlled for how long a person has lived in the community, how long the person has been in office, how many other elected or appointed offices the person has had, and so forth. There are no strong, consistent effects on any of our dependent variables.

Kenneth Prewitt: One problem, of course, is that everything in the society eventually aggregates to the national level, which means that disasters have to compete for policy space with unemployment, with inflation, with national security, and so forth. What differs, I think, between federal and local levels is the degree of differentiation and specialization. SADRI talks about disasters as being more serious problems at higher levels, but they are really not "more serious" compared to the whole agenda of problems that national leaders face. All problems are more serious at the federal level; the *relative* seriousness of hazards at that level is probably very similar to what you find at state and local levels. But at higher levels one finds the differentiation and the specialists, the advocates, who create a different kind of politics. My sense is that this is your major finding.

Frederick L. Bates: It occurs to me that solving many of the issues that this study raises, or understanding their implications, is dependent on developments in other areas of social science. What we are dealing with is a lack of information on what constitutes a problem, how it becomes salient, and how the politics that surround it work. These issues have simply not been researched. This suggests a need to do research that cuts across areas and that gives some comparative basis for saying where any one problem stands in relation to others.

Gary A. Kreps: Are the background characteristics of elites that predict salience ratings in any way similar to the background characteristics that influence other issues, such as fluoridation?

Rossi: We don't have that information. We asked our elites which groups in the community were active on natural disaster issues, and we also asked comparable questions about who is active on environmental issues. A very different constellation appears on environmental issues, one that is much more clearly structured than the disaster constellation.

Kreps: My question is whether there is any potential bridge between hazard issues in particular and environmental issues in general; is there any hope for a coalition?

J. Wright: We get an entirely different constellation for environmental issues as opposed to natural disaster issues, which is somewhat unexpected and which suggests that the answer is "no."

Michael Ornstein: I'm not sure what analysis SADRI has done of environmental coalitions versus natural hazard coalitions. On the basis of the reported factor analyses, there seem to be a lot of similarities. In fact, the coalitions may be quite similar, at least given the data you present.

Rossi: We are more impressed by the differences than the similarities. But we do have to look more closely at the factor structures for the two issues. To be sure, in both areas the elected officials are most important in getting legislation passed, so there will be at least some similarity. The question is how elites other than legislators coalesce.

Hirst Sutton: I react rather strongly to the word "apathetic" in the title of SADRI's report. We [the Council of State Governments] are coming out with a report soon that deals with the role of state and local government in hazard mitigation, and we are saying somewhat different things, namely, that there is a new environment for natural hazard programs and efforts at the federal, state, and local levels. We discuss in particular the new emphasis in Washington on mitigation, an emphasis that did not exist before the Carter administration. We are trying to persuade the states that now is an opportune time to explore their role in this new policy. While we are saying all of this, here comes your report saying that the politics are insignificant and that most people are not very concerned with this problem. I am not sure you do a service when you bring out the political realities of an issue that demands great leadership at state and local levels. I believe your report must deal very diplomatically with these issues.

Rossi: The viewpoint of the Council of State Governments on these issues, I agree, is not the same as ours. We will, of course, be as responsible as we can in presenting the material, but we will present it as we see fit. We do not have any stake in hazard risk mitigation policies; we see the advisability of such policies as an open question. We are not willing to close ranks behind the hazard mitigation movement to the extent of changing what we have to say. Your remarks seem somewhat censorial in context.

Coates: But is Sutton not really suggesting that the bull should feel some responsibility for the china shop? His point is that in going about your work according to your own inner dynamics, you are disturbing the work of large numbers of other people, creating unwanted side effects. I think what Sutton wants is to educate the bull about the china shop. Perhaps a little more caution would not destroy or damage your worthwhile efforts. The question is, how can you contain the secondary effects of your own presentation?

Rossi: I understand the point, that we have to present our results in a balanced, sensible, and responsible way. But understand that our sense of responsibility may be different from yours. We have a sense of responsibility to the policy *issue* that goes beyond partisanship for a particular policy approach. We agree: the nation should do "the right thing" about hazards. But we are less certain than you just what the right thing is.

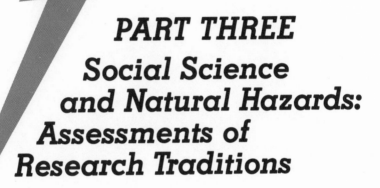

PART THREE

Social Science and Natural Hazards: Assessments of Research Traditions

THE WORTH OF THE NAS-NRC (1952-63) AND DRC (1963-present) STUDIES OF INDIVIDUAL AND SOCIAL RESPONSE TO DISASTERS

Gary A. Kreps

INTRODUCTION

The title of this presentation is presumptuous to say the least. A thorough assessment of the nearly three decades of social science research of disasters represented by the National Academy of Sciences-National Research Council (NAS-NRC: 1952-63)[1] and Ohio State University's Disaster Research Center (DRC: 1963-present) requires more than a brief paper. The NAS-NRC studies are reported in a 19-volume Disaster Studies Series, several related articles and books, and numerous unpublished documents. DRC has produced 27 publications in its book, monograph, and report series; 119 articles; and over 50 working papers. Accordingly, I will not provide a detailed summary of this work and will simply note that this has been attempted on several occasions (Fritz and Mathewson 1957; Fritz 1961; Loomis 1962; Barton 1969; Dynes 1970; Mileti, Drabek, and Haas 1975; Quarantelli and Dynes 1977; Stallings 1978). These previous state-of-the-art reviews have stressed knowledge developments and research gaps but have been largely circumspect about the applied, theoretical, and method-ological worth of work completed under various auspices. My primary purpose in this paper is to give greater substance to the latter, somewhat

---

[1] It should be noted that the academy's involvement in social science research on disasters did not cease completely in 1963. The social sciences were at least tangentially related to the work of the Advisory Committee on Civil Defense (1952-75) and the Advisory Committee on Emergency Preparedness (1965-75) and the Committee on the Alaska Earthquake (1964-69). The academy re-established a major interest in this area in the 1970s. Recent committees include the Committee on Mass Media Reporting of Disasters (present), the Committee on U.S. Emergency Preparedness (present), the Committee on International Disaster Assistance (1976-79), the Committee on the Socioeconomic Effects of Earthquake Prediction (1976-78), and the Panel on the Public Policy Implications of Earthquake Pre-diction (1974-75). However, the present paper deals only with the work done from 1952-63 under the Committee on Disaster Studies and its successor, the Disaster Research Group.

neglected issues. I believe that such an assessment is warranted, given the increasing importance attached to disasters (both domestic and foreign), the key historical roles of these two organizations in the development of social science research on disasters,[2] and the continuing need for reflection about the status and possible directions of disaster research as a field of inquiry.[3]

It is clear that DRC was able to build on the foundation established earlier at the academy, but the participants, research foci, and, of course, historical contexts of its work were different. Thus, although points of continuity will be noted below, the two research traditions will be treated as such in this paper. In both cases the assessment will revolve around the applied utility and theoretical and methodological yield of the respective work.[4]

On the applied side, attention is place on the possible relevance of the research to policymaking and policy implementation activities of public agencies. In this regard, it is important to keep expectations tied to disaster research in proper perspective. As noted in the recent NAS-NRC report on the socioeconomic effects of earthquake prediction (Committee on the Socioeconomic Effects of Earthquake Prediction 1978), application of social science research findings is seldom straightforward, even though government-supported "policy research" has grown substantially in the past decade or so. Recent studies of the use of social science research by government agencies suggest that it affects program development less through direct problem solving and more through the gradual assimilation of social science perspectives by government officials (Weiss 1977, Rein and White 1977).[5] There may be genuine worth in these indirect effects, but the "technology transfer" is subtle and therefore difficult to measure.

On the theoretical and methodological side, worth is perhaps best defined in terms of the contributions of these two traditions to basic research interests in sociology (development, refinement, and testing of theory). It was recently noted that there have been no startling theoretical breakthroughs in the

[2]Although not the focus of this paper, much of the recent social science research on hazards and disasters has been undertaken by other academically based research institutes. In the 1970s large-scale projects were funded at UCLA, University of Minnesota, University of Massachusetts, University of Denver, University of Georgia, University of Pennsylvania, Batelle Memorial Institute, and perhaps most visibly at the University of Colorado. However, prior to 1970, disaster research was dominated sequentially by NAS-NRC and DRC.

[3]The majority of support for academic social science research in this area has gone to the discipline of sociology. The NAS-NRC and DRC work falls predominantly within that field.

[4]I see theoretical and methodological issues as necessarily interrelated. I would also suggest that applied utility is not unrelated to the theoretical and methodological quality of research. However, I believe that application of social science knowledge to policy and program development implies a different set of issues.

[5]It also cannot be simply assumed that there are clear statements of agency problems and objectives that direct applied research or that research findings and recommendations can be readily implemented.

history of disaster research (Quarantelli and Dynes 1977),[6] even though the events studied number in the several hundreds and massive amounts of data have been collected. Of course, the need for breakthroughs is not unique to disaster research, but it is important to get a better fix on the theoretical and methodological returns of the research completed, to be specific about both progress and problems so that the field and the discipline involved can benefit from previous experience.

Finally, at some point in any assessment of this kind the costs of doing the research must be given consideration. I will largely skirt the issue in this paper, because I frankly don't know how to deal with it. It has been argued that support for social science research on disasters is inadequate to meet needs and capriciously determined (Quarantelli and Tierney 1979). However, beyond crude speculations about anticipated research costs and benefits (White and Haas 1975), there is a noticeable lack of precision about what an appropriate level of support would be and on what grounds one would argue for various levels and priorities in funding.[7] Taking it a step further, there is an inherent illogic to the funding of disaster research that is perhaps a combined function of the random occurrence of emergencies and major disasters, unpredictable political dynamics in funding allocation, and a general confusion about the boundaries of the field.[8] In any event, social science research projects on disasters have proven to be expensive. Current aggregate levels of funding may or may not be sufficient, but to argue for continuation or expansion is also to require responses to questions about the importance of the phenomena studied (eased by the elasticity of boundary definitions) and the worth or implications of what has already been done.

The primary objective of academy work appeared to be to develop disaster research as an interdisciplinary field that would be given credibility by both

[6]It should be added that these authors stressed the possibility that significant theoretical advances may be in the offing, particularly since the long sought "critical mass" of interested researchers and institutionalized research has come within reach.

[7]The most frequent comparisons are with funding for hazard research in the natural sciences and engineering fields and/or in terms of disaster impact data and aggregate expenditures for related disaster services. Another posssible point of comparison is with funding for other specialties in the same discipline. I know of no such comparison in sociology. By implication, the definition of how well served disaster research is is dependent, in part, on the points of comparison chosen. In all of this, of course, both the determination and seeking of funding are highly competitive processes.

[8]Precision in determining the boundaries of the field cuts both ways. The study by Rossi et al. (1978) suggests that precision in specifying hazards and levels of analysis leads to questions about funding priorities. On the other hand, ambiguity about hazard boundaries suggests possible funding benefits generated by rare events, such as the nuclear emergency in Pennsylvania. At a different level, a narrow research focus suggests an isolated specialty in the social sciences. A broad research focus implies greater integration with basic theoretical interests in the social sciences. The dilemmas in defining the field are obvious but their resolution is not.

scholars and government officials.[9] To that end the committee conducted its own research, provided a clearinghouse of disaster research, made small grants to encourage disaster studies, attempted to link interested researchers with other sources of funding, issued its own reports and other publications,[10] sponsored conferences and symposia, and in usual academy fashion provided advice to various interested government agencies.

Although not directly relevant to this paper, it seems that in addition to producing a considerable body of written material, the committee made significant progress in meeting its primary objective. By 1963 the field of disaster research had emerged (at least in sociology and psychology); it had an organized body of knowledge, a small but growing network of interested researchers, and a wealth of research interests. It had moved beyond description to theorizing and exhibited some reflection about methodological issues related to disaster research. It is important to add that not just the public but the broader disciplines involved in disaster research have a vested interest in responses to these questions.

THE NAS-NRC TRADITION (1952-63)

NAS-NRC became involved in social science research on disasters with the Committee on Disaster Studies (CDS: 1952-57). Prior to 1950 there was no significant program of disaster research in the United States. CDS was able to draw on the work of the World War II Strategic Bombing Surveys and a few earlier systematic studies of natural disasters, for a time a series of disaster studies undertaken by the National Opinion Research Center (NORC: 1950-54), and a limited number of smaller scale research projects located primarily in academic settings. But it is safe to say that at the time of the committee's formation in 1952, disaster research was not a well-known, let alone legitimated, specialty in the social sciences.

CDS was created as a result of a request made of NAS-NRC by the surgeon general of the Army, Navy, and Air Force to conduct research and monitor scientific developments related to "problems that might result from disasters caused by enemy action." The surgeon general was the chief source of funding for the committee from 1952 until 1955. From 1955 until 1963 the committee's activities were supported by grants from the Ford Foundation;

[9]Not all committee members were enamoured of interdisciplinary research. Janis (1954) argued that such an orientation was counterproductive to theory building. He suggested that the field be satisfied with piecemeal, discipline-based efforts.

[10]Of the nineteen volumes in the series, three were essentially inventories of previous research, two were conference proceedings, one was a specific attempt at modeling wartime evacuation, one dealt with methodological problems of disaster research, ten were case studies, and two were full-scale codification efforts. The latter two volumes are perhaps singularly important in terms of their respective push toward application (Fritz and Mathewson 1957) and toward theory (Barton 1963).

the National Institute of Mental Health; the Department of Health, Education, and Welfare; and the Federal Civil Defense Administration. The committee's name was changed to the Disaster Research Group (DRG: 1957–63), but its activities remained the same, with the exception that it became somewhat more active in fieldwork. Total financial support over the eleven-year period of the project was approximately $900,000.

Did the research have any relevance to the practical concerns of government agencies? A practical rationale, at least, was provided by the original funding agency — namely, to seek analogs to problems that might result from nuclear war — but there was (and still is) considerable confusion about both problems and analogs. Practical benefits were, of course, possible for both nuclear and nonnuclear hazards and disasters. Over time (and with changes in funding sources) a much broader interpretation of practical uses was evidenced in the reports (Wallace 1956, Fritz and Mathewson 1957, Moore et al. 1963).

Four of the nineteen volumes dealt specifically with the topic of nuclear war: two conference proceedings on shelters (Baker and Roher 1960) and the general civil defense problem (Baker and Cottrell 1962); a specific feasibility study of wartime evacuation problems (Ikle and Kincaid 1956); and a report summarizing survey analyses of individual responses to accidental air raid warnings in three cities (Mack and Baker 1961).[11] Perhaps the most specific social science–based recommendations made to government officials are found in the Ikle and Kincaid evacuation study and in a paper presented at the shelter conference by Fritz (1960).[12] The former report recommended (and showed by example) that ecological modeling should become a basic tool for evacuation, shelter, and transportation planning. The Fritz paper made a strong case against family shelters, promoted group shelters, and emphasized the problems of long-term shelter habitation and possible solutions. However, in all of the work noted above (and particularly the shelter conference) few questions were raised about alternative assumptions of the postattack environment.

In addition to these more focused works, several of the case studies made reference to possible links to the nuclear war situation. For example, Wallace (1956) suggested that victim behavior in response to a few seconds of warning in the Worcester tornado was perhaps analagous to responses to the blinding flash of a nuclear bomb. Moore et al. (1963), in their study of Hurricane

[11]There may have been other relevant but unpublished documents. There was at least one unpublished case study of shelter behavior in a snowstorm. This study was undertaken on specific request from the Federal Civil Defense Administration because of the perceived relevance of the incident to wartime shelter conditions.

[12]These are not assumed to be the only areas where findings and recommendations may have had some effect. They are used for illustrative purposes because they were the most obvious to me in reviewing the material.

Carla, suggested that problems of postimpact communications (for example, between shelters) were similar to those that might be anticipated during nuclear war. And so on. Thus, these and other implications were drawn in a discontinuous fashion from studies of events picked on a "catch as catch can" basis.

The committee and staff must certainly have been aware of and concerned about problems of discontinuity for both applied and basic research reasons (the latter to be discussed shortly). On the applied side, the monograph by Fritz and Mathewson (1957) was a clear attempt to synthesize findings on both convergence and other postimpact behaviors[13] and show the practical relevance of these findings to disaster management. Both specific disaster management recommendations (for example, mass media broadcast guidelines) and more general recommendations were offered, based on knowledge (translated as planning assumptions) of postdisaster environments. The authors simply assumed that their findings had relevance for both nuclear and natural disasters but stressed the latter.

What, then, were the practical results of this eleven-year research effort? In the case of the convergence monograph, some of the material was used in the preparation of Federal Civil Defense Guides. With regard to ecological modeling, this type of approach has apparently been used by federal civil defense agencies on a continuing basis. And, of course, the family shelter fad was short-lived. But are the control measures suggested in the convergence monograph effectively employed at various levels of disaster response? Is the country better prepared to cope with the evacuation, housing, and transportation problems associated with nuclear war? Have we developed a definitive and workable shelter program?

Both the implied benefits and criticisms suggested above are equally gratuitous. None of the studies undertaken by NAS-NRC was directed to focused problems or objectives, and the committee was in no way involved in program development or implementation. The point is that defining objectives, formulating problems, and enacting policies have independent dynamics to which research may be totally irrelevant. There is no fixed sequence of steps in policy and program development that can be assumed, and the role of research (even so-called policy research) in this process is seldom clear-cut.

Given confusion about the nature of the problems involved, it was inevitable that applications would be indirect at best. Perhaps the expansion of knowledge, combined with a growing number of formal and informal contacts between and among researchers and government officials, was

---

[13]I refer here to such general ideas as the absence of panic and looting in most disasters; the self-help orientation of disaster victims; the importance of individual and collective improvisation; the outpouring of altruistic behavior; and problems of communication, coordination, and control.

helping to dispel misconceptions about disasters and contributing to a more reasoned and reasonable approach to disaster demands. This notion of gradual diffusion of research findings and perspectives has never been documented even crudely in the disaster field, but it is consistent with studies (noted above) documenting indirect effects of applied research generally. I suspect that historically disaster researchers have hoped that this was, indeed, the case. However, what is most troubling about this optimistic view is not knowing what is being assimilated, how, and to what end. A related concern is the empirical foundation of what is being diffused.

Notwithstanding the practical rationale tied to its early funding, it is clear that the committee, staff, and other interested persons maintained a basic research orientation from the outset. Recall that the primary objective appeared to be to open up a new field of inquiry in the social sciences and give it theoretical and methodological substance. As time passed and new sponsors, such as the Ford Foundation and the National Institute of Mental Health were added, this basic research orientation was materially augmented. For perhaps less obvious reasons, the federal civil defense establishment (the Federal Civil Defense Administration, then the Office of Civil Defense Management) also contributed to this "normal science" approach, in part out of genuine confusion about what might be relevant to nuclear hazards (Garrett 1962). In any event, there were important theoretical and methodological issues facing the committee. The field had no clear boundary except as it could be loosely located as a social problem area (Merton and Nisbet 1961). The committee could shoot for any level of analysis (individual, group, organizational, community, society) and could mix levels virtually at will. All the methodological tools of the social sciences were relevant in one form or another. The committee also had a wealth of natural and man-made hazards to pick from, and the list was growing. The strategy taken was to forego defining the field (perhaps assuming a later crystallization) and to build inductively through exploration and description. In fact, it could be argued (and probably was) that the ambiguity of the nuclear hazard and the push for interdisciplinary work required depth of both domain and perspective. As noted earlier, however, the committee did not start from scratch, and its early activities were influenced in a major way by previous sociological research. The derived emphasis was on victim response and other forms of individual behavior.[14]

The primary methodological approach of the academy work was to describe events using field surveys (interviews) of disaster-impacted populations and public officials combined with analyses of secondary data.

---

[14]One of the key strengths of the case studies done under committee auspices was the simple fact that they reported marginals and cross-tabulations of individual status characteristics and behaviors, for example, postdisaster helping behavior by severity of injury (Wallace 1956).

All ten case studies of the nineteen-volume series involved some type of sampling frame of residents in impact areas, and in several cases random or saturation samples of victims were used. An important precedent for this approach to disaster research was the unpublished NORC study of the Arkansas tornadoes (five sites) of 1952. As implied earlier, events were chosen for study in happenstance fashion, depending on availability of funding, staff, and interested researchers. The most obvious point of similarity was that the majority of the case studies (seven out of ten) involved natural disaster agents.

The primary methodological themes were (1) the push for careful description of events regardless of how narrow the research focus, (2) continuing concerns about problems of doing disaster research in the field and the attendant need for more rigorous research designs, and (3) the effort to maintain at least some comparability in findings from disparate events. There were no instances in which direct replication occurred, but the researchers were always aware of related work and tried to build on it. The best examples of this were the two studies of disaster impacts on children (Perry, Silber, and Block 1956; Perry and Perry 1959) and the studies of Hurricane Audrey (Bates et al. 1963) and Hurricane Carla (Moore et al. 1963). In all of these instances the overlap of researchers across cases enhanced continuity.[15] It is interesting that discussions about research design and replication problems were not particularly reflective about prior questions of determining similarity of events. That is to say, the methodological benefits of boundary definition or taxonomy were not given much attention until the end (Barton 1963). Rather, thought was directed to more immediate problems of sampling individuals or informants (for example, convergers), gaining entree and access in the field, and developing measurement strategies (Killian 1956). To the credit of those involved, the research designs of the studies were for the most part presented in detail, with related difficulties explicitly noted.

The final issue concerns the theoretical yield of the research. Certainly a number of interesting findings and theoretical implications were generated. For example, the previously cited studies of psychological effects of disasters on children (Perry, Silber, and Block 1956; Perry and Perry 1959) documented postdisaster psychological symptom patterns and suggested explanations for their differences across the two events studied.[16] Clifford

[15] A related question is whether an institutionalized research capability (for example, a rapid response capability) is a functional imperative for doing and maintaining continuity in disaster research.

[16] The types of psychological symptoms were similar across the two events (tornadoes), but their distribution and severity were lower in the second event, even though the physical trauma was greater. Explanations for these differences generally revolved around implied rates of adult facilitative behavior, the degree to which role continuity of children was maintained, and the degree to which the disaster became a shared experience in the community.

(1955) did an interesting cross-cultural study of two communities in the United States and Mexico that were affected by the same flood and persuasively showed the relevance of predisaster cultural patterns in explaining differences in postdisaster attitudes and behaviors. The study was avowedly basic rather than applied in its explicit link to a Parsonian framework in sociology.[17] The Danzig, Thayer, and Galanter (1958) study of a false report of a dam break laid the groundwork for future studies of evacuation. The sampling plan was rigorous. Rates of warning confirmation and evacuation behavior were determined, as were sources of information used in making evaluation decisions, and a variety of hypothesized determinants of evacuation behavior (for example, proximity to hazard, role responsibility) were empirically examined.[18] The Beach and Lucas (1960) study of a coal mine disaster documented local convergence behavior that was effective and attributed this finding to the cultural absorption of both threat and appropriate response to this type of hazard.

The Bates et al. (1963) study of Hurricane Audrey merits special note because of its substantive breadth. It was a ground-breaking attempt to analyze long-term changes resulting from disasters. It made a serious effort to examine empirically previous hypotheses about mental health effects and the rise of the therapeutic community (Fritz 1961), as well as those dealing with occupational and family role conflicts (Killian et al. 1953, Form and Nosow 1958), and it invoked a sociologically based stress model, with particular emphasis on role strains (their sources and effects) in the emergency and rehabilitative phases of disaster response.

The above are only examples of the theoretical content of most of the work. As might be expected, there was theoretical progress but only modest overlap of research, some testing of hypotheses but few definitive findings, and of course the virtual absence of replication. But just as there was an attempt at applied synthesis (Fritz and Mathewson 1957), so too was this effort made, with some success, on the theoretical side. The theoretical results of this work are perhaps best expressed by two reports: the early case study by Wallace (1956) and the concluding codification by Barton (1963).

Wallace offered what he defined as a time-space model of disaster. Empirically grounding the model with research on the Worcester tornado of 1952, he argued that it had relevance for disasters in which "lethal impact is relatively sudden, brief, and sharply defined in area. . ." (Wallace 1956, p. 7). His time coordinates were labeled as (1) steady state, (2) warning, (3)

[17]The author focused on particularism and universalism (role orientations) in the two communities and showed how they affected a whole series of postdisaster responses (for example, family-based versus broader neighbor-based patterns of helping behavior and rates of complaints against public officials).

[18]For historical reference, it should be added that the importance and the calming effects of mass media activity were specifically noted in this study.

threat, (4) impact, (5) isolation, (6) rescue, (7) rehabilitation, and (8) irreversible change.[19] The spatial coordinates, expressed as widening concentric zones, were identified as (1) total impact, (2) fringe impact, (3) filter area, (4) organized community aid, and (5) organized regional aid. The basic purpose of the model was to distinguish areas both temporally and spatially in terms of their most marked disaster functions and problems. The case study material was then organized in terms of time phases that subsumed spatial referents.[20] For example, Wallace's now well-known notion of the "disaster syndrome" was tied to the total impact and fringe impact zones and given greatest prominence during the immediate aftermath of disaster, while the "counter disaster syndrome" was linked to the filter zone and area of organized community aid during the rescue phase.[21] The convergence problem was located in the filter zone during rescue and early rehabilitation. A so-called "cornucopia theory" of disaster relief was tied to the zones of organized community and regional aid largely during the rehabilitation phase of response.

Wallace's time-space model was important for three primary reasons. First, it provided some boundary definition for the field in terms of a particular type of disaster impact.[22] Second, it provided a framework for characterizing disaster events, thus opening the door to typologies of pre- and post-disaster functions and activities. Third, it offered a reasonably

[19]These were minor variations on time phases developed by Powell, Rayner, and Finesinger (1953).

[20]The integration of time and spatial coordinates was expressed only in terms of the threat, impact, isolation, and rescue time phases. The steady state, warning, and irreversible change stages implied only a vague system referent that was presumably the local community. Note that space was defined physically but not socially.

[21]The disaster syndrome was linked to victim response and said to involve four states: (1) a dazed, somewhat withdrawn reaction pattern lasting a few minutes to perhaps several hours; (2) a period of suggestibility, gratitude for help, and altruism lasting for several days; (3) a period of euphoric identification with the community and enthusiastic participation in repair lasting for up to several weeks; and (4) that point when the euphoria wears off and normal "ambivalent" attitudes return. The complementary counter disaster syndrome was said to affect those outside the impact area who had ties with those persons and places struck. Less precisely stated, this syndrome was characterized by extremely vigorous activity and other directed forms of behavior, motivated largely by concern or guilt. The determinants of both syndromes were said to be psychological, both positive and negative consequences were said to result, but the distribution of attitudes and behaviors implied by them were not documented. As far as I know, this still remains to be done.

[22]The fact that Wallace provided the defining properties of disaster events (simplifying assumptions really) is an important but generally overlooked point in the many restatements of his framework. For example, Bates et al. (1963) suggested that a necessary adjunct to Wallace's ecological model was a sociologically informed system stress model. However, they gave no heed to temporal-spatial determinants of stress or system level of stress as influenced by characteristics of the agent. Obviously, the framework has to be adjusted dramatically given different types of impacts. Wallace probably recognized that this adjustment wouldn't be easy and might not work.

precise conceptualization of what appeared, on examination of the Worcester case and related disaster literature, to be key behavior patterns in postdisaster responses. Many of the ideas and the observations expressed in this monograph had considerable influence on later work. But it is important to note that Wallace's study did not provide a systematic test of anything. Thus, the disaster syndrome and counter syndrome were potentially useful ideas about victim and nonvictim behaviors, but the distibution and determinants of those behaviors were obscure in his case study. And although convergence behavior and the massive outpouring of external aid were readily documented (as they continue to be in most disasters), patterns of individual and organizational behavior related to them were not.

The Barton monograph (1963), later revised as a book, *Communities in Disaster* (1969), was both a synthesis and an extension of disaster theory and research and can be seen as the culmination of the NAS-NRC tradition and the work that preceded it.[23] There can be no doubt that the report was an exercise in basic sociological theorizing about disasters. Indeed, Robert Merton, in his introduction to the volume, praised Barton's efforts to analyze the workings of social systems rather than the psychic processes of individuals collectively subjected to stress, and suggested that disasters were strategic sites for the development of middle-range sociological theories.

Barton's first contribution was to give greater precision to the boundaries of the field. He defined disasters as part of a larger category of collective stress situations that impinge on social systems. Employing the properties of (1) scope of system affected, (2) the speed and duration of impact, and (3) the degree of institutionalized preparedness, he developed a typology of collective stress situations. In so doing he was able to show that most previous disaster research fell within two clusters: (1) studies of disasters hitting without warning in small communities or small segments of cities that were little prepared (for example, studies of tornadoes, explosions, and flash floods); and (2) studies of World War II bombing raids where the system-level impact was cities or whole countries, where the impact was recurring, and where preparedness was high.[24] The research gaps were obvious and he quickly noted them (for example, a complete lack of studies of sudden disasters on a national level), but the typology also defined research areas (in effect, completed work) from which to build theory. To be specific, Barton began by theorizing from the individual level of analysis and focused on

[23]Baker and Chapman's edited volume, *Man and Society in Disaster* (1962), was intended as a companion state-of-the-art summary but was not published under academy auspices.

[24]Barton also developed a methodological classification of studies in order to distinguish the analytical power of anecdotal observations, careful qualitative descriptions, and quantitative surveys of single disaster situations. In the case of the latter, he characterized the NORC study of the Arkansas tornadoes as a prototype that much needed repeating.

postimpact emergency response, in large part because the field was preoccupied with individual behavior during that time phase. In a very real sense, Barton was imposing conceptual rigor (and simplifying assumptions) on a loose, inductive research tradition.

Barton's second contribution was to propose a general sociological framework for analyzing individual and organizational behavior in disaster situations. As stated earlier, the analysis began with a discussion of individual patterns of adaptive and nonadaptive reactions to stress. Attention was given to such concepts as role uncertainty (absence of defined action), role adequacy (possession of disaster-relevant skills), and role conflict (competing role demands) as possible determinants of postdisaster responses.[25] Based on past research, the rates of adaptive and community-oriented behavior were presumed to be high, but there was little empirical knowledge about the types of such behaviors, their distributions, and their causes. Barton gave particular attention to the motivational basis (for example, altruism, knowledge of victims, proximity to impact) of various types of helping behavior. He then argued that discrete patterns of individual behavior could be conceptually aggregated to reflect the community's informal mass assault on disaster-generated needs—in his terms, "one arm" of the emergency social system.

The "other arm" of the emergency social system was represented as the community's formal organizations. Here problems of mobilization of personnel, communications and coordination within organizations, and interorganizational relationships were examined. Links between informal mass assault and formally organized responses were defined in both positive (volunteers) and negative (mass convergence) terms, but the major practical problem seen was coordination and control of the informal mass assault (Fritz and Mathewson 1957).

Barton's third and major contribution was to develop an explicit systems model of processes related to the community's informal mass assault. By invoking earlier ideas about the therapeutic community (Fritz 1961), Barton essentially broadened his initial discussion of the individual basis of helping behavior by introducing a community model of the same. It was assumed that in large-scale disasters the community's formal organizations could meet only a fraction of the needs for disaster services and that the informal mass assault must be relied upon in coping with stress.[26] Stress was therefore

---

[25]Interestingly, Barton also introduced the notion of role improvisation as a way of handling uncertainty but implied that it had little value except as combined with disaster-relevant skills. Similarly, ad hoc organizational arrangements or informal leadership were given short shrift unless tied to disaster-relevant structures and roles.

[26]The absorptive capacity of the community system was therefore assumed to be highly elastic. Barton also suggested that the major portion of previous studies concerned events where this absorptive capacity was not severely tested.

expressed as an imbalance between disaster demands and organizational capability. The focus of the model was on rates of helping behavior as determined by disaster impact and community characteristics and a series of intervening interaction dynamics between victims and nonvictims. The relationships between the variable sets were formalized as a series of explicit propositions. Organizational processes related to helping behavior were not included in the model.

The model and previously developed ideas about the individual and community basis of action were then offered for testing. The principal types of studies recommended (there were others not mentioned here) were (1) systematic surveys of disaster-struck populations to determine rates of victim and nonvictim responses (the comparative benefits increase with each additional case); (2) surveys of organizational members in disaster-struck communities to study problems of mobilization, communication, and coordination; and (3) focused attempts to study the range of organizational and interorganizational patterns of action in different types of disasters. The research recommendations were explicit but unfortunately (perhaps intentionally) not assigned priorities. The strongest part of the book from a theoretical standpoint was the systems model of the informal mass assault. The best chance for continuity in the field, as well as a systematic test of this model, was clearly tied to surveys of disaster-struck populations along the lines of the earlier NORC study and several of the NAS case studies. Theoretically, the weakest part of Barton's argument, and obviously the least informed by past research, was his discussion of organized activity. The recommended organizational studies opened the door to the benefits of further exploration but at a potential cost of prolonging the discontinuity of theory and research in the field. As will be shown below, the Disaster Research Center chose the course of continued exploration.

THE DRC TRADITION (1963-PRESENT)

The NAS-NRC tradition was social psychological in both content and tone; that is, it explored individual effects and behaviors as influenced by the characteristics of disaster agents and by social forces in affected communities.[27] The field was developing a number of interesting findings and speculations along these lines and, with Fritz and Mathewson's (1957) and Barton's (1963) contributions, had formalized many applied and basic research questions. But the field was not well developed theoretically, and its domains were quite vague except for the obvious emphasis on natural disasters and emergency responses.

[27]This was not surprising given, first, the relative ease of thinking about disasters in these terms and, second, the importance of a social-psychological approach in sociology generally.

All of this was known by the founders of the Disaster Research Center. Perhaps the choices for future research were clear, but I suspect that they were not.[28] In any event, DRC chose a new level of analysis, the organizational level, while maintaining the exploratory research tradition established under NAS-NRC auspices. Since its founding, DRC's major objective has been to study local disaster-relevant organizations and emergent groups—with particular attention to emergency responses and the planning for such responses. The primary logic for this approach was that the organizational level of study had been virtually ignored by previous research and that efforts (like Barton's) to link ideas about individual and total system response theoretically would be unsuccessful without the full-blown development of an organizational framework.[29]

The primary approach of DRC research was to study the range of organizational and interorganizational response patterns in different types of disasters (recommended earlier by Barton). The center's initial funding (1963-68) came from the Office of Civil Defense (now the Defense Civil Preparedness Agency) and the U.S. Air Force Office of Scientific Research. This funding allowed the center to undertake both field and laboratory research on organizational behavior in collective stress situations. Possible application of findings to the practical problems of both conventional and nuclear hazards was of interest to all parties, but it was clearly understood that the effort would involve basic research on organizational behavior. That orientation has been maintained throughout the center's existence.

Civil defense and Air Force funding decreased substantially after 1968, but the center was able to compensate for this with a new five-year grant from the National Institute of Mental Health to study both natural disasters and civil disturbances. In this case the interests as well as funding requirements of the center dovetailed with a federal agency's interest in contemporary problems. The major effect, of course, was to expand the domain of DRC activity and provide for comparisons of different types of hazards (Veller 1973). The center also expanded its focus at this time to include studies of predisaster preparedness and planning and, secondarily,

---

[28]DRC was initially funded by the civil defense and the military. Their interests were, at least in part, tied to the nuclear hazard. However, links between natural disaster research and nuclear war were as confused as ever.

[29]It has been argued that there is a significant tendency to describe disaster response in terms of either the overall community or the individuals within it. To the degree that this tendency excludes the numerous organized responses characteristic of disaster, an element crucial to our understanding is omitted. Not only are various types of organized responses the primary means through which social systems respond to disasters, they also provide a shaping context for most individual responses. It has been suggested that the capacity of communities to withstand disaster impacts is to a significant degree a function of these discrete and in many ways autonomous organized activities (Kreps 1978, Veller 1972).

longer term organizational and community change. More recently, the center has undertaken large-scale research projects on special topics, such as emergency medical services (Public Health Service grant), mental health service delivery (National Institute of Mental Health grant and some state funding), and, most recently, chemical hazards and disasters (National Science Foundation grant). Since its inception, the center has conducted over 300 field studies of various types of natural and man-made hazards and disasters (about 180 actual disaster events). Total support for DRC research (the above-mentioned sources plus a few smaller grants and contracts) has been approximately $3,500,000.

In both philosophy and design, the DRC's work has been unabashedly exploratory. The center has not been noticeably concerned with defining the boundaries of the field, rather it has continuously attempted to break new ground. It has been more inclined to develop and empirically illustrate ideas than to test theoretical models. It has employed a variety of research strategies, but its studies have relied predominantly on unstructured and semi-structured data collection techniques. It has gathered large volumes of data (only some of which have been analyzed) and produced an abundance of written material. In what follows I attempt to discuss the appropriateness and utility of the DRC approach to disaster research. In so doing, I recognize that the approach taken reflects a long-standing and frequently debated view of the perceived need of developing a more sociological theory of disaster response.

With regard to the applied or policy implications of DRC's work, the same constraints noted in the discussion of NAS-NRC have also operated on the center. Thus, once again, there have been few direct applications, but the gradual diffusion of research findings and perspectives appears to have continued. In fact, the center's efforts to disseminate findings and ideas to public officials have been substantial. In addition to publishing a regular newsletter, the center's directors have given public speeches and lectures on many occasions, have been active organizers of and participants on committees and workshops related to disasters, have consulted widely in the area of disaster planning, and have regularly contributed to the training of civil defense and other disaster officials.

It is difficult to document precisely what is being disseminated or its empirical foundation. My impression is that DRC application attempts have been of two general types: first, to promote a particular perspective on disaster planning, based largely on its own research tradition (Quarantelli 1979; Tierney and Baisden 1977; Quarantelli and Taylor 1977; Dynes and Quarantelli 1977; Dynes, Quarantelli, and Kreps 1972) and, second, to provide a more realistic conception of pre- and post-disaster environments, based on a loose combination of inferences from its own research and that done under earlier NAS-NRC, NORC, and other post–World War II auspices (Quarantelli and Tierney 1979- Taylor 1977; Quarantelli 1973; Dynes and Quarantelli 1969, 1972, 1973).[30]

In my judgment the effort to promote a planning perspective has been the more coherent of the two types. The basic issue here has been to determine what can and should be done in advance of disasters to deal with their symptoms. The center has largely avoided the normative issue while arguing that what can be done is highly problematic. Although not systematically summarized in any single publication, the center's case materials have consistently shown relatively low levels of disaster planning and preparedness in local communities.[31] Useful disaster plans are difficult to come up with, but there is continuing interest in them by public officials because of the presumed benefits for emergency response. The center has shared this optimistic view, but its approach to planning has been informed by its own research, which suggests that much organized behavior in disaster is based on unpredictable but useful improvisations (Drabek 1968; Adams 1969; Paar 1969; Veller 1969; Drabek 1970; Brouillette 1970; Forrest 1972; Taylor, Ross, and Quarantelli 1976). In effect, it has been suggested that these improvisations are better seen as system strengths to build on than as weaknesses to be overcome by disaster planning.

As a result, the center has consistently argued for a flexible approach to disaster planning and preparedness at the local level. It has stressed planning principles rather than prototypes. It has recognized that disaster domains, tasks, resources, and activities cannot be fully anticipated by planning and therefore should be defined broadly. It has avoided the tendency of previous disaster research to interpret the complexity of local disaster response as social disorganization; rather it has interpreted this complexity, in part, as evidence of the community's absorptive capacity. Finally, it has admonished state and federal officials to get their own houses in order so that they can better serve local communities.

The empirical foundation of the planning perspective discussed above is potentially useful, but it unfortunately lacks rigor. Recommendations derived from it have therefore tended to be general rather than concerned specifically with the disaster agent, level of disaster response, or particular problems. In a few instances, however, DRC planning and preparedness recommendations have been more focused along these lines. The center's longitudinal study of mental health effects and mental health service delivery in the Xenia tornado of 1974 is a notable case in point. At the time of

---

[30]Given the center's primarily basic research interests, it is safe to assume that the attempts have not been strategically planned.

[31]This has been noted previously but not carefully studied. I would add that DRC archives are rich in data concerning local constraints on adopting and implementing planning and preparedness programs.

the study both policy and research issues concerning the mental health effects of disaster were becoming more pointed. Based on considerable field observation, intensive interviews with mental health and other disaster officials, and two random sample surveys of victim and nonvictim populations, the center produced findings and recommendations that were responsive to both types of issues (Tierney and Baisden 1977; Taylor, Ross, and Quarantelli 1976). Specifically, the center provided data on the types and distribution of psychological problems that occurred (generally problems of living rather than severe mental health pathology) and the crisis intervention efforts (in many ways ad hoc) that were responsive to these problems. The crisis intervention planning recommendations that followed reflected a sophisticated understanding of constraints on their adoption and implementation.

The second and more modest type of application involves the center's attempts to correct what are seen as widely held misconceptions about post-disaster environments, particularly as related to the reactions of individuals in impact areas. Assumptions of panic, looting, personal and social pathology, and the helplessness of disaster victims are treated as myths and replaced with assumptions reflecting the resourcefulness and resilience of affected populations, the rise of emergency consensus (at least in natural disasters), and the development of norms encouraging altruistic behavior. Much of what has been written or verbalized along these lines is not based on DRC research (except at a very impressionistic level), but rather derives from earlier social-psychological studies, such as those by NAS-NRC and NORC.[32]

There is a potential problem with this myth-breaking effort. The assumption of the predominance of adaptive rather than maladaptive response is based more on impression than evidence. Quite simply, the range and distribution of adaptive and maladaptive responses have not been fully conceptualized, let alone empirically documented. As noted earlier, there have been relatively few surveys of populations hit by disaster, thus little basis exists for comparisons of disaster reactions in terms of impact characteristics or community profiles. In most of the cases studied by social scientists the community's response capability was not seriously impaired and the likelihood of substantial and relatively quick outside assistance was great. Unfortunately, these very important qualifiers can be easily overlooked in discussions about the nature of postdisaster environments.

The danger is that a conventional wisdom can develop among both disaster researchers and users of disaster research findings (Kreps 1979,

---

[32]The previously noted DRC study of the Xenia tornado is the only case that I am aware of where systematic surveys of affected populations were undertaken. The findings of that study, although of direct relevance to the ongoing debate about the mental health effects of disaster, have not been used to verify other premises about victim reactions and behaviors.

Barton 1963). Of course, that conventional wisdom may be correct for a presently unspecified series of disaster events and behavior patterns.[33] However, in proffering it, the center raises fundamental questions about the nature of evidence in disaster research. For example, the London Technical Group (1974) has questioned the application of DRC and earlier social science research findings and perspectives to the problems of less developed societies. The specific view appears to be that assumptions about the viability of local response would have to be changed, principally because of the lower resource base of these societies. But the more general concern is the perceived lack of methodological rigor and theoretical precision of much social science research on disasters—problems that are felt to preclude generalization in any event. I now turn to these methodological and theoretical issues as they relate to the work of DRC.

As noted earlier, the NAS-NRC tradition involved a push for careful description of disaster events combined with more focused studies of patterns of victim and nonvictim behavior. Data collection was largely based on field surveys of affected populations, interviews with disaster officials, and secondary data.[34] DRC continued this exploratory thrust but changed the level of analysis from the individual to the organization. Purposive samples of disaster-relevant organizations and emergent groups have been selected in most of its studies and top organizational officials or group leaders interviewed in order to gather data on postdisaster activities (the main emphasis); predisaster planning; and, in some studies, longer term organizational changes.[35] Research results have generally taken the form of empirically based descriptions of disaster-relevant organizations and emergent groups (Anderson 1969, Brooks 1970, Adams 1972, Kreps 1973, Veller 1973, Waxman 1973, Forrest 1974, Wright 1976), more global conceptualizations of the behavior of these types of organizations (Warheit and Dynes 1968; Dynes 1968, 1970; Brouillette 1966; Stallings 1970;

---

[33]For example, I think that specification and empirical grounding are more definitive for panic behavior than for looting. Other patterns of response, such as helping behavior, remain obscure.

[34]One might argue that field observation was also a major data collection technique of both the NAS-NRC and DRC research. My judgment is that, although field observation played a role, it was generally a minor one given the necessarily delayed entry of researchers to affected communities. My own experience suggests that field observation was an important source of impressionistic but frequently useful background information. It became more directly relevant on those infrequent occasions when researchers were able to reach communities prior to impact.

[35]Random sampling of organizational members has not been employed, but frequently personnel from various levels of the organizational hierarchy have been interviewed. Saturation samples of members of emergent groups have, on occasion, been completed. Of the 6,000 or more interviews undertaken, the vast majority have been structured or semistructured.

Brouillette and Quarantelli 1971), and general discussions of organizational and community problems attendant to disaster response based on DRC and related research (Quarantelli 1966, Drabek and Quarantelli 1969, Wenger and Paar 1969, Dynes 1970, McLuckie 1970, Stallings 1970).

There are three important methodological implications of the DRC research approach that I think are reflected in the center's publications.[36] First, the quality of descriptions of disaster events has been very uneven, and this has probably resulted from the center's desire to study as many events as possible. Although in several cases events have been described in rich detail (for example, Drabek 1968; Taylor, Ross, and Quarantelli 1976), these have been the exceptions rather than the general rule. Several intensive studies of the behavior of a single organization (or a single type of organization) in a disaster have been completed (for example, Warheit and Quarantelli 1969, Adams 1969, Blanshan 1975, Smith 1977), as well as a few case studies at the community level of analysis (for example, Wenger 1970). However, overall, the primary emphasis has clearly been on breadth (number of events and organizations studied) rather than depth in the presentation of findings about organized behavior. The methodological wisdom of that strategy rests ultimately on the theoretical yield (discussed below) of the data collected.[37]

A second and certainly related methodological point is that links among conclusions, findings, and data collection are quite vague in many DRC publications, particularly those containing broad discussions of organizational problems and behaviors. To some extent, this is an inherent problem of qualitative research, but the problem has apparently been exacerbated by the center's attempts to generalize crudely from a large number of discrete cases. To discuss global problems and patterns of behavior (an implied strength of DRC's approach) is to raise questions about their marginal distributions over the large number of events studied. The center generally hasn't been able to answer these distributional questions except for small sets of studies in which there was some similarity in the events and/or some

---

[36]It is interesting that very few DRC publications have dealt specifically with methodological issues, particularly given the problems the center has faced in doing organizational studies. Those published initially (Dynes 1966; Dynes, Haas, and Quarantelli 1967) were largely restatements of previously expressed problems of doing disaster research (for example, unpredictability of events, lack of preimpact data, lack of methodological controls, problems in collecting ephemeral data). The most detailed and useful methodological paper dealt with the specific problem of simulating disaster experimentally and was based on an ongoing laboratory study (Drabek and Haas 1967). The most reflective paper was that by Drabek (1970b), who linked data collection problems with issues of taxonomy construction and model building.

[37]Note, however, that the potential of the center's data archives for producing qualitatively rich descriptions of events and organized behavior is far greater than has been evidenced in center publications. I have little doubt that data collection has exceeded data analyses since the center's inception.

consistency in the research questions addressed. Thus, the strength in the number of events studied is more apparent than real because of the exploratory, dicontinuous, and unstructured approach to data collection.

The third and final methodological point is that the center's research has evidenced only a small number of attempts at quantitative analysis, a few of which have been modestly successful (Drabek 1970a, Wenger 1970, Smith 1977). The probability of success has been low for at least two reasons: first, the chronic problems of measuring the key analytic properties of organized disaster response in other than qualitative terms (Kreps 1978) and, second, the continuing DRC emphasis on exploration and description rather than on hypothesis testing. The former reflects more general issues of developing sociological theories of human behavior.[38] The latter represents a long-standing view of DRC's proper role in disaster research.

My remaining points deal with the theoretical returns from the center's research. Had DRC continued in the social-psychological tradition of previous research, I suspect that hypothesis testing would have been more prominent (particularly given Barton's lead); data collection would have been more structured (via surveys of impacted populations); and, given the data collection and analysis costs tied to each case, a much smaller number of events would have been studied. It is, of course, impossible to say what the theoretical or practical yield would have been, but one obvious benefit would have been historical continuity of research. DRC took the different course of conducting exploratory organizational studies. As will be discussed below, the theoretical yield or potential of DRC research is uncertain, but a clear cost has been that some good leads have not been pursued.[39]

In a very real sense, the basic research problem that DRC has confronted implies a fundamental objective of sociology, that is, to develop theories of social organization at the organizational level of analysis. Postdisaster settings are potentially fruitful research contexts within which to pursue such an objective because they force us to deal with social structure (in this case

[38]For example, one could argue that, regardless of the complexity of the research questions, the emphasis on qualitative research makes it extremely difficult to separate fact from speculation. One could rejoin that crude quantification of structural properties is worse than none at all.

[39]Certainly these were not the only alternatives, and had the social-psychological approach been continued there probably wouldn't have been a Disaster Research Center. I also do not want to imply that DRC was given a blank check and a free rein to choose a course of action. The funding agencies had a distinct interest in organizational studies, probably because of anticipated returns for improved disaster management. However, it is arguable that continuing the social-psychological tradition was the "safe play" given the theoretical and methodological orientation of sociology to social-psychological issues; given the conceptual and empirical groundwork already completed; and given the difficulty of communicating within the discipline, as well as with disaster officials, in structural terms.

organized disaster responses) not in terms of status concepts tied to established organizations but as a series of analytical processes related to the creation, maintenance, and change of social structure (Kreps 1978, Drabek and Haas 1973, Veller and Quarantelli 1973, Dynes 1970, Veller 1969).[40] I am convinced that the development of a truly sociological theory of disaster response has been the primary rationale of DRC work. The attempt, although not yet successful, is a noble one. However, I have some doubts whether the center's historical research approach has been the most appropriate for the development and refinement of such a theory.

What has been accomplished so far? The most visible benefit has been the development of empirically based descriptions and conceptualizations of a wide range of organized behavior in a variety of disaster contexts (Quarantelli 1978, Veller 1973, Brouillette and Quarantelli 1971, Dynes 1970). This benefit is also reflected in DRC's historical orientation to such special topics as the following: laboratory studies of simulated disaster (Drabek 1970a; Drabek and Haas 1967, 1969); disaster warning systems (McLuckie 1970, Anderson 1969, Brouillette 1966, Adams 1965); mass media reporting of disasters (Kueneman and Wright 1975, Adams 1974, Waxman 1973, Quarantelli 1971); emergency medical services (Golec and Gurney 1977, Neff 1977, Tierney and Taylor 1977, Worth and Stroup 1977, Wright 1977); mental health service delivery (Taylor 1977; Taylor, Ross, and Quarantelli 1976); cross-cultural studies of disasters and emergencies (Quarantelli 1978, Anderson and Dynes 1975, Roth 1970, McLuckie 1970); and the handling of the dead in disasters (Blanshan 1977, Hershiser and Quarantelli 1976). These as well as other examples suggest that the center has provided small to modest amounts of information on a large number of topics as it has attempted to develop and refine ideas about organized disaster response.

The yield of this exploratory and in many ways disjointed effort is uncertain. I think that the hope has always been that DRC would open the door to more refined organizational analyses of these topics, presumably to be done by others as the "critical mass" of disaster researchers was achieved. I would further speculate that, given the capriciousness of funding for disaster research, the breaking of new ground was seen as increasing the probability of continued organizational studies of disasters by sociologists. In this sense, then, the theoretical return on the center's work can be seen only as indirect, and its determination must be based on subsequent studies.

But given the substantial and long-term support, there is the more basic question of DRC's direct theoretical contibutions. I will discuss two areas,

---

[40]In effect, the effort has involved trying to integrate and extend sociological theories of collective behavior and complex organizations (Dynes and Quarantelli 1968).

one briefly and the other in somewhat greater detail, where I think that some progress has been made but major problems remain.[41] First, the center has developed several related typologies or conceptualizations of the range of organized disaster responses (Bardo 1978, Veller and Quarantelli 1973, Brouillette and Quarantelli 1971, Dynes 1970). This is perhaps to be expected given the breadth of studies completed. The best known is Dynes's (1970) classification of established, expanding, extending, and emergent organizations based on a cross-classification of structures (old-new) and tasks (regular-nonregular). These classification schemes have been applied to a number of different disaster contexts and have proven to be descriptively useful. However, their utility is inherently limited because they are not exhaustive.[42] They are not exhaustive because they lack precision and depth in defining and specifying the conceptual properties of an organized disaster response. In effect, key problems remain in the definition and empirical grounding of what we are trying to explain (Kreps 1978).

Second, DRC efforts to account for these patterns of organized disaster response have most consistently revolved around what might be referred to as an organizational stress framework.[43] The framework gradually evolved at the center through frequent applications in various disaster contexts (Taylor, Ross, and Quarantelli 1976; Waxman 1972; Adams 1969; Dynes 1970; Drabek 1968, 1970a, 1971; Anderson 1969; Warheit and Quarantelli 1969; Yutzy 1969). The most detailed empirical examination of this framework was conducted in an experimental study of a simulated air crash (Drabek 1970a). Its most thorough conceptual treatment appears in a textbook on complex organizations (Drabek and Haas 1973). The framework has not been presented in the form of an explanatory or predictive model, and thus far only suggestive propositions have been offered.

Those using the stress framework generally assume a preexisting and open system (usually a formal organization) and focus on patterns of persistence and change in the system's performance structure. Social systems are said to exist routinely with a balance between environmentally based demands and internally based performance capabilities. But the balance can be altered by

[41]A relevant theoretical problem I will not discuss is that of taxonomy. In my judgment, little progress has been made in the development of a taxonomy of disasters based on the inter-relationships among agent characteristics. Such a taxonomy would provide an important foundation for comparisons of disasters in terms of individual and social impacts (Dynes 1970). This theoretical problem will not be solved simply, and it involves all disciplines in which disaster research is undertaken. It is exacerbated by the disinclination of the field to define its own boundaries.

[42]For example, classifications of emergent interorganizational networks (Drabek 1968) have received only modest attention (Dynes 1968, Brouillette 1970), even though they have much potential utility for discussions of communications, coordination, and control problems.

[43]The concept of stress has a long history in the social sciences and it was often invoked in early social-psychological studies (for example, Barton 1963, Bates et al. 1963).

changes in either demands or capabilities, and any resulting discrepancy between them is defined as system stress. The effects of stress on the system's performance structure are then examined.[44] Although stress is more often assumed than actually measured, in my judgment, the framework provides a reasonable way of describing disaster events and interpreting patterns of organized disaster response that result. Unfortunately, I seriously doubt whether its descriptive utility is matched by its explanatory power.

To be specific, the stress framework is inadequate because it virtually defines away the theoretical problem. The objective is to explain patterns of organized disaster response in terms of discontinuities between disaster demands and system capability. The mistake is in defining the interaction of demands and capability as *stress*. To make such an argument is virtually to destroy the independent explanatory power of each dimension in accounting for patterns of organized disaster response. What I think has happened is that a market metaphor (supply-demand intersection with two-way causation) has been unintentionally but inappropriately employed. If the intersection of disaster demands and system capability is defined as *patterns of organized disaster response* (the dependent variable with a price metaphor), then the conceptual independence of demands and system capability is maintained and the market metaphor is not violated. But to define their interaction as stress is to lose that conceptual independence and to introduce the methodological flaw of building interaction terms by addition and subtraction. A further risk is that cause and effect can become tautologically linked.[45]

In suggesting that a metaphor was mistakenly applied, I do not argue for its use—quite the contrary. I believe that the conceptual properties of organized disaster response, disaster demands, and system capability are of such complexity that a market metaphor quickly becomes useless. Similarly, to link the framework to psychological analogs of relationships between stress and performance is reductionistic and therefore ill-suited to the complexities of organizational study. A better approach is to work toward defining and empirically grounding key properties of organized disaster response, to treat disaster demands and system capability (really system states) as sets of

[44]The reader should note that the stress framework, particularly as it relates to the system properties of complex organizations, is far more complex than this brief description of it can convey. I simply decided to use scarce space to raise pointed criticisms for whatever utility they may have.

[45]To rejoin that the center has consistently argued for the importance of predisaster system characteristics (for example, routines, available resources) in explaining postdisaster responses is only to show the incompatibility of the stress framework with useful ideas about the elasticity of social structure (Burns 1958, Kreps 1978). Nor can stress be defined as an intervening but unmeasured causal property, because in this sense it lacks the conceptual independence to make it useful. And, as noted above, stress cannot serve as a statistical interaction term as presently defined.

independent causal properties, and to consider the interactions among these causal properties as statistical questions that can be deferred until logically prior measurement problems have been solved.

The DRC tradition has to overcome some difficult problems if it is to achieve a sociological theory of organized disaster response. The potential is there, but I believe that the historical approach to data collection and data analysis has not been fully responsive to theory-building requirements. Since a key problem involves defining and documenting the conceptual properties of organized disaster response, a strategy of fewer but more in-depth studies would have been more likely to reveal the range and complexity of response patterns. [46]The number of events studied would have increased more slowly, but the ability to generalize hasn't been good anyway. A saving grace is the continuing strength of the center's data archives. DRC publications don't begin to reflect the wealth of information that exists. The data are not well suited for testing theories, but they are well suited for revealing what active groups and organizations are doing, the processes related to social action, and the various contexts in which action takes place. It is here, working with the data already available, that I think genuine theoretical progress can be made.[47]

CONCLUSION

Both traditions have reflected a commitment to basic science. Both traditions have been concerned with the viability of disaster research as a field of inquiry in the social sciences and, in pursuit of that objective, have kept its boundaries as broad as possible. Both traditions have produced interesting theoretical leads but few definitive findings. In both cases the theoretical leads are still being pursued. Has one tradition been any better than the other? The NAS-NRC research approach had the advantage of coming first, had few specific theoretical or practical expectations tied to it, and had the ability to draw on a wider base of professional skill. I have been more critical of the DRC approach, but I think that the center chose the

---

[46]It has been suggested that there are four conceptually distinct elements of any organized disaster response — domain, task integration, human and material resources, and activities — but that no causal priority or assumption of dominance in their mutual effects is warranted. In this sense, organization is defined in terms of process. The theoretical problem is to establish empirically the various possible combinations of activation, maintenance, and suspension of the elements, then try to explain these patterns in terms of causal properties of the agent and the system level being analyzed (Kreps 1978, Veller 1972). Explanation of these patterns is perhaps most expeditiously obtained by purposive sampling of disasters in terms of points on a distribution of scope of impact.

[47]I have worked with these data long enough to know that success is no sure thing. I also appreciate the argument that DRC's historical approach was dictated by funding realities. I would simply respond that funding constraints were counterproductive to the center's primary purpose.

more difficult set of problems and that the theoretical and applied potential of its work is greater.

Do these traditions provide an important source of justification for continued or greater support of disaster research? The answer to this question depends on the case made for the importance of theoretical and/or practical issues related to disasters compared to the spate of other problems that compete for attention. I am an advocate on theoretical grounds, because I believe that disasters are fruitful contexts for studying fundamental questions in sociology. However, subsequent research should not be undertaken in the desultory manner represented by both of these traditions. One direction for NAS-NRC was well stated by Barton — namely, hypothesis-testing studies of disaster-affected or -threatened populations. Some of this type of research is currently being done. In the case of DRC there is much untapped potential in the mass of qualitative data already collected, and I think we have a good idea of what to look for in the archives. I would add that the large number of events studied may still prove to be an important strength.

Not surprisingly, I am more hesitant on applied grounds. The benefits of both traditions have been more indirect than direct and are not well documented. Admitting to a leap of faith, I think that these traditions have provided practitioners with useful ways of thinking about disaster environments, responses to them, and planning for them. They have pointed to the strengths of local improvisations that inevitably occur in disasters of selected characteristics and, in so doing, have provided a basis for a more informed approach to outside assistance. This has relevance for both domestic and foreign disaster assistance. I don't know whether these and related benefits provide sufficient argument for a large-scale applied research program. It depends on how one defines and documents the magnitude of the problem (and at what level) and the practical yield for improved disaster assistance. The magnitude of the problem is virtually indeterminate, because the domains of the field are defined as broadly as possible. The practical yield is unknown to me, but my experience suggests that we are better at suggesting what won't work than what will work. In this sense, disaster research is not unique.

REFERENCES

Adams, D. 1965. *The Minneapolis Tornadoes, May 6, 1965: Notes on the Warning Process.* Research Report 6. Columbus, Ohio: Ohio State University Disaster Research Center.

_____. 1969. *Emergency Actions and Disaster Reactions: An Analysis of the Anchorage Public Works Department in the 1964 Alaska Earthquake.* Monograph Series No. 5. Columbus, Ohio: Ohio State University Disaster Research Center.

_____. 1972. *Goal and Structural Succession in a Voluntary Association: A Constructed Type of the American Red Cross Chapter in Natural Disasters.* Ph.D. Thesis. Ohio State University.

_____. 1974. *A Description and Analysis of a Radio Station Operation During a Forest Fire.* Preliminary Paper 14. Columbus, Ohio: Ohio State University Disaster Research Center.

Anderson, W.A. 1969. Disaster Warning and Communications Processes in Two Communities. *Journal of Communications* 19 (June): 92–104.

Anderson, W.A. and Dynes, R.R. 1975. *Social Movements, Violence, and Change: The May Movement in Curacao.* Columbus, Ohio: Ohio State University Press.

Baker, G.W. and Chapman, D.W., eds. 1962. *Man and Society in Disasters.* New York: Basic Books.

Baker, G.W. and Cottrell, L.S., eds. 1962. *Behavioral Science and Civil Defense.* NAS-NRC Publication 297. Washington, D.C.: NAS-NRC.

Baker, G.W. and Rohrer, J.H., eds. 1960. *Human Problems in the Utilization of Fallout Shelters.* NAS-NRC Publication 800. Washington, D.C.: NAS-NRC.

Bardo, J.W. 1978. Organizational Response to Disasters: A Typology of Adaptation and Change. *Mass Emergencies* 3 (September): 87–104.

Barton, A.H. 1963. *Social Organization Under Stress: A Sociological Review of Disaster Studies.* NAS-NRC Publication 1032. Washington, D.C.: NAS-NRC.

_____. 1969. *Communities in Disasters.* New York: Anchor, Doubleday.

Bates, F.L. et al. 1963. *The Social and Psychological Consequences of a Natural Disaster: A Longitudinal Study of Hurricane Audrey.* NAS-NRC Publication 1081. Washington, D.C.: NAS-NRC.

Beach, H.D. and Lucas, R.A. 1960. *Individual and Group Behavior in a Coal Mine Disaster.* NAS-NRC Publication 834. Washington, D.C.: NAS-NRC.

Blanshan, S.A. 1975. *Hospitals in Rough Waters: The Effects of a Flood Disaster on Organizational Change.* Ph.D. Thesis. Ohio State University.

_____. 1977. Disaster Body Handling. *Mass Emergencies* 2 (December): 249–258.

Brooks, J.M. 1970. *A Sociological Study of Commercial Broadcast Organizations.* Ph.D. Thesis. Ohio State University.

Brouillette, J.R. 1966. *A Tornado Warning System: Its Functioning on Palm Sunday in Indiana.* Research Report 15. Columbus, Ohio: Ohio State University Disaster Research Center.

_____. 1970. *Community Organizations Under Stress: A Study of Interorganizational Communications Networks During Natural Disasters.* Ph.D. Thesis. Ohio State University.

Brouillette, J.R. and Quarantelli, E.L. 1971. Types of Patterned Variation in Bureaucratic Adaptations to Organizational Stress. *Sociological Inquiry* 41 (Winter): 39–46.

Burns, T. 1958. The Forms of Conduct. *American Journal of Sociology* 64: 137–151.

Clifford, R.A. 1955. *The Rio Grande Flood: A Comparative Study of Border Communities in Disasters.* NAS-NRC Publication 458. Washington, D.C.: NAS-NRC.

Committee on the Socioeconomic Effects of Earthquake Predictions. 1978. *A Program of Studies on the Socioeconomic Effects of Earthquake Prediction.* Washington, D.C.: NAS-NRC.

Danzig, E.R., Thayer, P.W., and Galanter, L.R. 1958. *The Effects of a Threatening Rumor on a Disaster Stricken Community.* NAS-NRC Publication 517. Washington, D.C.: NAS-NRC.

Drabek, T. E. 1968. *Disaster in Aisle 13: A Case Study of the Coliseum Explosion at the Indiana State Fairgrounds, October 31, 1963.* Columbus, Ohio: Ohio State University, College of Administrative Science.

_____. 1970a. *Laboratory Simulation of a Police Communication System Under Stress.* Columbus, Ohio: Ohio State University, College of Administrative Science.

_____. 1970b. Methodology of Studying Disasters: Past Patterns and Future Possibilities. *American Behavioral Scientist* 13 (January–February): 325–330.

_____. 1977. *An Assessment of Search and Rescue Missions in Natural Disasters and Wilderness Settings.* Research Project No. ENV 77-14162. Washington, D.C.: NSF.

_____. 1971. A Theoretical Framework for the Analysis of Organizational Stress. Paper presented at the meetings of the American Sociological Association, Denver, Colorado.

Drabek, T. E. and Haas, J.E. 1967. Realism in Laboratory Simulation: Myth or Method? *Social Forces* 45 (March): 337–346.

_____. 1969. Laboratory Simulation of Organizational Stress. *American Sociological Review* 34 (April): 223–238.

_____. 1973. *Complex Organizations: A Sociological Perspective.* New York: Macmillan.

Drabek, T. E. and Quarantelli, E.L. 1969. Blame in Disaster: Another Look, Another Viewpoint. In *Dynamic Social Psychology,* D.W. Chapman, ed. New York: Random House.

Dynes, R.R. 1966. Disaster as a Social Science Field. *The National Review of Social Sciences* 3 (January): 75–84.

_____. 1968. *The Functioning of Expanding Organizations in Community Disasters.* Columbus, Ohio: Ohio State University Disaster Research Center.

_____. 1970. *Organized Behavior in Disasters.* Lexington, Mass.: D.C. Heath.

Dynes, R.R., Haas, J.E., and Quarantelli, E.L. 1967. Administrative, Methodological, and Theoretical Problems of Disaster Research. *Indian Sociological Bulletin* 4 (July): 215–227.

Dynes, R.R. and Quarantelli, E.L. 1968. Group Behavior Under Stress: A Required Convergence of Organizational and Collective Behavior Perspectives. *Sociology and Social Research* 52 (July): 416–429.

_____. 1969. Dissensus and Consensus in Community Emergencies: Patterns of Looting and Property Norms. *Il Politico* 34: 276–291.

_____. 1972. When Disaster Strikes (It Isn't Much Like You've Heard and Read About). *Psychology Today* 5 (February): 66–70.

_____. 1973. Images of Disaster Behavior: Myths and Consequences. Preliminary paper. Columbus, Ohio: Ohio State University Disaster Research Center.

_____. 1977. *The Role of Local Civil Defense in Disaster Planning.* Report Series No. 16. Columbus, Ohio: Ohio State University Disaster Research Center.

Dynes, R.R., Quarantelli, E.L., and Kreps, G.A. 1972. *A Perspective on Disaster Planning.* Report Series No. 11. Columbus, Ohio: Ohio State University Disaster Research Center.

Form, W.H. and Nosow, S. 1958. *Community in Disaster.* New York: Harper and Row.

Forrest, T. R. 1972. *Structural Differentiation in Emergent Groups.* Ph.D. Thesis. Ohio State University.

_____. 1974. *Structural Differentiation in Emergent Groups.* Report Series No. 15. Columbus, Ohio: Ohio State University Disaster Research Center.

Fritz, C.E. 1960. Some Implications from Disaster Research for a National Shelter Program. In *Human Problems in the Utilization of Fallout Shelters,* G.W. Baker and J.H. Rohrer, eds. NAS-NRC Publication 800. Washington, D.C.: NAS-NRC.

_____. 1961. Disaster. In *Contemporary Social Problems,* R.K. Merton and R. Nisbet, eds. New York: Harcourt.

Fritz, C.E. and Mathewson, J.H. 1957. *Convergence Behavior in Disasters: A Problem of Social Control.* NAS-NRC Publication 476. Washington, D.C.: NAS-NRC.

Garrett, R.L. 1962. Social Science Research Program: Review and Prospect. In *Behavioral Science and Civil Defense,* G.W. Baker and L.S. Cottrell, eds. NAS-NRC Publication 997. Washington, D.C.: NAS-NRC.

Golec, J.A. and Gurney, P. J. 1977. The Problem of Needs Assessment in the Delivery of EMS. *Mass Emergencies* 2: 169–178.

Hershiser, M. and Quarantelli, E.L. 1976. The Handling of the Dead in a Disaster. *Omega* 7: 196–208.

Ikle, F.C. and Kincaid, H.V. 1956. *Social Aspects of Wartime Evacuation of American Cities.* NAS-NRC Publication 393. Washington, D.C.: NAS-NRC.

Janis, I.L. 1954. Problems of Theory in the Analysis of Stress Behavior. *Journal of Social Issues* 10: 12–26.

Killian, L.M. 1956. *An Introduction to Methodological Problems of Field Studies in Disaster.* NAS-NRC Publication 456. Washington, D.C.: NAS-NRC.

Killian, L.M., Quick, R., and Stockwell, F. 1953. *The Houston Fireworks Explosion.* NAS-NRC Publication 391. Washington, D.C.: NAS-NRC.

Kreps, G.A. 1973. *Decision Making Under Conditions of Uncertainty: Civil Disturbance and Organizational Change in Urban Police and Fire Departments.* Report Series No. 13. Columbus, Ohio: Ohio State University Disaster Research Center.

_____. 1978. The Organization of Disaster Response: Some Fundamental Theoretical Issues. In *Disasters: Theory and Research,* E.L. Quarantelli, ed. London: Sage Publications.

_____. 1979. Research Questions, Policy Issues, and Research Strategies on Mass Media Reporting of Disasters. In *Proceedings of the Workshop on Mass Media Reporting of Disasters.* Committee on Disasters and the Mass Media. Washington, D.C.: NAS-NRC.

Kueneman, R.M. and Wright, J. 1975. News Policies of Broadcast Stations for Civil Disturbances and Disasters. *Journalism Quarterly* 52 (Winter): 670–677.

Loomis, C.P. 1962. Toward Systemic Analysis of Disaster, Disruption, Stress, and Recovery—Suggested Areas of Investigation. In *Behavioral Science and Civil Defense*, G.W. Baker and L.S. Cottrell, eds. NAS-NRC Publication 997. Washington, D.C.: NAS-NRC.

London Technical Group. 1974. *Disaster Technology: An Annotated Bibliography*. London: Pergamon Press.

Mack, R.W. and Baker, G.W. 1961. *The Occasion Instant: The Structure of Social Responses to Unanticipated Air Raid Warnings*. NAS-NRC Publication 945. Washington, D.C.: NAS-NRC.

McLuckie, B.F. 1970. *The Study of Functional Response to Stress in Three Societies*. Ph.D. Thesis. Ohio State University.

_____. 1970. *The Warning System in Disaster Situations: A Selective Analysis*. Report Series No. 9. Columbus, Ohio: Ohio State University Disaster Research Center.

Merton, R.K. and Nisbet, R., eds. 1961. *Contemporary Social Problems*. New York: Harcourt.

Mileti, D.S., Drabek, T. E., and Haas, J.E. 1975. *Human Systems in Extreme Environments: A Sociological Perspective*. Boulder, Colorado: Institute for Behavioral Science.

Moore, H.E. et al. 1963. *Before the Wind: A Study of the Response to Hurricane Carla*. NAS-NRC Publication 1095. Washington, D.C.: NAS-NRC.

Neff, J.L. 1977. Responsibility for the Delivery of Emergency Medical Services in a Mass Casualty Situation: The Problem of Overlapping Jurisdictions. *Mass Emergencies* 2: 179–188.

Paar, A.R. 1969. *Group Emergence Under Stress: A Study of Collective Behavior During the Emergency Period*. Ph.D. Thesis. Ohio State University.

Perry, H.S. and Perry, S.E. 1959. *The School-House Disasters: Family and Community as Determinants of the Child's Response to Disaster*. NAS-NRC Publication 554. Washington, D.C.: NAS-NRC.

Perry, S.E., Silber, E., and Block, D.A. 1956. *The Child and His Family in Disaster: A Study of the 1953 Vicksburg Tornado*. NAS-NRC Publication 394. Washington, D.C.: NAS-NRC.

Powell, J.W., Rayner, J., and Finesinger, J.E. 1953. Responses to Disaster in American Culture: Groups. In *Symposium on Stress*. Washington, D.C.: Army Medical Service Graduate School.

Prince, S. 1920. *Catastrophe and Social Change*. London: Kind and Son.

Quarantelli, E.L. 1966. Organization Under Stress. In *Symposium on Emergency Operations*. R. Brictson, ed. Santa Monica, Calif.: Systems Development Corporation.

_____. 1971. Changes in Ohio Radio Station Policies and Operations in Reporting Local Civil Disturbances. *Journal of Broadcasting* 15 (Summer): 287–292.

_____. 1973. Human Behavior in Disaster. In *Proceedings of the Conference to Survive Disaster*. Chicago: IIT Research Institute.

_____. 1978. Cross Cultural Studies of Emergency Time Behavior. *Mass Emergencies* 2, No. 3 (September): 142–150.

_____. 1979. *Disaster Studies and Planning*. Columbus, Ohio: Ohio State University Research Foundation.

Quarantelli, E.L. ed. 1978. *Disasters: Theory and Research*. London: Sage Publications.

Quarantelli, E.L. and Dynes, R.R. 1976. Community Conflict: Its Absence and Its Presence in Natural Disasters. *Mass Emergencies* 1 (February): 139–152.

_____. 1977. *The Role of Civil Defense in Disaster Planning*. Report Series No. 16. Columbus, Ohio: Ohio State University Disaster Research Center.

Quarantelli, E.L. and Taylor, V.A. 1977. *Executive Summary: Delivery of Emergency Medical Services in Disasters*. Columbus, Ohio: Ohio State University Disaster Research Center.

Quarantelli, E.L. and Tierney, K. 1979. *Disaster Preparation Planning*. Columbus, Ohio: Ohio State University Disaster Research Center.

Raker, J.W. et al. 1956. *Emergency Medical Care in Disasters: A Summary of Recorded Experience*. NAS-NRC Publication 457. Washington, D.C.: NAS-NRC.

Rein, M. and White, S.H. 1977. Policy Research: Belief and Doubt. *Policy Analysis* 3 (Spring): 239–273.

Rossi, P.H. et al. 1978. Are There Long Term Effects of American Natural Disasters? Estimations of Effects of Floods, Hurricanes, and Tornadoes Occurring 1960 to 1970 on U.S. Counties and Census Tracts in 1970. *Mass Emergencies* 3: 117–132.

Roth, R. 1970. Cross Cultural Perspective on Disaster Response. *American Behavioral Scientist* 13 (January–February): 440–452.

Smith, M. 1977. *An Organizational Analysis of Disaster Response: A Study of Religious Organizations*. Ph.D. Thesis. Ohio State University.

Stallings, R. 1970. *Communications in Natural Disasters*. Report Series No. 10. Columbus, Ohio: Ohio State University Disaster Research Center.

_____. 1970. Hospital Adaptations to Disaster: Flow Models of Intensive Technologies. *Human Organization* 29 (Winter): 294–302.

_____. 1978. The Structural Patterns of Four Types of Organizations in Disasters. In *Disasters: Theory and Research*, E.L. Quarantelli, ed. London: Sage Publications.

Taylor, V.W. 1977. Good News About Disasters. *Psychology Today* (October): 93–96.

Taylor, V.W., Ross, G.A., and Quarantelli, E.L. 1976. *Delivery of Mental Health Services in Disasters: The Xenia Tornado and Some Implications*. Columbus, Ohio: Ohio State University Disaster Research Center.

Tierney, K.J. and Baisden, B. 1977. *Crisis Intervention Programs for Disaster Victims: A Source Book and Manual for Smaller Communities*. Columbus, Ohio: Ohio State University Disaster Research Center.

Tierney, K.J. and Taylor, V.A. 1977. EMS Delivery in Mass Emergencies: Preliminary Research Findings. *Mass Emergencies* 2: 151–158.

Veller, J.M. 1969. *The Social Organization of Disaster Response*. Master's Thesis. Ohio State University.

_____. 1972. Interorganizational Relations and Organized Response to Disaster Environments. In *Proceedings of the Japan-United States Disaster Research Seminar.* Columbus, Ohio: Ohio State University Disaster Research Center.

_____. 1973. *Organizational Innovation in Anticipation of Crisis.* Report Series No. 14. Columbus, Ohio: Ohio State University Disaster Research Center.

Veller, J.M. and Quarantelli, E.L. 1973. Neglected Characteristics of Collective Behavior. *American Journal of Sociology* 79 (November): 665-685.

Wallace, A.F.C. 1956. *Tornado in Worcester: An Exploratory Study of Individual and Community Behavior in an Extreme Situation.* NAS-NRC Publication 392. Washington, D.C.: NAS-NRC.

Warheit, G. and Dynes, R.R. 1968. *The Functioning of Established Organizations in Community Disasters.* Report Series No. 1. Columbus, Ohio: Ohio State University Disaster Research Center.

Warheit, G. and Quarantelli, E.L. 1969. *An Analysis of the Los Angeles Fire Department Operations during Watts.* Report Series No. 7. Columbus, Ohio: Ohio State University Disaster Research Center.

Waxman, J.J. 1972. *Changes in Response Patterns of Fire Departments in Civil Disturbances.* Report Series No. 12. Columbus, Ohio: Ohio State University Disaster Research Center.

_____. 1973. *An Analysis of Commercial Broadcasting Organizations during Flood Disasters.* Ph.D. Thesis. Ohio State University.

Weiss, C.H. 1977. Research for Policy's Sake: The Enlightenment Function of Social Research. *Policy Sciences* 3 (Fall): 531-545.

Wenger, D.E. 1970. *Toward a Comparative Model for the Analysis of Community Power: A Conceptualization and Empirical Application.* Ph.D. Thesis. Ohio State University.

Wenger, D.E. and Paar, A. 1969. *Community Functions under Disaster Conditions.* Report Series No. 4. Columbus, Ohio: Ohio State University Disaster Research Center.

White, G. and Haas, J.E. 1975. *Assessment of Research on Natural Hazards.* Cambridge, Mass.: MIT Press.

Worth, M.F. and Stroup, J. 1977. Some Observations on the Effect of the EMS Law on Disaster Related Delivery Systems. *Mass Emergencies* 2: 159-168.

Wright, J.E. 1976. *Interorganizational Systems and Networks in Mass Casualty Situations.* Ph.D. Thesis. Ohio State University.

_____. 1977. The Prevalence and Effectiveness of Centralized Medical Response to Mass Casualty Disasters. *Mass Emergencies* 2: 189-194.

Yutzy, D. 1969. *Community Priorities in the Anchorage Alaska Earthquake, 1964.* Columbus, Ohio: Ohio State University Disaster Research Center.

Commentary

E. L. Quarantelli

Kreps does three things: (1) he presents a selective history of social and behavorial disaster research in the United States during the 1950s and 1960s; (2) he highlights some of the Disaster Research Center's (DRC) major themes and orientations; and (3) he assumes and advocates a philosophy of research, and applies it to the disaster area.

Any outsider approaching a long-standing and continuous strand of research that has produced many studies and publications will see patterns that insiders may not be aware of, but there will also be misperceptions of things known to those involved. Thus, Kreps correctly notes the persistent attempt of DRC to maintain a social-organizational level of description and analysis in contrast to the pre-DRC dominance of social-psychological orientations. On the other hand, he tends to overstate the importance of DRC research objectives as a factor in the historical development of DRC and to overlook how much was guided by nonresearch factors, for example, DRC's very complex relationship to the sociology department and the college of which it is a part, as well as extrauniversity circumstances.

This only points to what is commonplace in the sociology of science and knowledge, namely, that research is social behavior and researchers are social beings, and as such they are subject to all the social factors that affect group and personal behavior. In that larger context such matters as scientific goals and substantive research questions are but one possible set of conditions influencing behavior and not necessarily of major importance at all times.

Thus, on all three matters the picture Kreps presents — especially of DRC, but also of the early National Academy of Science (NAS) disaster work — is, from my perspective as an insider, partially idealized in the following sense. The discussion assumes the perspective of what might have happened if the undertaking had followed the current ideal norms of scientific enterprise carried out by persons acting solely as professional social scientists. Kreps suggests a far more exclusively professional orientation and a considerably more organized enterprise than was actually the case, and he only hints at crucial extraresearch factors.

There are, of course, good reasons for these limitations. For one, discretion in reporting is often necessary. Kreps was constrained by both self-imposed and other discretions. Many of the involved parties, both individuals and organizations, are still active in disaster research. Thus, I would find it difficult at this time, for example, to be completely candid in reporting the significantly varying relationships, especially of an informal nature, that prevailed between DRC and about ten different research-sponsoring agencies. Most of these relationships were characterized by mutual respect and correct interactions, but at one extreme the sponsor was almost completely indifferent to anything that was done, and at the other extreme the sponsor attempted to manipulate field data and distort research findings.

Along other lines, obtaining a more accurate picture of what went on would have required intensive research totally beyond Kreps's mandate and resources. I was deeply involved in the birth of sociobehavioral disaster research in this country; however, I would have to ponder considerably, refresh my memory, and look up fugitive documents to make certain I was completely and correctly recalling both my own past activities and the early history of the area. In fact, in preparing for this presentation, long forgotten details resurfaced about the development of particular studies and the operative circumstances at the time when some data were obtained and analyzed. In one of the smaller scale DRC studies, in particular, I recalled how scientific norms and values were probably the least important factors at play.

We also cannot ignore the fact that there is a strong tradition among methodologists, in sociology at least, to attempt to deal with research issues as if they are solely technical matters in a social void, divorced from the realities of political and economic limitations and possibilities. Some of that orientation to means rather than context has rubbed off in the account by Kreps. For example, the federal civil defense agency, under a changing set of names, was the major sponsor of disaster research in the United States in the 1950s and 1960s. Its overall policies and internal politics did influence what types of research were done and what kinds of research reports were produced by disaster researchers. The agency and personnel involved were among those who maintained a generally correct "hands off" attitude toward research and researchers, but they had a major interest in only certain kinds of matters (for example, the immediate postdisaster period rather than the long-run recovery) and were uninterested in or actively avoided other kinds of topics (for example, disaster mitigation planning or in what way political considerations influenced federal-level decision making with respect to responding to state and local inquiries and requests at times of mass emergencies). Any complete and balanced assessment of the DRC research thrust would have to take seriously into account sponsor influence on the substantive questions addressed, the data gathering techniques that could be used, and the kinds of data analyses and reports that would become public.

Let me turn now specifically to the history, substantive orientation, and philosophy of research discussed in the Kreps paper, which, as a whole, I think is rather good. I do not have any major disagreements with most of what it states. It is more what it does *not* cover or examine that I want to address. I will note in my remarks some changes in emphases, certain qualifications, and the filling in of factual and other gaps, which, in my opinion, are necessary as corrective and balancing additions to the paper. Also, while I will make some passing references to the NAS work, my focus will be primarily on matters pertinent to the history of DRC and the studies it undertook.

HISTORY

On the selective history of disaster research presented by Kreps, I want to clarify some matters with respect to DRC. I want to note the peculiar organizational nature of DRC, which has existed since its establishment, some direct and indirect links in the past between DRC and NAS, and the two major phases in the historical development of DRC.

From the paper by Kreps, one might reach the conclusion that DRC is an organization that was deliberately set up to study disasters. That is not the case at all. What happened in historical terms was the following. Two rather different research projects on disasters were initiated at Ohio State University. The projects involved three faculty members and a number of graduate students. In addition, there was a university plan to centralize the facilities for certain research activities. The label of a center was advanced to cover the multiple but interrelated faculty and student studies, the physical location of the work, and the need for both the researchers and other university elements to have a single name for the collective activities. In other words, the establishment of a disaster research center at Ohio State University followed the ongoing work; sociological structure came after function.

Perhaps even more important, there never was a center established in the sense of an organization with full-time personnel and resources of its own, including a general budget. DRC does not exist in any formal sense at the departmental, college, or university level. Up to this day, almost all people working at DRC have been part-time personnel. Only infrequently have there been any full-time staff members, and then usually only for a year or two — the duration of a project. Even the directorship, which has never been a formal university position, has always been held by faculty members with other major and concurrent responsibilities for teaching and other activities in the sociology department. Funding for the center has come almost exclusively from external grants and contracts; there have been and are no general fundings or direct university financial support for center activities. The specialized library operation and the DRC publication program, as well as the personnel undertaking such activities, have been funded by bits and pieces from budgets for specific research projects. Thus, in many ways DRC has simply been a label covering sequential and concurrent multiple research projects on specific topics. There has never been a center with a formal structure, a regular staff of specialists, or resources for general center activities.

I emphasize all of this to point out that at no time did some people get together and say, "Let's create an organization to carry out disaster research." It just did not happen that way. Similarly, there is not to this day a formal group with a preplanned program of disaster research. The DRC label obscures the highly informal and unstructured nature of the whole enterprise. Statements in the paper by Kreps that DRC did this or that should be read with the understanding that the corporate existence implied by the name is more nominal than real.

The paper also seems to indicate that there are two separate traditions in the early development of sociobehavioral disaster research in this country, namely, the DRC tradition and the NAS tradition. There is an element of truth in stating there were two traditional paths of study, but the two paths have always been interrelated, and they have a common origin. The fountainhead of disaster research in the social area in this country was the work done from 1950 to 1954 by the National Opinion Research Center (NORC) at the University of Chicago. Charles Fritz was the work supervisor, and I was one of the staff members of the NORC disaster research project. We both learned the basics about disasters in the same context. Fritz went on to become a major figure in the early NAS disaster studies. I eventually helped found DRC (in 1963). However, our two careers continued to be in contact in a variety of ways. Most important, I served on a number of NAS committees, dealing with civil defense and mass emergencies of different kinds, in which Fritz had a leading role. Several times I also acted as an NAS consultant on disaster matters. Thus, while most of the NAS work preceded DRC, both had a common origin in the experience at NORC, as well as the contact provided by the continuing professional interaction between Fritz and me.

The importance of NORC as the breeding ground for most of the disaster research in the 1950s and the 1960s cannot be overestimated. For example, it was the NORC experiences of Fritz and myself that led us in our later work to emphasize field research and the need to maintain an openness and flexibility in field designs. From a substantive viewpoint, the NORC experience led to a focus on the group rather than the individual victim as the important unit of disaster study. Anyone at NORC also learned the basic principle that many of the central beliefs about disasters held by planners, operational responders, and even researchers were mostly mythological. For better or worse, the NORC experience provided both the methodological and theoretical guidance for most sociobehavioral disaster research in the United States for several decades.

Kreps implies that DRC has had substantive and methodological continuity in its research activities. But in looking back at the history of DRC, a case can be made that there had not been as total a continuity as might be thought. It is possible to see a pre-1970 phase and a post-1970 phase in the work at DRC. In his paper Kreps is primarily talking about the pre-1970 work of DRC. He does not take into account sufficiently the post-1970 work.

What is the difference between the two time periods? Up to about 1969 and trailing off in 1970, DRC concentrated its research almost totally on natural disasters and the emergency time period. From about 1968 to about 1973, DRC, although operative, was not doing much in the disaster area. This was not a deliberate withdrawal from the area but came about as a consequence of funding changes. Funded by a major grant from the National Institute of Mental Health, DRC for about five years looked primarily at a nondisaster category of mass emergencies, namely, civil disturbances. We partly rationalized what happened at that time by expressing the desire to study a kind of community mass emergency situation other than natural disasters. Whatever the reason, DRC did little work on disasters for a relatively long time. I was curious enough about this matter to go back and check the records. I found that in the three years from 1970 to 1972 DRC conducted only six field studies in the disaster area. In contrast, the center did fifty-five different field studies in the civil disturbance area. Thus, my feeling that DRC changed its work focus for about five years is confirmed by the record. Only since about 1973 has the center returned to working in the disaster area. In some respects, even this refocus on disasters is different, for we have extended our fieldwork to technological disasters, the emergency time period focus is no longer as dominant as it was in the pre-1970 era, and different field procedures have been instituted.

At any rate, the point is that the DRC research tradition, whether in terms of research focus or methodological orientation, is not all of one piece when looked at through time. The focus by Kreps on the pre-1970 period necessarily gives little consideration to the changes in the post-1970 period. If the full time period were examined, the description and analytical evaluation might be somewhat different. At the very least, the different post-1970 DRC research activities would have to be taken into account.

SUBSTANTIVE ORIENTATION

Let me turn now to the substantive orientation of the DRC work. There are two somewhat different positions about what determines, or should determine, the focus of a research effort. In some scientific circles there is the orthodox point of view that research ought to be guided by theoretical schemes or models. This is also sometimes voiced in the disaster area, although it has never been clear to me why this particular area should reflect such an orientation when much sociological research deviates sharply and often from such a stance.

The other point of view is that policy questions ought to dictate research efforts. This is a frequently asserted position in the disaster area. The focus sometimes is on how policy questions ought to structure research, sometimes on how research ought to feed back into policy issues. In the latter case the implication is that feedback will be better if policy questions are taken into account when research starts. While there are some major differences between starting with policy and ending with policy, in both views a direct connection is assumed between policy matters and research activities.

Undoubtedly there is some connection between theory and research and between policy and research. But my own view is that to think about the matter in such a way is rather unrealistic. A great deal of what happens in a research area is dictated by extraresearch considerations. In other words, the substantive questions addressed in many studies come out of other than practical policy questions or theoretical positions. Likewise, what is produced may be of little or no direct consequence to policy or theory. This is as true in the disaster area as in any other field of study.

On the basis of my experiences at DRC, I would say that the topic of study, the research findings that are produced, and utilization of the work are influenced by several factors. Important among these factors are what I would call organizational needs and constraints, which apply to both research sponsors and researchers. There are many reasons why sponsors fund disaster research. To obtain research findings on policy implications may be a reason, but in my experience this is seldom a major consideration. (I do not say research does not have policy implications, for it always does, but rather that this is seldom a major reason for research sponsorship.) Sometimes research is funded because it is seen as contributing to agency or group survival; in some cases it involves an attempt to win intra- or extra-organizational legitimacy or prestige. In still other cases research is supported because it is believed to be consistent with already prevailing organizational policies. There are even occasions when funds are given for studies because some administrator is genuinely interested in learning something that may be useful for his or her operation! My point, of course, is that there are multiple factors operative, all legitimate in their own way. What research topics will be examined are affected by these factors. To pretend, however, that most research is directly supported because of policy questions or implications, in my view, is rather naive.

I do not know what has been behind the rather substantial disaster research support DRC has enjoyed for over fifteen years. Others will have to explain the intent and reasons behind their research support of the center. I would be surprised, however, if our research funding as a whole was not generated by all the factors I mentioned, as well as by others that anyone knowledgeable about government bureaucracies can easily visualize.

The situation is somewhat the same on the other side, that of the researcher. Research groups also have their own varying organizational needs and constraints, which will influence the research questions posed and methodology used. This is clear in the case of DRC. In terms of its structural position in the university, DRC was and is informally a part of the sociology department. Very early in its existence an implicit decision was made to use the center to give sociology graduate students training in large-scale field research involving intensive interviewing and participant observing. The center, in other words, was to be used for graduate student training. One of the consequences of this decision was that DRC was committed from the very beginning to using primarily part-time staff members without specialized skills who would be available only for relatively short periods of time prior to graduation. DRC, therefore, never attempted to move in the direction of having career-oriented, full-time staff.

I suggest that the use of noncareer, nonspecialized, and part-time personnel has major implications for the kinds of research that can be conducted. For instance, since DRC was part of the sociology department and training sociology students, it was all but impossible for us to undertake interdisciplinary research. Structurally, in other words, it was very difficult for DRC to have on its staff either graduate students or faculty members from fields other than sociology. Even if we had wanted to, we were effectively barred from doing any but primarily sociological disaster studies.

To play my main theme again, research is never just research—it is social behavior in a social context. In a sense we all know this, but it might be wise to keep the point constantly in mind. Research values and the scientific subculture are only part of what is involved. Any assessment of the substantive or methodological focus of a research effort will be more sophisticated and closer to the reality of the situation if it assumes that there are always many extraresearch factors operative. Certainly the organizational needs and constraints of both sponsors and researchers influenced what DRC dealt with substantively in its studies. By now, the sociology of knowledge and science should have taught us the importance of nonresearch factors, and we would be better off applying scientific observations to the act of scientific research itself rather than simply expressing the ideology of science.

Other factors that affect research are the theoretical and methodological predilections of the people leading the studies. I doubt anyone would challenge such a statement. Certainly such predilections have been operative in the disaster area and are manifested in both the topics examined and methods employed in the DRC disaster work.

However, there are two rather different positions on this matter. First, there are the methodological or theoretical imperialists, who claim that only their methodology or their theory is acceptable. The other position, of course, is that, given the current status of the social and behavioral sciences, there can be honest differences of opinion as to appropriate theories and methodologies. Thus, it is seen as not possible at this point in time to rule out the potential value of different theories and methods. We find both positions — only one approach and openness to all approaches — expressed in the disaster area.

DRC has always strongly adhered to the latter position. We have never advocated only one particular theory or metholodgy. We have never assumed, for example, that only symbolic interactionism or quantitative surveys should be used to study disasters. In fact, we have assumed not only that several approaches are possible, but that using different theories and methodologies will lead to more interesting results.

For example, some researchers put a great deal of trust in attitude surveys. This is fine, except that I do not see much connection between attitudes and behaviors. I came out of the University of Chicago trained as a social psychologist, but I became disillusioned with social psychology because of its obsession with the study of attitudes and opinions. I could not see that much of what I was doing, including my disaster work, indicated a meaningful relationship between attitudes and behaviors. Therefore, I became interested in looking at behavioral activities rather than verbal utterances.

I do not deny that survey studies may find little change in attitudes toward disaster planning. On the other hand, I am sure that a pre-1970 and a post-1970 study at the community level using behavioral measures would show significant changes in disaster preparedness. DRC did such a study a few years ago, looking at twelve communities across the country. We found rather important changes in disaster preparedness planning in the last decade or so. There are, for instance, far more Emergency Operations Centers after 1970 than before 1970. There are far more written disaster plans at the community level than ever before. There have been considerably more risk assessment analyses made in recent years compared with earlier.

Thus, studies of attitudes and opinions give one set of results, and a behavioral assessment might give a different set. The important point is that if studies are conducted in different ways, making different theoretical assumptions and using different methods, they will produce rather different findings. This has always been a basic assumption at DRC, and our work should be read with that in mind.

Let me continue a little on this same point. Recently at DRC we have been doing content analyses of community disaster plans. One of the findings has been that in the last few years, insofar as disaster preparedness planning is concerned, two new components have been added to plans. One concerns the provision of disaster-related mental health services, and the other has to do with the handling of chemical hazards. Morelli said earlier that risk mitigation is being undertaken in Utah, California, and Boston, and he was worried because there does not seem to be a correspondence between this behavioral observation and what was reported in SADRI's studies. I do not think there is any incompatability here. SADRI found little attitudinal support of disaster planning. If some other researcher did a study in a different fashion, rather different results might be found. In terms of this example, it may well be true that official attitudes do not support community disaster planning. But it is also probable that observable changes in such planning can be found. The seeming contradiction is not found in the world of action, but results from the theoretical and methodological assumptions made by the social and behavioral scientists doing the studies.

There is much of this in the disaster area, its substantive questions, and its research findings. Different findings often simply reflect the theoretical and methodological predilections of the people involved. One can assume that one's own methodology is the best way of gathering data or that one's own theory is the best way of analyzing data, and that anything else is of little value. My own view, reflected in the substantive DRC findings, is that if we use different theories and methods, we are going to come up with both different questions and different findings, all with value in their own way.

I think also that in discussing conclusions, we sometimes ignore the fact that both researchers and research organizations almost always have multiple audiences for their products. Sometimes we address one, sometimes another, and what we say or write will differ as we change our targets. Usually changes in presentations are made because we assume our audiences have differential knowledge of what we are talking or writing about. Care, therefore, must be taken in the disaster area in assessing statements made for different audiences, especially those that are not research-oriented.

Let me put this in very concrete terms. Any experienced disaster researcher who knows the research literature would know that disaster experience per se is not crucial or even very important in itself in changing behavioral perceptions about disasters or initiating postdisaster organizational changes. The early (1950–1954) NORC studies reached that conclusion regarding disaster victims: there was no such connection. In 1968 DRC conducted a study of disaster-related organizational change or learning. We reached a similar conclusion about experience and organizational change. This followed a 1966 study by Anderson of organizational learning after the Alaskan earthquake which also found that experience provoked little change. In the mid-1970s DRC did a twelve-city study of changes in organizations at different time periods up to five years after a disaster. The same conclusion was reached: disaster experience in itself is not very important as a factor of change. This contrasts with studies, including one conducted by Kreps, showing that civil disturbance experience, when compared with disaster experience, does result in some kinds of organizational changes. Now the SADRI study finds that disaster experience is not crucial at the community level. The study was worth doing, if only to establish at the community level what was previously known at the individual and organizational levels. Experience of disaster by itself does not appear to have too many direct consequences for changes from predisaster states.

Is this counterintuitive? Certainly it is not counterintuitive among experienced disaster researchers. It may, however, be counterintuitive among others to whom the finding is presented for the first time. In other words, one must assess statements about disaster experience in terms of the knowledge of the audiences to which the statement is addressed. Disaster researchers are not going to be very impressed by the finding, but for other kinds of audiences, this may be a revelation of the first order.

The matter of different audiences also influences how findings are reported. When I talk to different people about research findings in the disaster area, I proceed as I do at the university in teaching students. I do not say exactly the same things to first-year students as I do to graduate students. It is not that I tell them different things, but I couch statements in different ways, assuming differential knowledge at different levels. The same is true when I present findings from the disaster area. For example, I have said as much as anyone else that panic and looting do not occur and are not problems in disasters. But I say this primarily to audiences inexperienced in disaster studies. The truer statement, that panic and/or looting occurs only in very limited kinds of circumstances, is what I say to audiences of experienced disaster researchers.

My point is that in trying to work against the stereotype of widespread panic and looting, I frequently make the flat statement that panic and looting do not occur. From my view, this is the best way of challenging existing beliefs and getting certain kinds of audiences to think in a different way. With more knowledgeable audiences, my statements are more qualified, more accurately reflecting the empirical data. In certain circumstances I oversimplify, in others I communicate a little differently. I do not say different things, but I use different strategies to communicate to audiences with different knowledge.

It is important, in looking at the DRC production of several hundred books, articles, and talks, to keep in mind they are *not* aimed at only one kind of audience, certainly not only a researcher audience. We have always assumed multiple audiences for the work of the center. The writings and speeches are at different levels and couched in different ways depending on the particular audience. To take the corpus of DRC work as a consistent whole assumes a homogeneity that is not there and overlooks deliberately heterogeneous products. What we have produced for operational personnel, for instance, is often of a rather different order than what we have addressed to sociologists. This, by the way, is not said as an apology but actually as recommended strategy for academicians. Too often, researchers write only for others like themselves and then wonder why they do not seem to be communicating to the rest of the world. A slight oversimplification in an initial communication is not too high a price to be paid to reach people who can actually do something with the findings.

Kreps applies certain evaluative standards to the DRC work with which I have absolutely no disagreement given a particular kind of audience. But these standards cannot be applied across the board, for there have been different audiences with which DRC has tried to communicate from its very beginning. I think, by the way, that the disaster literature as a whole should be treated in the same way. Something written to convince research sponsors that they are concerned with the wrong question in the first place needs to be assessed in a different way than an article attempting to show how a sociological specialty area ought to be restructured on the basis of empirical findings in the disaster area.

It is often said that policy recommendations should be based on hard data. That is a fashionable cliche but a questionable assertion, for it depends both on what is being recommended and to whom the recommendation is being directed. At times, disaster researchers may be trying to convince policymakers in the disaster area to adopt different perspectives on certain aspects of disasters. Or disaster researchers may want to raise questions about preparedness planning in the minds of disaster planners. These communications need not involve hard data at all. Other kinds of communications need not involve hard data at all. Other kinds of communications about certain topics should make use of hard data. But I would suggest the latter kinds of recommendations are usually the *least* important a researcher can make. There is also the danger that the researcher acts merely as a technician manipulating empirical data instead of as a scientist doing research. As the very word indicates, a researcher should be searching again for something different, be it a perspective, question, or whatever.

I conclude my remarks on substantive matters by touching on two specific points mentioned by Kreps. First, contrary to what he says, I think DRC has been far more successful in producing a realistic conception of pre- and post-emergency disaster environments than it has in getting people to develop a disaster perspective. If Kreps is right that we have communicated a disaster perspective, I would be most happy—for that has been one personal goal. But I do not think we have accomplished anything like that. My impression is that we have been far more successful in clarifying misconceptions and undermining myths about disaster behavior. The DRC mental health studies on both providers and receivers of services illustrates the point well. They have generated epidemiological studies that refute some myths of mental illness, but they have not led to changes in mental health delivery.

My second point has to do with Kreps's statement that DRC has attempted to develop typologies of disaster responses, as well as a sociological theory of disaster behavior. He may be giving us more credit than he should, for what we have accomplished on these two matters has fallen short of our aim. We have struggled with different kinds of typologies, but the end results have not been very satisfactory or useful. In fact, a very important typological question was approached in the early days of DRC and then, unfortunately, dropped: the question of what type of mass emergency or crisis constitutes a disaster. Failure to address the conceptual question of what a disaster is, in my view, is a major weakness of the disaster field, as Bates has also argued.

DRC has also not been very successful in developing a sociological theory of disaster behavior. Kreps is right that we have tried to operate at the sociological level, and we particularly have attempted to relate work in the disaster area to collective behavior theory and organizational theory in sociology. While the end results have been much more accepted and used than our attempts to develop typologies, we are still far from anything that could be characterized as a sociological theory of disaster response. Mostly what we have done is to move in that direction and to insist on a sociological perspective, but Kreps is right that we have not yet produced a sociological theory of the phenomenon. In fact, at least outside sociology, we have not yet adequately communicated the sociological perspective on disasters, that is, the notion of the interrelatedness of social phenomena, the latent nature of much social activity, the notion of unforeseen consequences, the idea of social emergence, and so forth.

RESEARCH PHILOSOPHY

I now take up three philosophical issues relevant to the DRC research. None of them is explicitly discussed by Kreps, but at least two are implicit in his remarks, and all three matters are raised in other evaluations of DRC's work.

One issue concerns the generally qualitative research work of DRC. In fact, DRC has undertaken far more quantitative work than is realized, including two of the largest disaster population field surveys ever conducted. Our survey after the Xenia tornado involved a strictly random sample of 600 households and obtained more in-depth, face-to-face interview data than most other field studies in the disaster area. Most of the several dozen Ph.D. dissertations using DRC data are quantitative studies as well. In its early days the center also conducted highly controlled laboratory experiments, including the fine work produced by Drabek.

Perhaps others lack knowledge of the DRC quantitative work because much of it has never been put into reports for general circulation. One reason is that a number of our quantitative analyses simply confirmed what was already generally known. For example, DRC examined in two major population surveys the extent and nature of looting behavior. The detailed statistical analyses reinforced our earlier impressions that, in general, looting is a very minor problem. Since I am not particularly impressed by numbers, I have not thought it necessary to publicize this quantified confirmation of what I and others have long called one of the myths of disaster behavior. But our failure to publicize such data and findings undoubtedly has led to the prevailing nonquantitative image of DRC.

Nevertheless, it is true that our work is generally more qualitative than quantitative. This reflects certain philosophy of science assumptions that are expressed in the particular methodological techniques we have used and in the theoretical questions we have asked. Thus, some of what we have examined, and found, simply reflects certain methodological biases. For example, the processes involved in the development of emergent groups, a prime focus of DRC research, have to be studied in a qualitative fashion. Similarly, my own interest in panic behavior in stress situations reflects my assumption that panic is intrinsically worth studying because it is an extreme case of human behavior, not because it is a practical policy issue or a crucial question in any current sociological theory. In fact, the standard theories are neither interested in nor do they account for panic phenomena. The research questions examined at DRC, and the method of examination, undoubtedly reflect our particular intellectual preferences. What others want to study, and how, in my view reflects other intellectual biases and preferences. Given the current disarray and controversy regarding all theoretical and methodological issues in the social sciences, I am unimpressed with arguments that there is one ideal path for disaster research.

These theoretical and methodological biases, of course, make a difference in what is studied and in the acceptability of research findings. The results of the DRC studies reflect the multiple methods orientation of the center. Thus, evaluations of the work will differ depending on what criteria of judgment are used.

Anselm Strauss and others have for some time been arguing that qualitative research comes out poorly when judged according to the criteria of quantitative research, and that quantitative research comes out rather badly if the criteria for qualitative work are used to assess its scientific worth. I do not fully accept this conclusion, but I do think the point is relevant to DRC's work. Questions that are sometimes raised about the nonrandomness of samples, the absence of frequency distributions, nonquantitative indicators, and so forth simply miss the point. In the qualitative studies we have done other matters of equal scientific value are reflected in the questions we posed and in how we went about obtaining data. Judged by the standards of qualitative work, this research has merit; to conclude otherwise is to adhere to the dogma that there is only one scientifically acceptable kind of data.

Let me touch briefly on two final philosophical points that are pertinent to the DRC studies. There is substantial controversy in sociology about whether research should give priority to theory and hypothesis *development* or to theory and hypothesis *testing*. DRC's work generally stands with those who argue that it is premature to attempt to test theories and hypotheses when we do not have even the most simple descriptive knowledge of a phenomenon. An in-depth study, in my view, is more meaningful when there exists a comprehensive general overview of the phenomenon being examined. The DRC work has therefore aimed at breadth rather than in-depth coverage of the disaster area.

There is a similar difference of opinion on whether a field of research should concentrate on particular topics or keep developing new topics. Our general position is that in an unexplored area, such as disaster research, it is far more important that new questions be raised, that new topics be explored, and that, generally, a sociobehavioral perspective be brought to bear on as many aspects of disaster phenomena as possible. In fact, for some years DRC stood almost alone in carrying out sociobehavioral research in this area, so we felt a professional responsibility to keep expanding disaster research into new topics and questions. Hence, our research forays into the handling of the dead during disasters; the role of financial institutions; the delivery of emergency medical services; the operation of the mass media; the role of religion and religious institutions; the provision of mental health services; legal problems; the diffusion of knowledge about disaster planning among emergency organizations; sociobehavioral preparations for and responses to acute chemical hazards; similarities and differences between civil disturbances and disasters; postimpact community conflict and cooperation; cross-cultural differences in national-level responses to catastrophes; and the operation of EOCs, hospitals, departments of public works, schools, and the military in disasters, to mention but some of the topics DRC opened up for study. It has been our policy to continue to move on to new questions and issues, leaving the more detailed in-depth work for others. We do this not because we think the detailed follow-up work is unimportant, but only because we are not interested in doing it.

Let me conclude with a more general observation. In another setting and for other purposes, I recently wrote that research in the disaster area was geometrically rather than arithmetically increasing. I cited that as an indication of the impressive growth of this research area. The effort at this conference to assess earlier disaster research is an even better sign. It indicates that the field has developed enough that systematic attention can now be turned to the quality of what it is producing. If my reading is correct, this conference may prove to have been a more significant event than was planned or envisioned.

Commentary

James Kerr

I would say that Kreps was quite courageous to write this paper, that Rossi had a lot of guts in asking him to do so, and I guess I must be nuts to stand up here and comment on it! Despite being a nuclear physicist, a registered engineer, and a municipal official, my principal concern involves the nuclear war case, because the legislation that set up my office directs our attention to that. I will talk later on about the metamorphosis of civil defense and disaster organizations, as I see them now and in the near future. Let us think first about the origins of some of what Kreps mentioned. In the early 1960s, when President Kennedy moved civil defense into the Pentagon, we had big events, such as the Berlin Crisis and the Cuban Crisis, to deal with. Up until then, I was in the Army, in the research and development business, and I was an avid reader of the National Academy of Science (NAS) output. I like to think that I used some of it beneficially in organizing the U.S. Army, but by the 1960s I, along with a number of other people, had concluded that the academy had told us more about individual behavior than we really needed to know. So, moving into civil defense as I did after it moved into the Pentagon, I learned that the academy research was winding down, and some reliable people came along and got my attention.

My conclusion was that we should support quite a bit more research but that, in view of our earlier conclusion about the individual studies, we really ought to start looking at organizations, because that was where we were defective. We were indeed pretty ignorant about that side of the question, and that was the rationale that led to my putting in the first dime. There were two deliberate exclusions from the program: one was studies of individuals, and the other was case studies (although we did support some case studies). The purpose of funding DRC was to study the functioning of organizations under stress. We wanted studies of various types of organizations. The support for each study was carefully orchestrated. The procedure was that one of the DRC codirectors would call me to discuss a disaster, and we would decide whether it was worthy of our attention. I would then touch base with the head of civil defense, to see whether there were political overtones that would prevent our going ahead with the study. Sometimes we went ahead and sometimes we didn't. When it was a foreign disaster, we would ask the ambassador. Sometimes he would say, "No way," and in other cases he would say, "Yes, it would help me know how to do my job if we had somebody looking around." As nearly as I can tell, the very first response to the Alaskan earthquake on the part of the federal government was our agreement that we would send somebody from DRC to the site. Later, we tried to get some interdisciplinary research underway, but that fell apart, as Quarantelli mentioned.

The criteria that we used to decide which disasters to study were very simple. First, we had to be sure that the organization that was out there was under stress. Second, the disaster had to be "juicy," that is, serious. If both of these held, then we would say, yes, and off DRC would go. Looking back now at what we did, whether it was right or wrong, I can think of a useful parable. A few hundred years ago, the Spanish came over from Europe and settled in North America. Eventually the English wound up in Bermuda. The settlement of North America by Europeans proceeded. As the settlers moved west, they debauched and betrayed the natives, the miners raped the land, the woodsmen deforested the mountains, the buffalo were killed, the water was polluted, and as a result we wound up with ecology people and Nader people. Now we look back over the sweep of history and ask, "What would we have done differently?" There is just no way that my great-grandfather, trying to build his cabin, would have done it any differently. And I do not regret that he cut down that wood. It is regrettable that the process of development had to victimize so many things and people, but looking back, I doubt that it could have been any different.

Likewise with the early history of disaster research: looking back, we may have some superficial regrets about what NAS and DRC did, and certainly some specifics could be debated, but we pretty well ended up where we wanted to be.

The example of nuclear war provides an explanation for the importance of disaster research. In nuclear war there is no we-they dichotomy of victims; everyone will be a victim. It is also tough to do applied studies, so we use disasters as a parallel to the problems of nuclear war. Thus, it is important to get DRC to focus attention on these problems and applications. Kreps perhaps underrates the utility or serviceability of the DRC research in this respect.

Civil defense is sometimes defined as government in action in an emergency, and civil defense rode in with the research of NAS-NRC. NRC, in short, got the point across regarding civil defense, and without the NAS-NRC programs, we would not have our present understanding of or involvement in civil defense. So the past is not all that bad. What we need to do now is build on what we have already learned. We need to set objectives. At the same time we need to consider which objectives are researchable and to determine the feasibility of research projects. We should consider interdisciplinary, rapid response problems, such as fire. We also need to blend the "patron of the arts" approach and the "pragmatic" approach to research and drop research programs in areas where we already know enough. We must also remember that no research contract comes back with a solution. It comes back with an answer, and it is then up to the sponsor to apply that answer to a policy issue. The criticism by Kreps that the benefits of the NAS-NRC program were weak is one I therefore disagree with. Those studies were used by their sponsors in a large number of ways. One should not underrate the applied benefits of the NAS-NRC and DRC work.

Discussion

Russell R. Dynes: Let me expand on some of Quarantelli's remarks. DRC grew through an evolutionary process and was aimed at a number of audiences. Kreps suggests that it was planned and rational, but that was not the case. The "exploratory" nature of DRC (a correct characterization) was caused by both the desire for flexibility and the anxiety about future funding. The plan was to develop new projects while continuing ongoing ones. Regarding the very different audiences, there was some effort to be interdisciplinary, so as not to be isolated from our academic colleagues. In addition, the needs of the funding agencies differ from the needs of the researchers, and there is also the need to be responsive to the public. Hundreds of visitations are made, taking time away from academic duties and research. We presented public talks, published in *Readers' Digest*, and so forth. I agree with Kreps that many of the problems with the London Technical Group arose because they were looking for an ideological base and for a funding organization.

Joseph F. Coates: Why did SADRI commission the Kreps paper, and how do you plan to utilize it?

Peter H. Rossi: Our hope was that this conference would consider all aspects of social science research on natural hazards. We have two papers on the major traditions, the second being presented later. From my perspective, these are important traditions worth discussing in detail.

Coates: As a user, I think Kreps's paper borders on being destructive. It almost denies any benefits and payoffs of the disaster research institutions. In terms of congressional oversight and funding, it is important to realize the parallels to other areas. We should temper these remarks with an identification of the benefits of the two institutions.

Gary A. Kreps: The benefits were largely indirect, and how they were felt is difficult to determine. There are many war stories about the DRC disaster manual being used in communities, and Kerr says that people in the government were influenced by the results. My remarks were not meant in a destructive way.

Fred Krimgold: From the point of view of NSF, SADRI's results were potentially threatening to accepted beliefs. Therefore, it seemed appropriate to have a broader forum to examine them. Since these results present a challenge to social science research on hazards, the Kreps paper and discussion are very valuable in providing the larger context for SADRI's studies.

Coates: I would like to challenge Kreps's judgment about costs. Disaster research is cheap, not expensive. We need to expand the criteria to make a judgment about cost. If this research is perceived as being expensive, less will be done. Kreps's point about costs should be withdrawn.

Kreps: I agree that we need to examine costs in context: cheap or costly compared to what?

William Anderson: We need to compare the amount spent on social science disaster research with the amount spent on other problems. NSF's involvement in social science disaster research is new, beginning in 1972-1975 with the White-Haas report. Comparing social science and engineering research on hazards, $2.5 million was spent on social science disaster research by NSF in 1977, $2.5 million in 1978, and $800,000 in 1979; at the same time, support for physical science and engineering increased. Funding for earthquake engineering research was $16 million in fiscal year 1979. The current sentiment is to maintain this relative division of resources, even though social science policy and planning issues are more difficult.

Rossi: The question has been raised about our and Kreps's "responsibility." Of course, we need to be concerned with what our responsibilities are, but at the same time we cannot give up our integrity or soft-pedal the findings just because they are anxiety-producing.

Dynes: Yes, but the tone is also important. We must remember there are unforeseen audiences that may use your results in ways you do not intend.

Hirst Sutton: I would further suggest that disputes be framed so as not to preclude further collaboration, discussion, or interaction. The nature of the scientific process is competitive and critical, but we must frame criticisms so that they do not destroy the possibility of future work.

Krimgold: NSF is more concerned with balance than with disputes over data, methodology, or technique. It is not SADRI's role to interpret; the interpretations will be given elsewhere. Crucial policy issues have both a scientific and a political basis for validity, which are independent of each other.

Rossi: I agree with the need for balance, but I think it is best achieved through tension and disagreement. I question whether we can or should ever fully satisfy all anxieties about the implications, or misuse, of our research.

Thomas E. Drabek: A researcher has more responsibilities than simply to satisfy anxieties, of course. For example, we are still waiting for your ideas about an agenda for future social science hazard research and what we need to do to improve our understanding of and ability to deal with natural hazards.

Robert K. Leik: I can speak to that. It seems to me there are three kinds of questions that need to be researched. First, what can be done in advance to protect against hazardous phenomena that cannot be directly controlled; that is, how do we mitigate the risk? Second, can we create an effective warning system? Can we get people to respond efficaciously to warnings once they are issued? Third, given that neither mitigations nor warning systems will ever work perfectly, and disasters will still continue to occur, what measures can be taken to mop up adequately after the event and return things to normal levels? Your results suggest, at least for the hazards you studied, that things return to normal quickly and the traces disappear. Therefore, local officials don't seem to be worried. I see nothing in either finding that suggests anything about the need for continued research on other important aspects of concern. Your research raises as many questions as it answers, in my judgment.

The tone of the discussion bothers me a little bit. It is almost as if you are being told, "You found what you found, but don't really say it in quite that way because we don't like what you've found — it seems frightening from our point of view." I don't think it is frightening in any way. It should encourage a lot more inquiry and essential redirection of future research.

Frederick L. Bates: What I hear being said is that SADRI's report needs to highlight some of the unanswered questions and the limitations of the research, so that unsophisticated readers will not jump to erroneous conclusions. As your report now stands, it is up to the reader to supply these caveats and provisos. Since this particular work is likely to become a landmark and may result in a lot of policy decisions about future research financing, some mechanism needs to be found to bring the limitations forcefully to the reader's attention.

James D. Wright: Let me respond with three comments. First, we are at this point discussing only the first draft of the preliminary report of findings. The purpose of having this conference is in part to air the research, find out what the sensitive and interesting issues are, so we can deal with legitimate concerns in the final draft. Second, most of you have seen only the first chapter of the preliminary report, a highly condensed summary of a very detailed and complex analysis. The full report, even in its current preliminary form, contains most of the caveats that are being suggested. Finally, just as one can lead a horse to water but not make it drink, so can one prepare a report but not make people read it. In my opinion, our reports go out of their way to stress the (serious) limitations of the studies. If, in their haste to achieve a policy conclusion, users ignore these limitations, it is not our responsibility. We lead them to the water patiently and cautiously, in my view. Whether they choose to drink is their own business.

ASSESSMENT OF RESEARCH ON NATURAL HAZARDS REASSESSED IN LIGHT OF THE SADRI DISASTER RESEARCH PROGRAM

Peter H. Rossi, James D. Wright, and Sonia R. Wright

INTRODUCTION

As with much other ongoing or soon-to-be completed research on the social aspects of natural hazards, SADRI's research program can be traced back, intellectually if not genealogically, to White's and Haas's *Assessment of Research on Natural Hazards* (1975). With the exception of Rossi's short stint on the National Research Council's Disaster Research Committee, none of the project investigators had any previous interest or experience in natural hazard research. One of us (James Wright) was primarily interested in political behavior; another (Sonia Wright) was interested mainly in applied social research, especially the evaluation of social policies; and the third (Peter Rossi) had long-standing professional interests in both these fields, as well as in communities and urban sociology. So, while each of these areas of specialization and expertise relates at least tangentially to issues in disaster research, it would have been very hard to predict SADRI's disaster research program from the backgrounds and interests of the people involved.

In 1975 the three of us developed a strong interest in collaborating on a research project, and, in casting about for a suitable topic that would appeal to our disparate areas of specialization, we were introduced by George Baker to White-Haas's *Assessment*. What *Assessment* made clear in our minds was that natural hazards and the policies employed to deal with them have distinctive and essential political elements that were, at the time, not very well understood; further, that the social policy issues posed by natural hazards had scarcely been adequately enunciated, much less thoroughly researched; and finally, that in working in this area we would be involved in applied research on a problem of considerable significance to the larger society, namely, the loss of life and property resulting (often needlessly) from natural hazard events. Working directly from *Assessment,* we proposed a two-study research program to the National Science Foundation (NSF), the outcome of which was the research discussed at this conference. Our initial debt to *Assessment* is thus that it demonstrated to our satisfaction a very intimate connection, or at least the possibility of such a connection, between our professional interests and the substantive problems of natural disaster research.

When *Assessment* was first published, the hope was that it would stimulate a "new generation" of social science research on natural hazards. Indeed, the research agenda proposed in *Assessment* has served, essentially, as a guide to NSF funding of social science research on hazards. In this respect, *Assessment* has been quite successful. Both the amount and the quality of social science research on natural hazards have increased perceptibly since the publication of that report.

By now at least some of the research called for in *Assessment* has been completed, and so it is instructive, some five years later, to reconsider its themes and emphases from the comfortable vantage point of new knowledge that has been generated. When we first read *Assessment,* we were novices in disaster research, and so we accepted its contents at face value. The research designs that we proposed reflected a certain naivete of which we were quickly disabused. Now that we have acquired a modest level of sophistication in the substance of the disaster research area and have a few reasonably firm findings in hand, a reappraisal of *Assessment* is in order.

What follows is generally critical of *Assessment.* In many cases our findings seem hard to square with the themes of that report. On the other hand, we are quick to acknowledge that hindsight is an easy vantage point from which to be critical and, further, that our research has revealed some things that were unknown to White, Haas, and their collaborators at the time. The critical tone of our remarks, then, does not in any sense belie our judgment that *Assessment* was and remains an important document and an excellent model of how social science theory and research, intelligently and properly applied, can make genuine contributions to the development of public policy.

HIGHLIGHTS OF ASSESSMENT

It is important to recognize that *Assessment* is intended to serve at least two distinct and in some ways contradictory purposes. First, it is meant to be a scientific document assessing the then current state of the art with respect to natural hazard knowledge and research and directing attention to potentially fruitful new research leads. But second, it is also meant as a consciousness-raising document calling attention to the seriousness of the natural hazard problem and spurring recalcitrant decision makers to action. We suggest throughout this paper that these consciousness-raising efforts sometimes work at cross-purposes with the more strictly scientific goals.

It is also important to distinguish between tone and emphases on the one hand and detailed substantive content on the other. Most of our quarrels are more with the emphases than with the detailed content of *Assessment.*

The main message of *Assessment* is that the hazards of the natural environment pose a serious and considerable problem to society. Each year persons are killed or injured and much property is destroyed by the ravages of natural disasters; these losses are increasing over time as the size of the population grows and the human uses of the environment increasingly encroach upon inherently hazardous areas. Much of the human and property loss due to natural hazards could be prevented by appropriate policy measures, most of all by stricter land use management in hazardous areas.

Assessment contains little concrete information about the actual costs of natural hazards to society. Several estimates of costs, injuries, and deaths from past disasters are presented, always with an acknowledgment that these estimates are plagued by potential errors of considerable magnitude. Early in the report natural hazards are characterized as a billion-dollar-per-year problem, but White and Haas acknowledge that estimates of economic losses from disasters can be off by as much as a factor of two or three. The volume does not attempt to estimate the annual per capita costs of natural hazards to the society at large or trends in per capita costs over time. As we have since learned in painful detail, *Assessment* does not present better data on these matters simply because better data do not exist.

Lacking the evidence necesssary to assess the *actual* costs of natural hazards to the society, *Assessment* depicts something of the *potential* costs through the mechanism of scenarios. The second chapter presents three such scenarios, a superforce hurricane striking Miami, a flash flood raging through Boulder, and a major earthquake in San Francisco. Each scenario depicts the worst possible outcome: every decision made is the wrong one and the worst possible luck is encountered at every juncture. Given these worst-possible-case assumptions, the scenario for San Francisco projects total losses of $10 billion, 8,750 deaths, and 22,000 injuries — a serious problem indeed!

The problem with these scenarios is certainly not that they depict events that could never happen; indeed, each of the three scenarios is not only possible, each is entirely inevitable given a long enough period of time. Rather, what is missing is a sense of the *probability* that such events will occur in any span of time relevant to human society. If it were the case, for example, that the probability of a superforce Miami hurricane occurring within the next 50 years was very close to 1.0, then the scenario would suggest a basis for immediate action. If, on the other hand, the probability of such an event over the next 50 to 100 years is very close to zero, then the scenario is less informative. The problem, of course, is that nobody knows for sure just what the probabilities are.

Admittedly, immense natural catastrophes of the sort depicted in *Assessment* have happened in the past and will happen again; it is also undeniable that the seriousness of such catastrophes would be exacerbated by human folly or bad luck, as the scenarios depict. But these scenarios obviously do *not* present an empirical picture of the natural hazard problem in the United States; they are used as a consciousness-raising device in that they depict the worst imaginable, rather than most probable, situations. Our feeling is that "most probable" situations represent the firmer basis for policy considerations.

Assessment recognizes the distinction between "catastrophes" and "average disasters," but says little about the distribution of hazardous events across these two categories. The distinction arises mainly in tables projecting the benefits of research for each class of events; interestingly, most of the projected benefits for research on average disasters are larger. But these average disasters contribute little to the overall tone of the volume: the tone is set instead by the depiction of hypothetical catastrophes. Lacking an empirical notion of the shape of the severity distributions for natural disasters, *Assessment* is somewhat misleading; it tends to depict how serious the natural hazard problem in the United States *could* be, rather than how serious it actually *is*.

This distinction between catastrophes and average disasters has proven to be a crucial one in our research. In some respects, of course, every disaster event is a catastrophe to its specific individual or family victims. The seriousness of any particular event is very much a function of the perspective from which it is viewed. A flood that wipes out a family is, without question, a catastrophe to that family, but it is not necessarily a catastrophe to the community in which it occurs, much less to the nation as a whole. In short, the distinction between average disasters and genuine catastrophes is very hard to draw in an absolute sense; the measure of disaster severity is relative to the viewpoint employed.

To deal with this relativity, our volume on long-term disaster effects develops the concept of an "impact ratio." The ratio is defined simply as the losses suffered by a social unit from a disaster divided by the total resources at the command of the unit and that can be brought to bear on the unit's recovery (in short, resources lost as a fraction of total resources). For obvious reasons, this ratio is typically very high when the unit in question is the individual or family affected by the disaster, but is not nearly so high when the unit is an entire community or the nation as a whole. Indeed, there are very few events, short of an all-out nuclear holocaust, that would be catastrophic to the nation as a whole, in other words, that would destroy anything more than a trivial fraction of the national resources.

An implication of these considerations is that catastrophic disasters tend to have intense localized impacts, overwhelming, at least temporarily, the recovery capacity of local social systems. The most catastrophic disasters are thus large events striking small and isolated places—in short, the Cameron Parishes, Big Thompson Canyons, and Buffalo Creeks. It is interesting that the case study literature on community-level disaster effects is dominated by disasters occurring in small communities of this sort. In the larger cities disasters rarely achieve the status of catastrophes, simply because larger cities have adequate resources to handle all but the most extreme disaster events.

These relativistic considerations are for the most part missing from *Assessment*. The San Francisco scenario, for example, projects 8,750 deaths and 22,000 injuries, or 30,750 human casualties altogether. In absolute terms this would be a staggering toll. Relatively speaking, however, 30,750 casualties would represent only about 4 percent of the city's 1970 population; the remaining 96 percent of the total human resources of the city, in short, would be unharmed. Should we assume that this 96 percent would be unable to undertake any creative or useful postdisaster response? Probably not. The fact is, the vast bulk of San Francisco's human, social, political, and economic resources will survive even the most catastrophic earthquake. *Assessment*, however, says little about the resources that these communities could and would bring to bear on their recovery even from a cataclysmic disaster event.

There are several other relativities that *Assessment* might have considered. One is the simple relativity of time. The San Francisco scenario, for example, projects the events of the first three to five days and ends with the California National Guard holding "a tight grip on the city." Everything is in a mess and the entire situation is as bad as one can imagine. But what might the city look like, say, a month later, or five years later? Our research on long-term disaster effects suggests that within a very short time the city would look very much the same as it looked before the disaster struck. Other research suggests the same thing. The Friesema study, for example, found no effects attributable to the disasters studied that lasted for more than six months to a year. The Bowden, Kates, and Haas study estimates that the functional recovery time for the 1906 San Francisco earthquake was about one year. Given the present-day resources of the city and the many sources of disaster aid for which it would be eligible, one can easily imagine that the functional recovery today from a repeat of the 1906 quake would be substantially quicker.

A second important relativity is what might be called the "relativity of political aggregation." What this means is simply that the presence of natural disaster problems and the frequency of disastrous events both tend to increase as one moves from smaller to larger aggregates or units. To illustrate, very few families actually experience damage or injury from a natural hazard over the course of any typical decade; for the decade 1960–1970, the figure would be on the order of 5 to 10 percent. The proportion of local communities that experience such a disaster in a typical decade, of course, would be considerably higher; and the proportion of states, even higher. Finally, when we aggregate the disaster problem over the whole United States, serious, even cataclysmic, disasters become relatively commonplace events.

Since attention and appropriate policy with respect to natural hazards are very much a function of the seriousness of the problem, it follows that different units of political aggregation will have very different views about what policies to undertake and their urgency. For example, the federal viewpoint on land use management in flood hazard areas reflects the unfortunate fact that 100-year-or-greater floods happen somewhere in the nation all the time; for the United States as a whole, in short, 100-year-or-greater floods are commonplace occurrences and thus justify aggressive policy measures. To any particular community with a flood hazard potential, in contrast, the 100-year flood is, by definition, a once-per-century event. And what one is willing to do to prepare for an event that happens every other day is very much different from what one might be willing to do to prepare for an event that happens less than once in a human lifetime. From the federal viewpoint, land use management and building code mitigations may appear to be a rational and sensible approach to the problem; from the viewpoint of the local community that has to adopt and enforce these regulations (for which the return periods are measured not in months or years but in centuries), they may appear irksome, restrictive, even wasteful of scarce community resources. The viewpoint adopted in *Assessment* is very much a federal viewpoint; that the states and communities, whose responsibility it would be to implement many of the policy recommendations of *Assessment,* might have an entirely different outlook is not systematically considered.

The state and local viewpoint on the seriousness of hazard problems, as measured by the key persons survey, points up yet a third relativity, namely, that every state and community faces a wide range of problems that threaten the quality of life and compete for a share of state and local resources, and that, within this range, natural hazard problems are not among the most serious. Indeed, *all five* of the natural hazards we asked about — floods, fires, hurricanes, tornadoes, and earthquakes — were seen by our respondents to be less serious than pornography and very much less serious than inflation, unemployment, crime, housing, and so on. Moreover, our respondents are not obstinately refusing to face the facts of the natural hazard risk when they tell us that these problems are much more serious, because by any reasonable standard they are. What they are telling us is that natural hazards do not rank high among the many threats to the quality of life in the society and that our policy recommendations and initiatives should be cognizant of this fact. Our expectations about what states and local communities will be willing to do with respect to hazards, in short, must be tempered by a realistic appraisal of all the other things they must also do and by some recognition that many other serious problems are competing for the same meager resources. This sensitivity to the *relative* priority that states and communities can afford to give to natural hazard problems is largely absent from *Assessment*.

Assessment's disaster scenarios tend to imply that much of the havoc could be avoided if only the proper policies were in place; the volume therefore reveals little sensitivity to the very real limitations of policymaking. Given the evident impossibility of controlling the disaster events themselves, all policy measures must of necessity deal either with predisaster preparations or with the postdisaster response mechanism. And there are limits to what can be achieved on either side, limits imposed first by the uncertainties of disasters themselves and second by the finite resources available to states and communities to be spent on mitigating hazard risk. *Assessment* scenarios imply that cities facing a serious hazard risk should prepare for a possible event of large magnitude and maintain a high level of preparedness. But from the cold and calculating viewpoint of a state or city budgetary process, such readiness is rational only if the expected benefits exceed the expected costs. The expected benefits are, of course, virtually impossible to calculate since they must be multiplied first by the probability that the disaster will actually occur and again by the probability that the mitigations being undertaken would actually work if such a disaster did occur. Neither of these probabilities is known with any assurance, although it is certain that neither equals 1.0. *Assessment* thus deals more with *hypothetical* gains to be achieved by disaster policy innovations than with the likelihood that these innovations would actually work or with the associated costs.

In sum, *Assessment*'s depiction of the nation's hazard problem is designed more to stimulate concern and action than to provide a sober or empirical picture. The volume tries, quite effectively, to impart a sense of urgency to the situation, but for the most part it does not provide an accurate empirical impression of the dimensions of the natural hazard problem in the United States.

THE POLICY EMPHASIS OF ASSESSMENT

The policy emphasis of *Assessment* is that nonstructural risk mitigations, for example, land use management and building code regulations, are the policies of choice. The best technique for reducing loss of life and property from natural hazards is reducing the exposure of the population to risk by regulating the uses of land in hazardous areas and by requiring the construction of safer buildings.

Alternative policies are viewed with considerable suspicion because they often pose perverse incentives that increase, rather than reduce, exposure to risk. For example, hazard insurance, unaccompanied by mitigation requirements, may cause people to become complacent about the true risks to which they are exposed. Structural mitigations, such as flood control dams, levees, and seawalls, are possibly counterproductive for the same reason: areas protected by structural mitigations appear to be safer than they actually are; the existence of such structures encourages the habitation of hazardous areas, thus worsening the disaster potential. And postdisaster relief policies foster the complacent view that whenever a disaster does occur, somebody will come along with the funds to rebuild and restore the community to its predisaster condition. Of the major policy emphases available, then, only nonstructural mitigations avoid these possibly perverse incentives.

Another distinctive characteristic of nonstructural mitigations is that they require the cooperation and support of states and local communities. Structural mitigations can be instituted at the federal level; likewise, the federal government could market hazard insurance nationally independently of communities and states. And if the federal government wants to come into a community in the disaster aftermath and provide assistance, there is little the state or community can do to stop this intervention, even if it wants to. But land use management and building code requirements are different: the right to regulate such matters is left to states by the Constitution; most states, in turn, delegate this authority to local communities. Thus, the federal government can suggest these mitigations, can offer certain incentives to states and communities that undertake them, can even dole out some punishments for the states and communities that do not, but the federal government cannot *command* states and communities to institute these policies.

The political feasibility of *Assessment*'s policy emphasis thus turns critically on the willingness of states and communities to adopt and enforce nonstructural hazard risk mitigations. Our research provides little optimism on this score. The political influentials in the sample were presented with five alternative hazard risk policy emphases and asked to state their agreement with each. The most popular emphasis (by a wide margin) was structural risk mitigations, favored at some level by more than 70 percent of the respondents. The second most popular policy was one focusing on postdisaster relief (favored by 55 percent). In contrast, a policy emphasis on nonstructural mitigations (land use and building code requirements) was *dis*favored by the majority (53 percent), and an emphasis on compulsory hazard insurance was somewhat less popular (rejected by 59 percent).

The preference for nonstructural approaches varied in the sample according to political position. Local influentials specializing in hazard problems, such as Red Cross or civil defense respondents, tended to be most in favor of such approaches; respondents representing real estate and development interests were least in favor of them. In general, the more political clout a group of elites could be expected to have, the *less* favorable they were to nonstructural hazard mitigations.

These data suggest that the implementation of nonstructural mitigation measures may well prove to be an arduous political struggle, most of all because political elites at these levels do not regard hazard problems as especially serious in the first place. *Assessment* tends to treat the benefits to be derived from these policies as self-evident, but the political leadership of states and local communities has a rather different view. Our findings, of course, say nothing about the intrinsic value of this policy emphasis, only about its likely political acceptability.

On the other hand, the skepticism expressed by our respondents is not entirely without justification. Properly employed, land use management will reduce, but not eliminate, exposure to risk. The concept embraces a wide variety of specific measures, some of which may prove adequate for any specific hazard, others of which may not. Prohibitions against building in the 100-year floodplain do not protect against a 500-year flood any better than a dam designed to protect against a 100-year flood will. Thus, the drawing of boundaries on flood hazard maps may well induce the same false sense of security as structural mitigations might induce. How many homeowners have breathed a sigh of relief upon learning that their homes were, say, across the street from the 100-year floodplain demarcation? And is this naive feeling of safety any more productive than that of other risk management policies?

The same applies to hazard-sensitive building code requirements. A mobile home outfitted with tiedowns for severe winds remains, nonetheless, hazardous during severe winds. Hurricanes often wreak utter devastation on "hurricane-proof" buildings. There seem to be no such things as hurricane-proof, flood-proof, wind-proof, fire-proof, or earthquake-proof structures. If hazard-sensitive building codes cause people to believe otherwise, a false sense of security may result.

Assessment recognizes the importance of reliable risk mapping in implementing nonstructural mitigations and calls for additional research on the topic. The sciences involved are inexact. Hydrologists are asked to define flood hazards with an accuracy so fine that the maps can be used to zone land use. Seismologists and other earth scientists are asked to do the same thing. This risk mapping cannot be done very accurately without prohibitive measurement costs. Inaccuracy in risk mapping produces possible inequities: when one may do certain things (build, develop, and so forth) on one side of a risk line but not on the other, an inaccurate placement of the line will produce inequity. Until the relevant sciences develop more accurate measures, such inequities must be calculated as a cost incurred by this policy emphasis.

The costs associated with land use management as a means of risk mitigation receive less attention than the potential benefits. One important cost is the opportunity cost: a dollar spent mitigating hazard risk is no longer there to spend on crime, malnutrition, housing, and so on. It is not obvious that the dollar spent on risk mitigation will return more to the overall quality of life than the same dollar spent elsewhere.

The dollar costs of implementation are potentially substantial. Federal purchase of the flood zone of Rapid City at predisaster values cost $12,000 per capita; the *New York Times* estimated that a similar effort in New York City would cost billions.

There are other costs. When development in one area of a city is prohibited, the alternatives are not to build at all or to build elsewhere. The first is a policy of no growth and is therefore politically problematic. Among local respondents in our survey, the problem "too little growth" ranked eighth in aggregate seriousness; the problem "too much economic growth" was seventeenth, just ahead of earthquakes. The second alternative—build elsewhere—may be equally unacceptable, since it favors urban sprawl, especially in areas that are already highly developed, and thus increases ugliness, transportation and energy costs, and other negative social and economic externalities.

Similar cost considerations apply to building code restrictions embodying hazard mitigation features. *Assessment* notes that mobile home tiedowns would cost less than $200 per structure, a seemingly trivial amount, and that seismic stress–resistant features could be designed into buildings for less than 5 percent of the total building cost. But $200 may not be trivial to families residing in mobile homes, least of all when the expected loss being mitigated (the value of the structure times the probability that it would otherwise be destroyed by disaster times the probability that the tiedown will prevent the destruction) amounts, over the structure's lifetime, to nearly nothing. Independent evidence reported by Petak and associates indicates that building code hazard mitigations may not be cost-effective in all cases. For example, the cost-benefit equation for hurricane risk mitigation favored the mitigation only when a zero discount rate was assumed (that is, when it was assumed that the capital expenditures would otherwise not appreciate with the passage of time). Any realistic assumption about the discount rate tips the cost-benefit equation *away* from the mitigation, even during the initial construction. As for retrofitting existing structures to new hazard-resistant standards, the evidence is that the costs greatly exceed the likely benefits.

One final cost incurred by nonstructural mitigations is the potentially high administrative cost. Unless these measures are enforced at the local level, they will obviously have no effect on exposure to risk. Little is gained when variances and appeals are routinely granted, or when inspection cycles are so infrequent that violations go unnoticed, or when regulations are applied inconsistently, and so on. These risk mitigation policies rely very heavily on administrative devices for their effectiveness. Perhaps nothing has been quite so disappointing to those of us with some fondness for the welfare state as the recognition that government agencies at all levels often prove incapable of effective administration of any human service.

In sum, nonstructural mitigations may be cheaper or more effective or less perverse than any existing policy alternative, but they may also not be. There are costs associated with these policies that have, so far, not been thoroughly assessed. The desirability of nonstructural mitigations, relative to alternative policies, can be known only through an intelligent cost-benefit analysis — one in which all the costs associated with the policy, both direct and indirect, are arrayed against all the anticipated benefits. Until better research is done, nobody will know whether *Assessment*'s emphasis on nonstructural approaches is justified.

A word of caution is in order: cost-benefit analyses can be only as good as the assumptions made about anticipated costs and benefits. The best cost-benefit equations are calculated on the basis of costs and benefits determined through empirical research; the worst are calculated on the basis of assumed or anticipated benefits and costs. In the hazard area there are far more assumptions than data, and it would be premature and potentially misleading to undertake these analyses with presently available data.

ASSESSMENT'S *RESEARCH PROGRAM*

The social science research program proposed by White and Haas in *Assessment* is advanced because the authors believe that social scientists can provide information on critical social aspects of natural hazard management. It would be useless, for example, to develop better methods of forecasting disasters if the resulting warnings were not efficiently disseminated or if communities or individuals failed to respond appropriately. Similarly, land use management will never reduce hazard risk if local communities and states refuse to pass the necessary legislation or fail to enforce the measures they do pass. It is precisely because the management of natural hazard risk requires more than technological innovation that social science research becomes potentially important.

Applied social research (research directed toward assisting in the formation and testing of social policy) generally takes one of three forms: *model building,* or construction of abstract theoretical representations of the social phenomenon in question and accompanying policy measures; *monitoring,* or collection of data that describe the course of the social problem in question or the implementation of a social policy; and *evaluation,* or assessment of the impact of policies on the social phenomenon. The studies suggested by *Assessment* also fall roughly into these categories, although monitoring and evaluation, rather than model building, receive the greatest emphasis.

Model Building

The two types of model building stressed in *Assessment* are computer simulation models and scenarios. Computer simulations play a prominent role in some of the *Assessment* subprojects. These models are used to simulate the impact of alternative futures and policies. Thus, a computer simulation model was constructed by Friedmann to generate assessments of the expected damages from hurricanes, given past experiences, current and projected future distributions of coastal plain populations, and so on. White and Haas recognize that these models are inherently no better than the data fed into them, the parameters assumed, and the underlying algorithms. Indeed, the major problem with computer simulation models is that much of the data necessary to develop good parameters do not exist.

Much the same is true of scenario methodology. A scenario can be no better than its writer, can contain no more information than the writer possesses, and has the distressing characteristic of being bounded only by the writer's imagination. A scenario would be a useful descriptive device if all relevant underlying processes were very well understood, if all the key decision points could be anticipated, if the relative probabilities of one decision over another were known, and if the unavoidable stochastic components of all elements of the process could be modeled. Since none of these conditions hold in the case of modeling a community's disaster response, the scenario writer is thus driven toward a description of the worst imaginable situation, which may (but probably does not) provide a sound basis for decision making.

Assessment speaks at several points to certain basic (versus applied) social science concerns. Thus, there is favorable mention of studies of decision making in high-loss/low-probability circumstances, which speaks to a key issue in information science. Another area suggested for research is political decision making in communities, knowledge of which would presumably aid in developing strategies for the dissemination and adoption of appropriate risk mitigation measures. Indeed, this second suggestion led to our study of state and local elites.

Political decision making is worth studying whenever decisions are being made; when we first proposed to study the politics of natural hazards, we assumed this was the case. What we learned is that natural hazards are nearly invisible on the political agenda of states and local communities. Hence, our study is at best a study of how hazard-related decisions in local communities *might* be made, as seen by the people we interviewed.

Monitoring

Most of the research agenda proposed in *Assessment* calls for better monitoring of natural hazards, disasters, and attendant policy processes. The descriptive studies that constitute this class of applied social research can be of considerable or even overriding importance in areas where little is known about critical topics or parameters, since it is difficult to make sound decisions in the absence of sound information. In general, too little monitoring is done in all areas of public policy, and the call for more activity along these lines is much to *Assessment*'s credit.

Most early social science research on disasters was cast in the postaudit tradition. We now have considerable information on what happens in the narrow time frame immediately following a disaster, thanks to the tradition of response studies going back to the early 1950s. *Assessment* rightfully urges this tradition to drop its case study approach and move toward comparative studies that systematically contrast numbers of communities, and also to enlarge its time frame to include the period of reconstruction.

Although we are quite sure that White and Haas did not mean to suggest the kind of postaudit that we conducted in *After the Cleanup*, that study was designed as one form of postaudit assessment of long-term disaster effects.[1] Also, the research currently underway at the University of Minnesota on responses of communities to warnings undoubtedly derives from *Assessment*'s call for longitudinal studies where a sample of communities is studied both before and after the disaster. Turner's study of reactions to earthquake prediction is also a longitudinal study that closely resembles what White and Haas had in mind.

Postaudit studies of many disaster agents (floods, hurricanes, and tornadoes in particular) present no special technical problems as far as locating sufficient cases is concerned, since there are usually enough disaster-stricken communities around for postaudits. The main problem is that such studies will be biased toward small places. Since it is more likely that a disaster event will be catastrophic in a small place than in a large one, social science knowledge of reactions to disaster in small cities and towns has been perpetuated as the dominant perspective in this field. This is especially true of the single-case, postdisaster study in which researchers are looking in advance for a "juicy" disaster to study. Small town disasters just happen to be the juiciest. One of the virtues of *After the Cleanup* is that it tends to redress the small town imbalance by its focus on larger metropolitan areas.

In contrast to postaudits, for which postdisaster measures are sufficient, longitudinal studies that require both pre- and post-disaster measures are difficult to design efficiently, because the frequency of catastrophes is so low that it is extremely difficult to anticipate which places will be hit. Hence, large numbers of wasted observations are necessary in order to obtain a

---

[1] Indeed, Gilbert White in several communications expressed considerable skepticism concerning our approach, being especially worried that the units we chose — census tracts — would not fit closely enough to the areas directly affected by disaster events. This was a well-founded skepticism, although the problem ultimately proved more annoying than fatal.

relatively small number of places with both pre- and post-disaster data. The cost per bit of useful data thus tends to be inordinately high in longitudinal studies of the sort *Assessment* recommends.

Evaluation

Evaluation research is designed to estimate the effectiveness of particular programs or policies, net of confounding issues. The evaluation question, in a phrase, is, will it work? Definitive evaluations of social policies are extremely difficult to execute, and even nondefinitive but convincing evaluations require considerable skill and technical expertise. Although *Assessment* calls in many places for policy evaluations, there is relatively little emphasis on the evaluation of nonstructural risk mitigation, *Assessment*'s policy of choice. It is, however, as we have already argued, not clear that a rational cost-benefit assessment would favor nonstructural mitigations over alternative approaches. Certainly some evaluation of these measures would be useful *before* national implementation.

AN AMENDED SOCIAL SCIENCE
RESEARCH AGENDA

Since the studies we have carried out over the past three years were profoundly influenced by *Assessment*'s research agenda, it is useful to consider how we would modify that agenda now that we have completed our project. Our studies have uncovered some research needs that were not identified by White and Haas. We have also found that some of the problems have been misidentified. Finally, certain research strategies that we would advocate receive little attention in *Assessment*.

Perhaps the most serious research problems are those generated by the extremely poor quality of the existing natural hazard data base. *Assessment* rightly notes on several occasions the thinness and poor quality of existing data on the distribution of natural hazard events and resulting damages and injuries. Although the National Severe Storm Forecast Center's tornado tape comes closest to providing a fairly good historical record of tornadoes, for floods, the most serious natural hazard, nothing even approaching adequacy exists. The available data on damages resulting from natural disasters are often simply a congeries of rumors, clippings from old newspaper stories, and guesses, more or less educated. We do not yet know the precise magnitude of the natural hazard problem, nor do we have any precise idea of how many victims are claimed, who bears the costs of damages, or how the costs are redistributed through relief measures. Much less do we have any good sense of how the objective seriousness of hazard problems compares to that of other problems in the society, which should be essential information in setting relative levels of national effort.

It is especially important to sort out the untoward effects of disasters from the untoward effects of ongoing processes that increase the impact of disasters. Thus, if we have more deaths from riverine floods because we have more people in the society, then it is not the flood problem that is increasing but the population. It is tempting to use natural hazard mitigation to accomplish other ends, a kind of spreading out of the aims of natural hazard mitigation to serve a variety of other social goals, for example, protection of the environment or preservation of life-styles. The inclusion of other issues in natural hazard mitigation efforts is aided by assessments of the natural hazard risks that do not carefully distinguish between the effects of the hazards themselves and the associated processes that interact with hazard events.

We believe that the assessment of the extent and distribution of natural hazard events and the associated losses is an activity of such importance that it should be given priority over other research efforts. Until we know precisely what we are dealing with, it will be impossible to design appropriate social policy or appropriate social science research.

A second set of implications from our research concerns the identification of nonproblems. Perhaps the leading nonproblem is that of long-term disaster effects. There are many defects in the research we conducted on the long-term effects of disasters that occurred between 1960 and 1970, defects of which we are very much aware. However, we simply found no evidence that there are long-term effects of any appreciable magnitude, and we are quite certain that if such effects existed, they would have surfaced in at least some of the effect estimates we computed. We are bolstered in this interpretation by the failure of Friesema and collaborators at Northwestern to detect any but very short-run effects in detailed studies of catastrophes and near catastrophes in smaller places. In the United States the typical disaster event is well within the capacity of local communities to absorb.

It is important to keep in mind that our findings do not necessarily apply to extremely severe disaster events or to events occurring in societies and communities with few or no resources. We do not mean to imply that the San Francisco earthquake would be entirely within the capacity of San Francisco to absorb, or that earthquakes, typhoons, and the like occurring in societies with lesser resources are not important events. But it is also important to keep in mind that the vast bulk of the hazard problem in the United States consists of events very much less serious than these. The *worst* empirical disasters in the decade we studied — Hurricane Betsy and the Topeka tornado — were not nearly as serious as the disasters depicted in the *Assessment* scenarios.

A second important implication of our research stems from the low salience of natural disaster problems among the issues that agitate local and state elites. For the people we interviewed — a sample that was heavily weighted toward places with relatively high risk exposures — the problems posed by natural hazard events are simply not very important. We included pornography on the list of community problems because we assumed that pornography would anchor the salience hierarchy on the low end. That pornography routinely outranks natural hazards in attributed seriousness provides dramatic evidence that the politics of natural hazards are typically the politics of low-salience issues. This is a characteristic shared with other policy areas, the most studied example of which is fluoridation of water supplies. Studies of this topic have shown that the outcome of such issues is often determined by small groups to which the issue becomes, for one reason or another, of critical importance. The adoption of fluoridation in many communities was held up for a number of years by the appearance — usually unexpected — of a small but highly articulate and vocal opposition. The controversies that these antifluoridation groups managed to stir up led city councils and voters to give the opposition the benefit of the doubt and to turn down fluoridation proposals even when backed by the strongest possible advocates in the dental and medical professions.

Hazard risk mitigation has some potential to become locally controversial in the same way. "Experts" in technical positions within city and state governments may be strong advocates, but mayors, city councilmen, and other public officials are typically not and may well back off if vocal opposition arises, for example, from real estate and development interests or from homeowners who feel they are being treated unfairly.

These findings imply that research on the politics of disaster mitigation should be framed as studies of the politics of low-salience issues. A special research opportunity is going to be provided over the next decade as local communities move from the emergency to the regular phase of the National Flood Insurance Program and attempt to regulate more closely land use in floodplains.

It is important to appreciate that floodplain management is not a cut-and-dried application of relatively fixed procedures and rules. One community's floodplain regulation may be a model of adequacy, while another's may be a model of ambiguity that is designed to provide the appearance, but not the reality, of compliance. The implementation of complicated social programs with large administrative components is always problematic. Hence, good studies of implementation and attendant problems will need to be undertaken. Monitoring the progress of these policies in the postimplementation phase will also be essential.

Finally, there is a strong need to bring social science research on natural disasters into line with the current state of the art of social science research. Too much research still employs the technology and designs of the immediate postwar period. There is simply no need for additional case studies of this or that. If social science research on natural disasters is to pay off, it will have to be comparative in design, employ more sophisticated statistical techniques, and have case bases large enough to support adequate statistical generalizations. The research model of times past — get to the disaster site as soon as possible and scrounge up whatever information is available, in the hope that something of interest may eventually surface — will not advance our knowlege of community response to natural disasters much beyond its present state.

In short, social science research that will be useful to the formation of adequate and cost-benefit–conscious social policy should evidence a healthy skepticism about *all* policy alternatives, consider the full range of natural disaster events — average disasters as well as catastrophes — and employ social science research paradigms that are among the most sophisticated currently available.

REFERENCES

White, G. and Haas, J.E. 1975. *Assessment of Research on Natural Hazards.* Cambridge, Mass.: MIT Press.

Commentary*

Thomas E. Drabek

I found SADRI's *Assessment* paper perceptive and very insightful. I agree with many of the points made. There are several places, however, where I favor alternative interpretations. My comments should not be construed as a defense of White and Haas; they are, rather, first impressions and reactions to some of the larger issues posed in the paper.

It is very important that this paper not be misread. It is generally critical of *Assessment*, but early on the authors make a very clear statement:

> The critical tone of our remarks, then, does not in any sense belie our judgment that *Assessment* was and remains an important document and an excellent model of how social science theory and research, intelligently and properly applied, can make genuine contributions to the development of public policy.

Let me, then, address myself to what I see as the important conceptual and research questions that have been raised, of which I think there are four:

1. Do natural hazards constitute a social problem?
2. Have past research efforts brought us closer to identifying key elements in alternative solutions and more informed policy?
3. What implications emerge when we juxtapose SADRI's findings and conclusions against this past legacy?
4. Can future social research efforts make positive contributions to the development of more informed policies regarding natural hazard mitigation?

DO NATURAL HAZARDS CONSTITUTE A SOCIAL PROBLEM?

Until recently, hazards have been assumed to be social problems. Some will recall the value of Fritz's chapter on "Disaster" in the early Merton and Nisbet *Social Problems* text. Without question, White and Haas argue in *Assessment* that we have an increasingly hazardous environment in terms of both potential and actual losses. There are a variety of reasons, for example, invasion of floodplains and the mobile home sales curve. Their detailed presentation gives a much broader perspective than had ever been available

---

*I thank the Social and Demographic Research Institute, University of Massachusetts, Amherst, which provided a transcript of this portion of the conference, and the staff of the Department of Sociology, University of Denver, who typed this version.

in the past. More recently, other elements, for example, increased nuclear, chemical transportation, and other technological risks, have made us even more vulnerable. Largely because of these increasing risks, in the last ten years both the public and government officials have probably greatly changed their views of the responsibilities of government agencies regarding natural hazards. All this suggests, of course, that hazards *are* social problems of considerable magnitude.[1]

The question is, is this view of hazards anything more than a convenient assumption? Do our data support the view that hazards are indeed social problems? I would argue that most disaster researchers made this assumption until SADRI's studies started to challenge it.

One major contribution of *Assessment* was that White and Haas pulled together for the first time a massive amount of existing data. The only precursor to this kind of effort was the U.S. Office of Emergency Planning's *Report to the Congress: Emergency Preparedness* (1972). Having done this, White and Haas could then point to some holes in the data base, both in *Assessment* and at conferences and workshops they sponsored. SADRI's conclusions about the inadequacies of the data base only extend themes that are emphasized throughout *Assessment*: the existing data bases are highly incomplete; they are fragmented; they are noncumulative; they are exceedingly difficult for most researchers to use. These inadequacies, as SADRI notes, make it difficult to use existing data to assess the general dimensions of the hazard problem in this country.

But that is only one dimension of the problem. The second is that event frequency is an absolute measure, whereas evaluation of the seriousness of any problem is relative. And as to the relative seriousness, "all five of the natural hazards we asked about—floods, fires, hurricanes, tornadoes, and earthquakes—were seen by our respondents to be less serious than inflation, unemployment, crime, housing, and so on." These findings should help us place environmental hazards within a more general social problem context.

SADRI explicates several different kinds of relativities. One has been discussed quite a bit during this conference—the relativity of time. SADRI argues that the severity of impact in the emergency period has to be juxtaposed against the recovery capacity of communities and the residual impacts that might be detected a year or more later. In that sense, they confirm what several streams of past research have concluded. However, in my judgment, the specification of that confirmation of past research is not

---

[1]A recent book by Kates, Burton, and White, *The Environment as Hazard,* makes the point in the following way: "In a time of extraordinary human effort to control the natural world, the global toll from extreme events of nature is increasing. Loss of property from natural hazards is rising in most regions of the earth, and higher loss of life is continuing or increasing among the poor nations of the world" (Kates, Burton, and White 1978, p. 1).

stressed sufficiently. There are many who have reached similar conclusions in the past, but they remain unrecognized.

Second, SADRI tells us of the relativity of political aggregation. This is a more complicated point: both the presence of natural disaster problems and the frequency of disaster events tend to increase as one moves from smaller to larger aggregates, or units. Thus, in regard to mitigation efforts, various federal regulations may appear to be irksome, restrictive, and even wasteful of scarce resources, when viewed by local community elites. In contrast, the viewpoint adopted in *Assessment* is very much a federal perspective. Mitigation remedies that seem most desirable when viewed from this systemic level may not have the same relative valuation when one shifts to a smaller unit.

Both these relativities give us a great deal to ponder. But we should ask whether these notions of relativity are unique to natural hazards. They would, I think, tend to be true of all problem areas, irrespective of content. The question then becomes whether SADRI has learned about *natural hazard* politics, or just about state and local politics in general. With no indication of the context (in this sense), the data are very difficult to interpret. SADRI's report on the findings should supply the context for interpretation.

There is one potential misinterpretation of their results that should be noted. Because of this aggregation process, SADRI argues, natural hazards are more salient problems at the federal level than at the community and state levels. Clearly there is greater functional differentiation at the federal level. But this does not necessarily mean that on the federal level, vis-a-vis other federal issues, natural hazards have any higher priority. In fact, I seriously doubt whether natural hazards occupy higher priorities within the mix of issues comprising the current federal political agenda. *All* problems are more serious at the federal level, and the *relative priority* of hazard problems may be just the same as at the lower levels.

A third notion is the relativity of competing resources. Certainly this is very important if we assume that resources are allocated politically according to the relative seriousness with which problems are viewed. But is this a correct assumption? The fact is, we really don't know very much about the resource allocation processes actually used by communities for hazard mitigation or any other policy activity. This, I suggest, is a key research question for future inquiry.

What, then, do these observations suggest about the larger question of whether natural disasters constitute a social problem? First, it is clear that extreme disaster events do and will continue to occur. Second, the evidence, though poor, is that populations are more at risk today than ever before. But third, this question can only be judged relative to other concerns and other public issues. Most local elites—and probably federal elites too—give natural hazards a relatively low political priority in an attitudinal sense.

One possible reaction to these points is that we ought to accept this view of the nonseriousness of hazard issues and, being wise people, focus our resources and thinking on whatever the elites think are the most serious problems. This reaction seems implicit in SADRI's report. Note, however, that in this view a "social problem" is defined as whatever the elites decide to call a problem.

In contrast, there is a second position which is in the best tradition of social problem research, one stated best by Robert Lynd (1948) and more recently by Gresham Sykes (1971): social scientists have a responsibility to define social problems. There may well be social trends that exacerbate structural strains. And in the process segments of the population suffer. The pain of private troubles reflects larger public issues, although it is seldom linked to them in any direct way (Mills 1959).

Thus, the real issue raised by SADRI's study, it seems to me, is whether the social scientist has a responsibility to define issues, not just study what a segment of the public, at a given point in time, might think is important. For the social scientist who acknowledges this responsibility, the assessment of what constitutes a social problem is quite independent of the perceptions held by the population. Rather it is based on a larger understanding, a sensitivity to the absolute losses that are occurring and, equally important, the potential losses that could occur.

CONTRIBUTIONS OF PRIOR RESEARCH

Have past research efforts brought us closer to identifying alternative solutions and more informed policies? If we use a highly idealized model of tightly controlled, policy-oriented research as our standard, the answer is, probably not. Natural hazard research has been somewhat erratic, somewhat discontinuous, and somewhat opportunistic. Seldom have research issues in this area been defined with a specific policy objective in mind.

Disaster research in the social sciences has too often been designed in isolation from practitioners. Many of our colleagues (for example, Benson 1977) would argue that this is a good thing—it ought to be even more isolated. Depending on the values of the researcher and a complex set of epistemological assumptions, we can argue about the desirable degree of isolation. But most of us would agree with Kreps's conclusion that most research on natural hazards for the past twenty years has been conducted by scholars working in relative isolation from practitioners.

Clearly, applied or policy-oriented research is something we need to understand much better—the barriers, the constraints, the cases that worked, and so on. And here, it seems to me, White and Haas broke new ground. As SADRI's paper acknowledges, *Assessment* is for all practical purposes the first sustained effort to examine the whole of existing social science disaster literature for the purpose of illuminating major policy questions.

However, intentionally or not, the legacy of previous resesarch *has* contributed to more informed natural hazard policies. Let me illustrate with six different points, each exceptionally important to planners and others concerned with improved management of emergency responses.

First, through a variety of studies reflecting several social science disciplines, we now have a greatly improved understanding of basic human responses during the immediate postimpact period, rather than a cluster of mythologies. Furthermore, we now know a great deal about primary group bonds and their importance in structuring responses. This information can and ought to be used as a basis for planning and emergency response training. But today, in my judgment, we still lack adequate translation and dissemination of these findings to persons confronting the task at the local level.

Second, we have an improved understanding of the organizational complexity that characterizes community response systems and subsystems. We have a good sense of the design requirements for community warning systems (and are learning more each month), as reflected in the work of Mileti (1975); Perry (1979); and especially Carter, Clark, and Leik (1977) and Carter and Clark (1977).

Third, there have been emergent efforts at application, for example, White's Natural Hazards Research and Applications Information Center and the workshops conducted there. These workshops have made it clear that the dissemination task is highly complex given current disciplinary provincialism and a multiplicity of political priorities. Yet at least we have begun to experiment with both interdisciplinary perspectives and different models of dissemination. More attention to both of these issues is essential in the immediate future.

Fourth, we need more comprehensive and comparative analyses, as SADRI underscores. In a comprehensive sense, the White-Haas volume (1975), and earlier the U.S. Office of Emergency Planning's *Report to the Congress* (1972), were the first efforts to break this ground. More work must be done within this kind of global perspective. But one cannot do studies such as SADRI's on a shoestring budget. And certainly ample research funds have not been uniformly available for hazard research, even for a visible center like that at Ohio State.

Fifth, and extremely important, the Boulder workshops and a few other efforts have begun to identify some fundamental policy tensions in the hazard area. We need a better understanding of those tensions if informed policy is to be made. Here, perhaps, is where SADRI's paper is most relevant. I think back to workshop discussions three or four years ago, when people were just beginning to raise questions such as:

"Is any type of regulation of land use a restriction on human freedom?"

"How far should any unit of government go to protect people from potential risks?"

"How are these costs to be assessed and juxtaposed against any benefits that might be gained?"

The workshop, of course, did not provide answers to these questions, but there was some fundamental growth in the ability of the participants to raise them and to begin to sense the inherent complexities of the answers.

Hazard planning does cost money. And there are competing priorities in any community. How does one find a middle ground between negligence and overprotection? What is a reasonable balance? These are not uncommon questions for an emergency preparedness director to ask. But they lead to an even more important matter. Any significant adjustment, be it flood insurance, a new dam, or what have you, is going to affect some vested interest group. How do local officials establish the politically possible, vis-a-vis the best desirable mix of adjustments, as they might be viewed by various scientific experts? This seems to me to be a crucial question—in both the behavioral and normative senses.

Sixth, we need to recognize that within the scientific research community there are competing claims of legitimacy regarding research priorities. This is especially true of allocations between the physical and social sciences. It is one of *Assessment*'s major virtues to have identified a strong imbalance disfavoring social research, and to have called for redress:

> Research today concentrates largely on technologically oriented solutions to problems of natural hazards, instead of focussing equally on the social, economic and political factors which lead to non-adoption of technological findings, or which indicate that proposed steps would not work or would only tend to perpetuate and increase the problem. In short, the all-important social, economic, and political "people" factors involved in hazards reduction have been largely ignored. (White and Haas 1975, p.1)

THE IMPLICATIONS OF SADRI'S STUDIES

Given this brief overview of the legacy of natural hazard research, where does SADRI's research take us? First and unequivocally, we should recognize the contribution made by these two projects. I personally commend Rossi, the Wrights, and the SADRI staff for both the rich data they collected and the rigor of their analysis. Clearly, in terms of both methodological rigor and innovative applications, this work represents something never before done.

However, as with all other major studies, SADRI's projects have raised more questions than they have answered. Given the methodological rigor of their work, there is a temptation to conclude that there is nothing else of interest to be studied. But this is, of course, a seriously mistaken conclusion. We need to go beyond the question they posed and take the next steps. For example, we should next ask whether unique changes in population levels over a ten-year period are to be expected given the class of phenomena selected for study. In short, how can we demarcate classes of disasters in order to look for long-term effects? This again raises the issue of the appropriate taxonomy of hazard events.

SADRI's laudable effort to get a larger number of cases has at one level blurred the research focus. By dropping their event threshold to pick up adequate numbers of cases, they include large numbers of relatively trivial events. According to their criteria, a disaster would be included if it destroyed only ten houses and seriously damaged thirty others, and this over an entire county. Could we really imagine that such events would register impacts on the population base of any county over a ten-year period?

What is a reasonable threshold level? That really is the fundamental question, and to answer it most easily, we ought to turn it around; that is, what threshold level, if any, is required to register various types of effects with given degrees of precision in measurement? Additional relevant questions are: what about microsystems; are effects detectable here that may not be registered at more aggregated units; is it likely that long-term effects are differentially distributed? These and many other criticial research questions are suggested by SADRI's results.

Or consider the notion of "impact ratios." This is a useful concept but not a panacea, and much more research will be necessary to give it concrete meaning. Even if we could get more standardized measures of loss, the notion of "resources available," or "recovery capacity," is very complex and difficult to operationalize in a satisfactory manner. Furthermore, counting bodies or destroyed dwellings does not capture the symbolic meanings of these physical losses, and these symbolic meanings may be very important. While quantification of damage is possible and desirable, understanding social factors requires that elements of sentiment be included as well.

As SADRI has emphasized, the politics of disaster is a critical area that should be a top priority for future research. We need to know much more about the transformation processes whereby an issue of low salience becomes a key issue receiving considerable attention. And we need to know how, in the case of a low-salience issue, some things nonetheless get done. More important, how can hazard mitigation be encouraged?

What, now, of SADRI's policy conclusions? SADRI suggests that the so-called average disaster ought to be the basis for federal policy rather than more extreme cases. "Perhaps the most reasonable policy may be simply to admit in advance that such catastrophic events cannot be prepared for and to expect that special measures would have to be taken ad hoc if such events were to occur" (Rossi et al. 1978, p. 130).

This recommendation is intriguing, but the notion of an average disaster is rather vague. We still need to know more precisely the full spectrum of losses due to natural hazards before an average can be meaningful. And we know little about the aggregation effects. How many average tornadoes do we have to have before we get a loss equivalent to Topeka? SADRI's "two-tiered" policy sounds good on paper, but just how would it be implemented?

To some degree, the 1974 Disaster Relief Act established just such a policy. I suggest we need a critical evaluation of that act and the way in which it has been implemented. What we need, then, is more research on the execution of programs operated by the Federal Disaster Assistance Administration and other federal agencies.

Let me take this point one step further. Local units do differ greatly across numerous structural characteristics. Whether they are rural or urban, for example, makes a major difference in their recovery capacity and in the organization of their emergency services (Drabek et al. 1979). By implication, then, future research ought to seek insight into the feasibility of alternative federal policies, not just for varying classes of disasters, but for varying classes of local communities as well.

One theme in SADRI's *Assessment* paper is that White and Haas failed to recognize and emphasize the costs of various policies, especially non-structural mitigations. As the paper notes, many of these costs are hidden: risk mapping, for example, is imperfect and may therefore introduce important inequities. Also, all communities confront many other problems that require resources. So we cannot assume that communities will go very far in hazard mitigation on their own. Furthermore, the *real* costs for most of these nonstructural adjustments may have been underestimated.

Certainly we have to agree that we need better data on the potential costs of all hazard adjustment options, including nonstructural options. But it is unfair to say that White and Haas are not aware of these cost issues. For example, in their discussion of new research strategies the authors note: "It seems desirable to designate a few lines of work that deserve early initiation in the face of severe budget constraints" (White and Haas 1975, p. 223).

The *Assessment* paper is basically hostile to the notion of scenarios, treating them as a nonscientific methodology. In contrast, I suggest that the scenario analysis can be very helpful for certain purposes. It is an invaluable aid in explicating aspects of *potential* interdependence among units, for example. Any such hypothesized interdependence still requires empirical verification, but this form of analysis can be most helpful in sorting things out and identifying potential linkages and sequential impacts.

White and Haas do *not* stress scenarios as a new research strategy, contrary to implication. Rather they are used as a teaching tool. This point is made repeatedly in *Assessment*. For example: "One sobering lesson from past experience with hazards is that the nation has difficulty visualizing the human suffering and economic disruption which will result from events whose coming is certain, but whose timing is completely uncertain" (White and Haas 1975, p. 29). Scenarios are used mainly to facilitate this visualization.

It is also incorrect to say that *Assessment* does not recognize the problem of doing longitudinal studies. Quite the contrary: the problem is explicitly acknowledged:

Because it is impossible to predict areas in which the extreme events will occur over the next ten years, ingenuity is required in design (Baker and Chapman, 1962). A program might provide for base observation for a large number of communities supplemented by intensive studies in those where events occur. (White and Haas 1975, p. 229)

Predisaster data, where available, provide an invaluable context for interpretation. I am particularly sensitive to this because of the mental health and family interactional data we collected following the Topeka tornado (for example, see Drabek and Key 1976; Sterling, Drabek, and Key 1977). If we had presented our findings using only the postdisaster data, they could have easily been misread; that is, some might assume that our percentages of mental pathologies or kin detachment resulted directly from the event. But once we had looked at the pretornado data obtained from the Menninger Foundation, our interpretation was very different. It is, as SADRI argues, difficult to execute pre- and post-test hazard research designs. But it is essential that such studies be done.

THE FUTURE OF SOCIAL SCIENCE RESEARCH ON HAZARD MITIGATION POLICIES

Let me conclude with some summary comments about the future of social science research and the development of more informed hazard policies and applications. First, any applied or policy-oriented research must be conducted with the realization that value choices, not solely technical expertise or better data, are part of the research process. This starts with the question, what is to be studied?

Second, we academics should not masquerade as wizards or prophets whose truth is revealed only in complex correlation matrices. We cannot work in total isolation. We have a clear responsibility both to publish in technical and trade journals and to meet with practitioners, translating and disseminating our findings. In general, social scientists in our fields do much too little of this.

Third, we need more of what I would call two-way research, that is, research informed by continuing interaction with practitioners. That's not to say that our own independence and autonomy ought to be abandoned. But I am convinced that we are capable not only of better research, but also of better dissemination if a genuine two-way process is encouraged.

Fourth, more methodological rigor is clearly required. But we should not overreact to criticisms that challenge past work. Rossi and the Wrights conclude, "There is simply no need for additional case studies of this or that." In contrast, Quarantelli has argued persuasively for the desirability of multiple methods. I suggest that case studies, like everything else, can be done well or poorly, and that there *is* a continuing use for good case studies.

My own field of complex organizational analysis, for example, leaped prematurely into quantification and produced an excessive number of rather poor studies that gave wrong inferences based on low levels of correlated variability. Now, after some ten years of this emphasis, some critics (for example, Benson 1977) are claiming that case studies do have a place in the research process. We should not eliminate them from the research enterprise.

Let me conclude by noting that the structural strains within American society — and especially between our society and other sectors of the world — are intensifying. Thus, the general public perceives many problems with a sense of urgency. But should we define what constitutes a social problem — or what might be the best candidate for research — on the basis of an opinion poll? I think not! Prior to the mid-1960s, many Americans did not view race relations as an important social problem. Prior to Three Mile Island, few gave any thought to the safety of nuclear reactors. In my judgment, what we need from Rossi and the Wrights at this point is a more elaborate analysis of the research agenda that their data suggest.

REFERENCES

Baker, G. and Chapman, D., eds. 1962. *Man and Society in Disaster.* New York: Basic Books.

Benson, J. 1977. Innovation and Crisis in Organizational Analysis. *Sociological Quarterly* 18 (Winter): 3-16.

Bond, C.E. 1979. The Energy-Environment Crisis: Values and the Social Structure of Social Problems. *Sociological Focus* 12 (April): 125-139.

Carter, T. and Clark, J.P. 1977. Disaster Warning Systems: Implications from a Formal Theory of Inter-Organizational Relations. Paper presented at the annual meeting of the American Sociological Association, Chicago, September.

Carter, T., Clark, J.P., and Leik, R.K. 1977. Social Factors Affecting the Dissemination of and Response to Warnings. Paper presented at the Eleventh Technical Conference on Hurricanes and Tropical Meteorology, Miami Beach, December.

Drabek, T.E. and Key, W.H. 1976. The Impact of Disaster on Primary Group Linkages. *Mass Emergencies* 1: 89-05.

Drabek, T.E. et al. 1979. *The Flood Breakers: Citizens Band Radio Use During the 1978 Flood in the Grand Forks Region.* Boulder, Colo.: Institute of Behavioral Science, University of Colorado.

Fritz, C.E. 1961. Disaster. In *Contemporary Social Problems,* R.K. Merton and R. Nisbet, eds. New York: Harcourt.

Kates, R., Burton, I., and White, G.F. 1978. *Environment as Hazard.* New York: Oxford University Press.

Kilijanek, T.S. and Drabek, T.E. 1979. Assessing Long-Term Impacts of a Natural Disaster: A Focus on the Elderly. *The Gerontologist* 19: 555-566.

Lynd, R.S. 1948. *Knowledge for What?* Princeton, N.J.: Princeton University Press.

Mileti, D.S. 1975. *Natural Hazard Warning Systems in the United States: A Research Assessment.* Boulder, Colo.: Institute of Behavioral Science, University of Colorado.

Mills, C.W. 1959. *The Sociological Imagination.* New York: Oxford University Press.

Perry, R. 1979. Evacuation Decision-Making in Natural Disasters. *Mass Emergencies* 4: 25-38.

Rossi, P.H. et al. 1978. Are There Long Term Effects of American Natural Disasters? *Mass Emergencies* 3: 117-132.

Sterling, J., Drabek, T.E., and Key, W.H. 1977. The Long-Term Impact of Disaster on the Health Self-Perception of Victims. Paper presented at the annual meeting of the American Sociological Association, Chicago, September.

Sykes, G. 1971. *Social Problems in America.* Glenview, Ill.: Scott, Foresman and Company.

U.S. Office of Emergency Planning. 1972. Report to the Congress: Emergency Preparedness. Volumes I, II, and III. Washington, D.C.: Office of Emergency Preparedness, Executive Office of the President.

White, G.F. and Haas, J.E. 1975. *Assessment of Research on Natural Hazards.* Cambridge, Mass.: MIT Press.

Commentary*

Gilbert F. White

SADRI's appraisal of *Assessment of Research on Natural Hazards* raises several major questions about the lines of research currently pursued with respect to natural hazards in the United States, offers cautions at a few methodological points, and provides the background for what one may hope will be a more thoughtful appraisal of suitable ways in which to assess research needs in a field of public policy. It is helpful to have these issues raised in the light of work completed by the SADRI research program, but it is unfortunate that a number of the judgments and propositions are flawed by inaccurate presentations of data or findings from other sources.

To clear the ground, attention is directed first to points at which SADRI's assertions about *Assessment* are at variance with statements in *Assessment*. This comparison is difficult because assertions are not accompanied by quotations or specific references: where SADRI states that *Assessment* presents some specified position, it is difficult to identify the evidence on which the judgment is based. In the following paragraphs the comparison, wherever practicable, is made by direct quotes.

SADRI states that:

> ...*Assessment* is intended to serve at least two distinct and in some ways contradictory purposes. First, it is meant to be a scientific document assessing the then current state of the art with respect to natural hazard knowledge and research and directing attention to potentially fruitful new research leads. But second, it is also meant as a consciousness-raising document calling attention to the seriousness of the natural hazard problem and spurring recalcitrant decision makers to action. We suggest throughout this paper that these consciousness-raising efforts sometimes work at cross-purposes with the more strictly scientific goals.

This does not conform to the *Assessment* authors' opening statement:

> In undertaking our *Assessment of Research on Natural Hazards* we had two broad aims. The first was to provide a more nearly balanced and comprehensive basis for judging the social utility of allocating funds and personnel for various types of research on geophysical hazards. The second was to stimulate,

---

*The author was not able to take part in the conference. This commentary reflects a later comparison of SADRI's paper with the content of White and Haas's *Assessment of Research on Natural Hazards*. The first draft benefited from helpful comments by Thomas Drabek, Howard Kunreuther, Adam Rose, and Susan Tubbesing.

in the process of that analysis, a more systematic appraisal of research needs by scientific investigators in cooperation with the users of their findings. (White and Haas 1975, p. xvii)

The difference between these statements of aims is important, because, in preparing *Assessment,* heavy stress was placed on a method that would involve both producers and users of research in an improved, cooperative assessment of research needs.

SADRI at a number of points asserts that *Assessment* makes "policy recommendations." *Assessment* makes no explicit policy recommendations. It does recommend research on policy options that appear promising and have been neglected. The stress accordingly is on examining the full range of research opportunities and on those least explored. Thus, in dealing with floods, the authors of *Assessment* stress not the engineering aspects of flood control, but research on urban drainage, warning response, land management, building codes, and related measures. For example:

> The most promising short-term research thrust is testing and refining new approaches to land use management by studying ways to speed up the adoption of sound land use schemes and to measure their social effectiveness. Land use management can be significantly advanced by coupling relief and rehabilitation efforts and insurance regulation with plans for community preparedness and long-term reconstruction.

> All of this work is dependent to some extent upon improving methods of estimating flood hazards. These activities should be accompanied by basic research on variables affecting flood damage. Fresh analysis should be made of public participation in project choice with an eye to helping communities arrive at workable methods of choosing the optimal mix of adjustments for their particular locations. (White and Haas 1975, p. 19)

The same general approach, which seeks to build a practicable range of choice for local administrators, is exemplified in *Assessment*'s summary of research needs:

> In the United States there are five major methods of adjusting to natural hazards common to all or most of the hazards covered in this study. Sometimes they are used in combination, but the utilization of one adjustment, such as insurance or relief and rehabilitation, may work against utilization of another, such as land use management, even though the latter may hold a greater long-term potential for reducing danger and loss. These five adjustment methods are:
> 1. relief and rehabilitation;
> 2. insurance;
> 3. warning systems;
> 4. technological aids (protective works, etc.); and
> 5. land use management.

Depending upon local conditions, it may be most productive to promote protection works in one area while planning open space in another, or to mix warnings with a scheme for widened insurance coverage.

With the currently increasing natural hazard losses and loss potential, and the move towards national and state-wide land use management efforts, the nation would benefit substantially from comparative investigations of these adjustment processes and of the effects of different mixes. There is much to gain by examining insurance experience across the whole range of hazards, or by asking why land use regulations are acceptable in some flood plains but not in an earthquake zone, or why people will vote for a levee construction bond issue in one area while in another they will walk through the after-shocks of an earthquake to vote down a bond issue for strengthening the earthquake resistance of a local school, even though such strengthening is required by law. (White and Haas 1975, pp. 14-15)

To emphasize that the opportunities, difficulties, and implications of a given type of adjustment should be investigated is quite different from saying, as asserted by SADRI, that this is considered to be "the best technique."

At a more restricted level of generalization, SADRI states: "The volume does not attempt to estimate the annual per capita costs of natural hazards to the society at large or trends in per capita costs over time...." In fact, Figure 3-4 of *Assessment* gives estimates of deaths per 10 million, injuries per 10 million, and property damage in dollars per capita for 15 hazards (p. 68). Estimated trends based on time series in supporting monographs are shown graphically in Figure 3-5 (p. 70). Estimates of aggregated adjustment costs are given wherever practicable. For example: "In the aggregate, the adjust-ment costs may account for at least 50% of the direct property losses. As already noted, it is 60% or more for floods" (p. 74). There is no doubt that the basic data are miserable. SADRI stresses this more strongly than *Assessment* does, and the center has taken a few steps to try to improve the data base.

A major observation is that the findings show that the total and long-term effects of a natural disaster in a community are not "of any appreciable magnitude" except in those instances where the community is small in size and population and the area struck by the natural disaster represents a com-paratively large proportion of that community and population. This has been a part of the conventional wisdom about disasters for a long time: the smaller the community the more likely the total amount of disruption from an extreme event in a significant part of it. SADRI's interpretation of these findings is that because the gross social impacts seem to be relatively small and because selected people in a community are reported to regard natural hazards as low in any list of priorities for community action, the national problem of dealing with such extreme events has been exaggerated and is less demanding of attention than might otherwise have been believed to be the case.

It is helpful at this point to ask, what are the national as well as distributional consequences of the repetition of the sort of events occurring during 1960-1970, both of low frequency and of high frequency, that have been studied by SADRI? Rose suggests a 2 percent or greater reduction in level of local, regional, or national output as an operational tolerance level during a period of disruption. The largest single natural catastrophe that has occurred in recent decades was Tropical Storm Agnes, which in 1972 caused an estimated property damage in excess of $3 billion, accounting for a $1.8 billion loss in direct output. This would be 6 percent of gross national income. For the 2.8 million people in the affected region, the relative income loss, assuming a labor-output ratio of 1/$4,500 and direct and indirect (1/2.8) output losses of $5.18, would be about 4 percent. Given the figures that have accumulated from the rough estimates of property damage, as cited both by SADRI and the *Assessment* authors, it appears that the effect of all natural hazards is on the order of .5 to 1 percent of gross national income in an average year in the United States. Is this significant? As Rose has pointed out, a reduction of as much as 2 to 4 percent in level of output has been a distinguishing feature of recessions in recent decades. Disruption at the regional level may be more severe. Should not a nation that is worried about the approach of another recession be concerned with events that can generate interruption in regional economic income flows of the same magnitude?

Should it not also be concerned about effects that may be severe or tragic for some people and slight for others? *Assessment* suggests that distributional differences require more attention than they receive in aggregate studies.

Economic effects on communities that receive little of SADRI's attention are income flows and transfers. When it is asserted that a community has experienced relatively modest economic impacts in the wake of a flood or hurricane or tornado, nothing is said about the ways in which income flows have compensated some people and not others for the damages resulting from property loss or from dislocation of economic and social activities. As cited in *Assessment*, the magnitude of these flows is large, and the trend over recent decades has been toward increasing the proportion that comes from the national treasuries of either government or nongovernment agencies, such as the American Red Cross. If the economic impact of a tornado on a community turns out to be relatively modest, this is due to some extent to the transfers from government and nongovernment sources to compensate for local losses and dislocations. To pursue the argument further, it might be asserted that if only the modes of making income transfers in the wake of disaster could be improved, there would be virtually no significant economic losses in the communities affected and only a much greater drain on the national treasury. It should be noted that while a variety of nonstructural measures call for administrative expense, so also do measures for making these income transfers through insurance, relief payments, and emergency expenses.

The criticism that *Assessment* is geared to a federal view is correct in part. *Assessment* attempts to look at the net impact of extreme events on the nation as a whole, as well as on individual communities. In these circumstances it is to be expected that the concerns of federal agencies might in many instances seem more prominent than those of local agencies. Insofar as local and state groups can transfer costs to the national income, it is likely to be the federal agencies that are the instruments for such transfers and that are sensitive to their magnitude. *Assessment* suggests inquiry into possible cooperative measures by federal, state, and local agencies (White and Haas 1975, pp. 15-16).

The lack of saliency of many natural hazard issues in the interim between extreme events in local communities has long been recognized, and it highlights the need for relating the concern with hazard adjustments to other policies and programs that claim attention in the communities. This suggests a paradox. On the one hand SADRI reports that many communities do not regard natural hazards as high on the list of salient issues confronting the community. On the other hand it is evident that many communities in some fashion exert sufficient pressure upon federal agencies to obtain elaborate and costly programs to deal with those natural hazards. This is attested to by the volume of expenditures for national programs for flood control, for beach protection, for earthquake prediction, and the like. There has been enough concern on the part of local agencies to lead them to push for federal funds in the directions noted and to insist on an increase in the efficiency and diffusion of federal emergency measures in the aftermath of disaster. This could hardly be viewed as an exclusively federal bias.

The federal legislative and executive agencies are sensitive to state/local demands, and a repeated criticism of expenditures for flood control, drought relief, and emergency rehabilitation activities is that they are unduly responsive to the pressures of local groups.

Although a community leader may regard pornography as more urgent than floods, the community may agitate for a flood control project and be prepared to take on the local costs of lands and damages that are a normal and often substantial part of any federal nonreservoir project. Is community concern to be judged by what influential people say or by what the community seeks and pays for? The aggregate demand for federal funds is large and increasing.

The scenario methodology is strongly criticized on the grounds that it is unrealistic. There is much merit to such criticism. The conventional wisdom is that all our knowledge is about the past, all our decisions about the future.

It should be noted that the scenario methodology was developed in order to deal with the problem of presenting the likely social impacts of high-magnitude, low-frequency events that do not lend themselves to customary statistical analysis. Had the reliance been on statistical averages from a very short period of record, it would have been impossible to suggest the magnitude of the kinds of catastrophes that can be envisaged in San Francisco and that certainly will occur within a matter of tens or hundreds of years. Wherever possible, the calculations are more precise. For example, by consulting Figure 11-1 (White and Haas 1975, p. 245), it is possible to read, on the basis of statistical analysis, the percentage probability that a great hurricane will strike in one year in the fifty-mile segment of the Miami coastline. The scenario method also was intended to specify significant decision points, as illustrated in the Rapid City scenario, which estimates mean annual damages under alternative policies (p. 142). The method is far from satisfactory, but it is one way of suggesting answers to such questions as: what are the alternatives, and how can they be fashioned?

SADRI makes incisive comments on two of the five general research recommendations put forward in *Assessment*. Postaudits and longitudinal studies are noted, but nothing is said about recommendations for a clearing-house, early action by states, and congressional overviews (pp. 229–235). It would be helpful to have comments on the suitability of at least the clearing-house and congressional overview in light of the SADRI research.

It is to be regretted that while *Assessment* is cited as "an excellent model" of assessment of research needs, there is no searching examination of whether it was indeed such a model and whether the results have been productive on balance. It might be argued, for example, that if the research that has been generated has led to the sort of questions posed by SADRI, the model has precipitated new thinking about the way in which the field of public research and policy is viewed, and therefore it is beneficial. It could also be argued that a more prescient review might have foreseen likely conclusions from such investigations and avoided them in the first instance. In any event, it is important to note that *Assessment* represents a high degree of consensus at the time of its writing among people in both the research and administrative communities dealing with the problems of natural hazards.

While a number of judgments are primarily those of the authors — senior and junior — who participated in *Assessment*, the recommendations as to emphasis and type of program are represented in the views of a large number of people participating in the field from one vantage point or another. The text sums up the group judgment at the time, leavened with the views of the principal investigators, but in most instances paralleling or converging on those that grew out of the analysis conducted in the course of the review. Might it have been more nearly prescient if there had been less direct involvement by research users and producers?

Assessment represents a process rather than a single independent measure. It was designed to generate and stimulate thinking within the agencies that use research and those that produce research as to objectives and appropriate methodologies, and it probably would have had some major effects simply as a result of the participation of users in our workshops and manuscript reviews, even if no documents had ever been published. It is this aspect of *Assessment* that deserves critical examination. Should similar exercises be promoted? Is it an effective way in which to carry out such an exercise? Would some other format have been more effective in influencing the course of research activities and the application of research results?

REFERENCES

White, G.F. and Haas, J.E. 1975. *Assessment of Research on Natural Hazards.* Cambridge, Mass.: MIT Press.

Discussion

Peter H. Rossi: To respond to one of Drabek's points, I think we are at a very primitive stage in understanding the nature of the disaster problem. I do not think we can say for sure that the problem is truly increasing. To be sure, there *are* more people living at risk from hazards than before, but there are also more people than before. The question is whether the growth of the population at risk has exceeded the simple growth of population. I don't think we know the answer, and until we do, the focus on an increasing population at risk is somewhat alarmist.

Thomas E. Drabek: I think that is a very important point. It would require better data than now available to provide a definitive answer. But I do feel there is more to the problem than population increase. Use of the environment by that population is also an important factor.

Joseph F. Coates: Your review of White and Haas is completely ungenerous. It makes no concession that readers, much less the authors, are able to fill in any gaps. Furthermore, your review, with the exception of the last part and one or two minor points throughout, in no way depends upon the research you did. Your criticism is largely canonical. You review the difficulties of cost-benefit analysis; you did not have to do any work to know those difficulties. You review the difficulties of scenarios; you did not have to do any new research to know about them, and so on. I am struck by the complete lack of generosity in your review.

A subsidiary point: I think you have overlooked the growing complexity of society as an important factor affecting future disasters. There is an interesting, albeit small, body of work suggesting, for example, that the effects of the San Francisco earthquake will not be limited to San Francisco or even California, but because of the integration of the economy will have multiplier effects, ripple effects, throughout the whole society.

Rossi: Our purpose was not to be generous. This is not an eleemosynary activity. Much of the tone and emphasis of the volume now strike us, in retrospect, as misleading, and our critique was intended to set at least some parts of the record straight.

On another point: Drabek has raised an extremely important criticism of our study in observing that we should have asked questions concerning the regulatory philosophy of the respondents with respect to several content areas, just as we did with seriousness. That would have enabled us to calibrate the responses. To say that 30 percent of the elites believe in the free market philosophy with respect to natural hazards means very little unless we know what proportion supports the free market philosophy in matters of food additives, abortions, and so forth.

Charles Fritz: I would like to make one final point: you should place your own work more in the tradition of the entire literature. I think what you have done is to document and confirm many of the ideas that appear in the literature. I have a sense that you do not recognize the confirmatory nature of your research, so I think that broadening the context to include some other relevant literature would be helpful.

PART FOUR
Epilogue

IMPLICATIONS OF THE CONFERENCE FOR HAZARD POLICY AND RESEARCH

Peter H. Rossi and James D. Wright

Nearly a year and a half have passed since the conference was held on which this volume is based. Had this epilogue been written immediately after the conference ended, its tone in all likelihood would have been quite different, possibly more concerned with answering the criticisms leveled at our research than identifying the highlights of the conference themes that emerged. Although the pressure of other commitments may have been the major reason for postponing its writing, the passage of time has given us a more dispassionate and balanced view of what was said.

The purpose of this epilogue is to extract, highlight, and evaluate the main themes that arose in the conference. Because the conference considered three bodies of social science materials—the work produced by SADRI, the long series of immediate postdisaster studies, and the White-Haas *Assessment* volume—the epilogue naturally divides along the same lines. This is not to say that the three topics were unrelated, but only that different themes emerged from the sessions that were concerned with each of the topics.

Before proceeding, a comment may be in order about the participants. All of the persons invited to the conference had long-standing commitments to the study and/or management of societal responses to natural disasters. Some had been members of the advisory committee to SADRI's disaster research group. Others were connected with federal disaster relief agencies. Still others had participated in disaster research. Many were acquainted with some of our work before coming to the meeting; others had their first contact with SADRI disaster studies at the conference.

If there was any enduring difference among participants, it was between those who identified themselves mainly as social science researchers and those who identified themselves with the management of societal response to disasters. Researchers commented mainly upon the fit between our findings, our data, and other findings derived from previous work. Those with operating responsibilities were more concerned with the policy implications of our findings.

While the division between researchers and persons with operating experience held for the first day's discussion of SADRI findings, this division was hardly as clear-cut during the second day, when the discussion turned to the two other bodies of research materials. Indeed, most of this dialogue was carried out by the researchers, perhaps because they were more familiar with the content of the two traditions that were being discussed.

CONCERNING THE SADRI RESEARCH

It was gratifying to read through the prepared commentaries and the conference discussions and to find that few comments took our studies to task for lack of technical quality. Perhaps the researchers present felt that such comments were out of place in the conference context. Whatever the reason, comments on the SADRI research focussed more on substance and the policy implications of the two studies.

The Long-Term Effects Study

Some commentators were apparently reluctant to give up the search for long-term effects, pointing out the dated character of our data and the fact that some critical potential long-term effects could not be indexed by the census data we employed. Others were concerned that the level of aggregation was too great: long-term effects on individuals and households were quite possible, even though tract and county growth trends in population and housing were hardly affected.

There was considerable discussion about whether our definition of disaster really isolated serious natural hazard events for study. The very real danger of producing tautological results, were one to move toward a higher threshold (or a lower threshold), was also discussed.

The policy implications of our study received possibly the greatest attention. Several persons expressed the fear that the results might be mis-interpreted to mean that all sorts of long-term effects, including those experienced by individuals and households and types of effects our data could not deal with, did not exist. Disaster relief efforts might suffer because of overgeneralization of our findings.

Perhaps the strongest message of the conference was the consensus that the search for long-term effects ought to be pursued further. Our research had fairly well crossed out significant community-level effects for all places except those experiencing natural hazards on a catastrophic scale. An extremely important direction in which future research should go is to estimate effects at the level of households and businesses. Partially as a consequence of the conference and partially as an outgrowth of discussions we had been holding ourselves, we subsequently designed a household study and have recently received a grant to carry it out. Our plans call for screening a large number of households to locate those that have suffered damages or injuries from natural hazard events. Such households will be interviewed to derive estimates of the costs inflicted, periods of time over which damages or injuries were experienced, and coverage of private and public disaster relief efforts. Results from this survey should be available toward the end of 1981.

The Politics of Disaster Mitigation

While many of the participants had seen earlier versions of the long-term effects study, few had been acquainted with any of the results of our interviews with community leaders. Hence there were stronger reactions to these findings, especially from the disaster mitigation managers.

Kenneth Prewitt's prepared remarks on our summary paper set the tone, at least for some of the reactions. Prewitt saw the study as a somewhat desperate attempt to study a nonexisting political process. The level of salience of disaster mitigation to the political elites of local communities and states was so low that whatever political alignments existed were at best only faint lines of coalition and opposition. The question the study raised was why anything at all was done about disaster mitigation when so many of those who presumably are at the heart of local and state concerns thought the problem was trivial and scarcely worthy of concern. Prewitt saw the policy area as being maintained by the steady and determined work of "social engineers," those who manage the disaster relief and mitigation programs of the federal government and their local and state counterparts.

Reactions from other conference participants were quite strong. The social engineers who were present were concerned about the impact of a study that showed so little state and local concern with natural disasters. At least part of their pitch to the Congress and to the executive branch was that among the grass roots there was considerable sentiment that "something must be done." There were more than a few suggestions that the findings be somehow toned down or brought into line with "other" knowledge.

Reading over the transcripts and papers within the last few days brings about the same sense of bafflement that we experienced during the conference. There is simply no way in which our data could be interpreted to show that there was any more than a very weak level of concern for natural disasters as an important topic on local and state political agendas. Even the "disaster experts" (Prewitt's social engineers) apparently could not place natural hazards ahead of what they saw to be the more pressing local problems of inflation, employment, and economic growth. Nor was there any way in which we could make a case for strong levels of support for nonstructural disaster mitigation measures. Yet some of the conference participants were asking us either to downplay our findings or to qualify them drastically. We were asked to consider the impact of those findings if placed in the hands of persons who might not understand them.

This has not been the first time that social science findings went against the conventional wisdom held by experts, and no one should have been surprised by the reactions our findings provoked. Nevertheless, some commentators came close to asking for suppression of our findings. A consoling thought is that, at least in our society, the bearers of bad news are not summarily executed!

The criticism that we took most seriously was Prewitt's questioning of the value of studying the political alignments related to an issue of such low salience. The faint traces of political alignments that we did see are not necessarily those that will be strengthened in the event that natural hazard mitigation rises higher on local political agendas. Hence the meaning of our findings is unclear. Certainly direct extrapolation of our findings to other historical circumstances appears unwarranted and is made possible only by employing quixotic assumptions of heroic magnitude.

There also appears to be no easy way to retrofit our research design to provide remedies. Clearly, additional research is called for. It would be particularly important to monitor the development of political controversies over the National Flood Insurance Program, the major item that will be forced onto local agendas as each community moves from one stage of the program to the next. It is likely that as this occurs conflicts will sharpen that are inherent in the issues surrounding land use control in floodplains. Land use management issues may rarely become as important as inflation, but the political alignments of the business class and the social engineers are likely to be different from those we portray in our findings.

STUDIES OF INDIVIDUAL AND ORGANIZATIONAL RESPONSES TO DISASTER EVENTS

A long and extensive history of "firehouse" research on natural disasters has been one of the main contributions of sociologists to the study of natural disasters. Starting in the 1950s and continuing to the present, such studies have been concerned with reconstructing the behavior of individuals, households, and local organizations in the immediate postdisaster period. The evolution of such studies over time was the subject of the paper by Kreps and the commentary by Quarantelli. In an attempt to make the evolution understandable, Kreps saw more structure in the changes than could be acknowledged by Quarantelli, a major figure in this research.

Reading over the transcript, we find it hard to draw one or two central points from the paper and the ensuing discussion, not because so little was discussed, but because of the contrary condition. The series of case studies constitutes so long a research tradition, has led to so many publications, and has so profoundly influenced our understanding and knowledge of disaster events, that the discussion necessarily covered a great deal of territory, ranging from basic scientific philosophies to specific findings.

Perhaps a central issue is whether or not such case studies remain an efficient research method at this point in time. While no one disputed the fruitfulness of case studies under circumstances in which very little empirical knowledge was at hand, the issue is whether each additional case study has a drastically lowered marginal return.

THE ASSESSMENT OF ASSESSMENT

The final session of the conference was devoted to an attempt on the part of the SADRI principal investigators to reassess the White-Haas monograph concerning social science research on natural hazards. This item was placed on the agenda of the conference in the first place because the SADRI research was sparked by reading that volume. The major criticism made by our paper was that the volume not only surveyed existing knowledge about the social aspects of natural hazards but also presented an advocacy viewpoint. *Assessment*, in our view, made a stronger case for regarding natural hazards as a social problem than could be supported even by data existing at the time, but also showed a bias toward nonstructural mitigation as a policy designed to lower the costs of such events.

The reactions to our paper were quite strong, as some of the comments undoubtedly convey. In his rejoinder comment Gilbert White claimed that we misread and exaggerated the policy biases of *Assessment*. Drabek was much kinder to our paper but certainly tried to correct what he saw as misinterpretations on our part. One participant accused the SADRI researchers of lacking charity.

The comments were well taken. We did draw a more slanted view of *Assessment* than is warranted by a close reading of *all* sentences in the text. We were concerned more with the predominant tone, discounting quiet disclaimers as not fully counteracting such general messages. A careful line-by-line reading of *Assessment*, we claimed, may lead to different conclusions.

Overall, we learned a great deal from the conference. First, we began to appreciate in a very direct way Prewitt's remarks about the social engineers and their role in the definition of low-salience issues. We would extend that notion to identify a "disaster industry," one subdivision of the more general enterprise that might be called the "social problem industry." The extension is meant to express that around a recognized social problem there arises a set of interests that have stakes in providing publicity for the problem, and hence raising its salience to decision makers, in designing programs, in obtaining funds, and in building organizations to deal with the problem. Perhaps each social problem industry also develops a stake in the intransigency of the problem in question. After all, no problem equals no industry. The disaster industry consists of the agencies—federal, state, and local—that deal with disasters, the researchers who receive grants and contracts to study disaster, and the contractors who do the work that is involved in introducing disaster mitigation measures.

Of course, the disaster industry is quite small potatoes when compared, say, to the "military industrial complex" that President Eisenhower identified. Yet it is no less concerned with staying in business and receiving its share of attention, funds, and public power.

The concept of social engineers and that of the disaster industry were brought home to us in a very direct way at the conference. For one thing, most of the strongest statements about our research came from disaster industry members who were concerned that our results would be "misunderstood" by decision makers and would lead to a reduction in the effort to mitigate natural hazards in this country. For another, we learned that, had we not taken the disaster industry's hyperbole seriously in the first place, we might not have undertaken the research to begin with. Especially had we realized that there was only a latent politics of disaster mitigation, we might not have conducted the survey of local and state elites, or at best would have redesigned it to take that prior information into account.

Second, we learned that it takes a long time for research findings to filter into the policymaking process, especially if the studies are not performed directly for agencies and persons engaged in the political process. The message that natural disasters have no long-term community effects is filtering only gradually into the thinking of the disaster agencies. It may never get established as conventional wisdom. We venture that no one knows (or can even make a reasonable guess) when our study of local and state elites will enter the knowledge pool upon which disaster policy is based. It may never make it.

Finally, we did learn that an extremely useful purpose could be served by conducting additional research on the household-level effects of natural disasters. Our current research will pursue this line. We expect to find that many households have been close enough in space to have "experienced" a disaster, fewer will have suffered any injuries or damages, and even fewer will have suffered high levels of either. We also expect to find that current and recent disaster relief programs provide relief for only some victims. Of course, we anticipate the disaster industry will have some difficulty assimilating our findings.

ACKNOWLEDGMENTS

The first debt of anyone who tries to put together a published proceedings volume is necessarily to the secretarial staff whose dedicated labors transformed the oral testimony of the participants into documentary material. For the especially cheerful and able discharge of the tasks of taping the proceedings, transcribing and editing the tapes, typing and retyping the manuscript, and tending to the details of organizing the conference in the first place, we thank Cindy Coffman, Jeanne Reinle, and Laura Martin.

The Disaster Research Program of the Social and Demographic Research Institute, the results of which are presented here, was funded by Grant No. ENV-76-15441 from the National Science Foundation, Research Applied to National Needs. The same grant also paid for organizing the conference. We are grateful to the foundation for the lavish funds provided for our research, and to our program managers at NSF, Dr. George Baker and Dr. Fred Krimgold, for their advice and assistance in all phases of the research. The opinions expressed in this volume, whether by SADRI staff or other conference participants, of course do not necessarily reflect the views of the National Science Foundation.

SADRI's Disaster Research Program began in 1976 and has continued for the ensuing four years, and such success as it has enjoyed is due in large measure to the cadres of research assistants who have worked on the project at various times. Special thanks to Marianne Pietras and William F. Diggins for their contributions to the report on the study of state and local disaster politics, and to Anne Shlay, Susan Marshall, Jerry Wilcox, Steve Nock, Narayan Acharya, Anita Sinha, Judith Mark, and Marsha Gordon for their generally excellent contributions to the project.

Every active social science research shop has its computer person who sits at the interface between the thinking of the investigators and the numbers coming off the machine. No expression of gratitude could ever possibly convey a proper sense of the debt owed by all SADRI research personnel to our Director of Data Base Management and Software Development, Eleanor Weber-Burdin, who not only makes our CYBER sit up and sing on demand, but is also one of the good people of the earth.

Finally, we are grateful most of all for the time and energy expended by the participants in the Conference on Social Science and Natural Hazards, whose names and affiliations appear on the List of Participants that follows.

The willingness of the participants to be frank and critical in their commentary is the ultimate source of whatever value this volume may contain.

James D. Wright and Peter H. Rossi
Amherst, Massachusetts
August 1980

Conference Participants

William Anderson
Program Manager
Division of Problem- Focused
    Research Applications
National Science Foundation

Frederick L. Bates
Professor
Department of Sociology
University of Georgia

T. Michael Carter
Coprincipal Investigator
Natural Hazards Warning Systems
University of Minnesota

Walter D. Castle
National Oceanic & Atmospheric
    Administration
U.S. Department of Commerce

John Clark
Professor
Department of Sociology
University of Minnesota

Joseph F. Coates
Office of Technology Assessment
U.S. Congress

Hal Cochrane
Department of Economics
Colorado State University

Cynthia J. Coffman
Administrative Assistant
Social and Demographic Research
    Institute
University of Massachusetts,
    Amherst

William F. Diggins
Social and Demographic Research
    Institute

University of Massachusetts,
    Amherst

Thomas E. Drabek
Professor
Department of Sociology
University of Denver

Russell R. Dynes
Executive Officer
American Sociological Association

William Fitzgerald
Federal Disaster Assistance
    Administration
U.S. Department of Housing and
    Urban Development

Calvin Frederick
Mental Health Disaster Assistance
    Administration
National Institute of Mental Health

Charles Fritz
Committee on Socioeconomic Aspects
    of Earthquake Prediction
National Research Council

Ralph Garrett
Emergency Operations Systems
    Division/Research
Defense Civil Preparedness Agency

John Gibson
Federal Disaster Assistance
    Administration
U.S. Department of Housing and
    Urban Development

James Huffman
Director
Natural Resources Law Institute
Northwestern School of Law

James Kerr
Emergency Operations Systems
    Division/Research
Defense Civil Preparedness Agency

Gary A. Kreps
Department of Sociology
College of William & Mary

Fred Krimgold
Program Manager
Earthquake Hazards Mitigation
Division of Problem-Focused
    Research Applications
National Science Foundation

Howard Kunreuther
Chairman
Department of Decision Sciences
The Wharton School
University of Pennsylvania

Robert K. Leik
Director
Minnesota Family Study Center
University of Minnesota

Michael Massie
Small Business Administration

Clifford McLain
Emergency Operations Systems
    Division/Research
Defense Civil Preparedness Agency

Dennis S. Mileti
Associate Professor
Department of Sociology
Colorado State University

Ugo Morelli
Federal Disaster Assistance
    Administration
U.S. Department of Housing and
    Urban Development

Annabelle B. Motz
Sociology Department
American University

Roy Newsome
Federal Disaster Assistance
    Administration
U.S. Department of Housing and
    Urban Development

Michael Ornstein
Institute for Behavioural Research
York University

William Petak
Vice President
J.H. Wiggins Company

Janis Pieper
Federal Disaster Assistance
    Administration
U.S. Department of Housing and
    Urban Development

Marianne E. Pietras
Social and Demographic Research
    Institute
University of Massachusetts,
    Amherst

Roy Popkin
Assistant National Director
Disaster Services
The American National Red Cross

Kenneth Prewitt
President
Social Science Research Council

Daniel O. Price
Burlington Industries Professor
Department of Sociology
University of North Carolina

Henry Quarantelli
Professor of Sociology
Director, Disaster Research Center
Ohio State University

Peter H. Rossi
Director
Social and Demographic Research
    Institute
University of Massachusetts,
    Amherst

Claire B. Rubin
Fellow in Public Management
The Academy of Contemporary
    Problems

Anne B. Shlay
Social and Demographic Research
    Institute
University of Massachusetts,
    Amherst

John Susich
Federal Disaster Assistance
    Administration
U.S. Department of Housing and
    Urban Development

Hirst Sutton
Emergency Preparedness Projects
    Office
The Council of State Governments

Charles Thiel
Director
Division of Advanced Environmental
    Research and Technology
National Science Foundation

Eleanor Weber-Burdin
Social and Demographic Research
    Institute
University of Massachusetts,
    Amherst

Russell Whitney
Federal Disaster Assistance
    Administration
U.S. Department of Housing and
    Urban Development

James D. Wright
Social and Demographic Research
    Institute
University of Massachusetts.
    Amherst

Sonia R. Wright
Social and Demographic Research
    Institute
University of Massachusetts,
    Amherst

INDEX